THE EARLY CHURCHES OF ROME

THE EARLY CHURCHES OF ROME

EMILE MÂLE

Translated by DAVID BUXTON

CHICAGO QUADRANGLE BOOKS INC 1960

First published by Flammarion et Cie, Paris
under the title *Rome et ses Vieilles Eglises*

Quadrangle Books, Inc., Chicago 1
Ernest Benn Limited, London, EC4
Printed in Great Britain
Library of Congress Catalog Card Number 60 – 7082

Contents

List of Illustrations

[Photographs not otherwise attributed are by D. R. Buxton]

Author's Preface

On ne trouvera pas dans ces pages une suite d'études consacrées à toutes les vieilles églises de Rome; on n'y trouvera même pas l'examen complet de toutes les œuvres d'art que contiennent les églises dont nous parlons. Nous n'écrivons pas un guide du voyageur. Nous avons choisi, de siècle en siècle, jusqu'au XIIIe, quelques antiques sanctuaires dont les uns nous ont séduit par leur beauté, les autres par leurs souvenirs, d'autres par des fresques ou des mosaïques liées à l'histoire et ouvrant de vastes perspectives à l'imagination. Il en est qui nous proposaient des problèmes que nous avons essayé de résoudre. Ces quelques chapitres, qui ne forment pas une histoire suivie de l'art romain, permettront cependant d'en apercevoir les différents aspects depuis l'âge des persécutions jusqu'aux approches de la Renaissance.

Ce livre a été écrit à Rome pendant les années qui ont précédé la guerre; un séjour de quatorze ans nous a permis d'y examiner à loisir tous les monuments que nous décrivons. On trouvera peut-être, dans ces jours de tristesse, quelque consolation à s'associer à cette grande histoire du christianisme et de la papauté, qui ont connu tant d'épreuves, dont l'art porte témoignage, mais qui n'ont jamais cessé de créer et d'espérer.

1942

Emile Mâle

Translator's Preface

THERE ARE surprisingly few books for the general reader on early-Christian and medieval Rome, but I discovered Emile Mâle's splendid little work soon after arriving in Italy, and quickly came to prize it. It seemed to me a pity that the book should be available only in a too-modest war-time edition with few illustrations. I therefore offered, after toying with the idea for two or three years, to prepare a new, fully illustrated version for English readers, for it is well known that many Englishmen are reluctant (even if perfectly well able to do so) to read for pleasure and profit in a foreign tongue. I would have wished to discuss this project with the author himself – the tall, aristocratic figure of martial bearing who was one of the most eminent scholars of his day. But he had died (at the good old age of 92) on October 6, 1954, which happened to be the very day on which I in turn became a resident in Rome.

Mâle's own brief foreword includes the necessary statement that his book was not intended as a complete or systematic guide to the early churches of Rome. He set out to describe, and to relate to the history of their times, those ancient Roman churches which had most appealed to him for their beauty or their associations. However, his readers' tastes are likely to coincide with his own, and very few favourite buildings of his chosen period (from early-Christian times to the 13th century) are altogether missing from his text.

Perhaps the leading characteristic of this book is the synthesis of viewpoints it presents, for Mâle was a many-sided medievalist, at once historian and art-historian, an unrivalled specialist in iconography (including, of course, its theological background) and a biographer of profound human understanding. Parts of his text would make good reading as history pure and simple, even if they did not illumine – like a shaft of sunlight in surrounding darkness – those monuments of art which form the main theme of his discourse. An example is his masterly study of the great iconoclastic dispute, of which the horror and the tragedy, as well as the justification, are brought vividly home to us, and of which our own 'Protestant iconoclasm', some eight hundred years later, was a faint but faithful echo.

The book has another attraction, for it reveals, incidentally, the workings of a great scholar's mind. In each of these essays Mâle pursued the thread of his enquiry, in spite of his advanced years, with truly youthful zest, rejecting no material, however unpromising, undeterred when seemingly defeated, turning aside with eager curiosity to explore by-ways and side-issues, always taking delight in the adventure of research. And his writing, lucid as the best French always is, and free of all jargon, has that liveliness, and those occasional touches of humour, which ensure that hardly a page shall be dry or tedious.

A few words seem called for on one of the recurrent themes of this book – the basilican church, which in Rome (and Rome alone) maintained its ascendancy throughout the Middle

Ages, indifferent to the challenge of the medieval styles. Much has been written about the original meaning and the correct definition of the term 'basilica', and further confusion arises because the word is often applied, in Italian usage, to churches which are not (architecturally speaking) basilicas at all. In this book, however, the word is applied only to the typical early-Christian church with the following characteristics: a broad nave leading up to an apse and flanked by two (occasionally four) aisles; colonnades formed of closely spaced classical columns bearing either a flat architrave or arches, carrying in turn the upper nave wall which is pierced by windows; timber roofs either exposed or hidden by a flat ceiling. When a transept intervenes between nave and apse it is separated from the nave by a great transverse arch, locally called the 'triumphal arch'. This term seemed to me ambiguous and I have used the expression 'sanctuary-arch' instead, on the grounds that the transept is (or at least was originally intended as) a sanctuary.

At one stage or another the book has been looked through both by Mr. L. Russell Muirhead (whose excellent Blue Guides will be in the hands of many visitors to Italy) and by Mr. J. W. Franklin (author of Batsford's recently-published *Cathedrals of Italy*). I am grateful to them both for many useful comments, some of which have found their way into the new footnotes (distinguished by square brackets) which I have added where necessary. I am also deeply indebted to my friend and neighbour Mr. G. U. S. Corbett, an expert on early-Christian architecture, whose advice I sought on several points, and who very kindly lent me his old-fashioned plate-camera, which was just what I needed for some of the architectural photographs.

As for the illustrations, which I think constitute the main justification for this edition, they are strictly documentary, and I have resisted the temptation to admit subjects merely because they were pretty or picturesque. Two-thirds of the plates are reproduced from my own photographs, taken for this purpose in the summer of 1958. The other photographic illustrations are derived from professional sources and are duly acknowledged in the list of plates. We have also used several fine old engravings. Although they have lost a great deal in the reproduction they demonstrate once again the excellence, for architectural illustration, of this beautiful but almost forgotten technique.

Emile Mâle spent fourteen years in Rome as Director of the French Archæological Institute (l'Ecole Française de Rome) at the Palazzo Farnese, a post he relinquished in 1937 at the age of 75. Mâle in his old age, with faculties unimpaired, alive as ever to intellectual and emotional stimulus, became enamoured afresh of the Rome he had loved in his youth. This book proves how greatly he enjoyed the long years, how rewarding he found them and made them. I believe those who use the book will find (as I have found) that they share his enjoyment, while their experience of this unique city will certainly be enriched by the delightful learning he distilled from its various elements. And some may be left with a feeling of affection for the distinguished author whom they were never privileged to meet.

D. R. Buxton

Rome, July 1959

THE EARLY CHURCHES OF ROME

INTRODUCTION

Rome and the Roman Campagna

TO SEE Rome as a whole we must climb the Janiculum in the hours before sunset. From the terrace of San Pietro in Montorio we overlook almost the entire city, and from the first glance our eyes are charmed by its sweeping lines and tawny hues. Ancient Rome with its painted houses had the same colour, was set in the same gracefully undulating landscape. As in the times of the Caesars, magnificent gardens crown some of the heights with sombre green. Martial, who described this very view, would recognise it again; only the domes would cause him astonishment, for the many temples of his day have been succeeded by a greater multitude of churches. Just when the sun is about to disappear we see the town transfigured, wholly clothed in pinkish gold – wonderful moments which Claude Lorraine has perpetuated. A splendid semicircle of mountains, deep blue or palest sky-blue according to the time of day, closes in the distant horizon.

From the Janiculum one sees the city, but we must climb the Monte Cavo, highest summit of the Alban Hills, to enjoy a bird's-eye view of the surrounding plains where the life of Rome was lived in the first centuries of her history. It is a grand panorama, extending well beyond the limits of southern Etruria as far as the misty Ciminian mountains, that formidable barrier which the legions for long years dared not attempt to pass. All around there rose hostile heights from which a fierce enemy might descend: the hills of the Sabines, of the Aequi and Hernici, and the long range in the country of the Volsci. One needs to see these lonely hills, these stony valleys and dried-up streams, these wretched villages clinging to hill-top and hill-side, to understand why hunger so often drove the mountain people towards the rich harvests of Latium. The great plain, now again intensively cultivated, as it once was, slopes down insensibly to the sea. The Monte Circeo, farthest limit of Ulysses' voyages, raises its double summit low in the western sky. Beyond is the Mediterranean of Homer, with all its enchantments.

The traveller who would explore this ancient world of central Italy must, if he proceeds chronologically, begin with the coastal belt – that legendary region immortalised by Virgil. These still solitary reaches of forest and scrub are the setting for the last songs of the Aeneid. It is without doubt most difficult, on the modernised bathing-beach of Ostia Lido, to think of Aeneas; nevertheless, if the poet is to be believed, the Trojan camp stood near by – the new Ilium, where the exiles dwelt. Pratica di Mare, the big Borghese stronghold with its surrounding village, is the old Lavinium. Ardea, where Turnus lived, still dominates the plain and has preserved its great name, *magnum Ardea nomen*. In the distance, on the mountainside, we can just distinguish Privernum, birthplace of the amazon Camilla, who was raised on the milk of a mare. Virgil is possessed with holy horror when he names the antique gods of these remote ages, and when he describes their fabled inhabitants: those of Praeneste and Anagnia with their wolf-skin helmets; those of Soracte and the Monti Cimini who sang as they walked; the Hirpini, armed with bronze swords, and the Marsi, whose priests were charmers of serpents. Virgil thought he had reached back to the beginning of time, but the study of prehistory has revealed a much longer past. Today we know about the inhabitants of Latium in Neolithic times, who buried their dead in the posture of the infant in the womb, believing no doubt that man could as well be born twice as once. Later on we can follow the wanderings of the Bronze Age invaders from northern Europe: they brought with them the language one day to be Latin and the art of building villages on piles – whether over water or on the dry land. These square villages – terramari as they are called – face the four points of the compass.

Such was the Rome of the Palatine, the *Roma quadrata* of Romulus. The town, related as it was to the cardinal points of the heavens, was the image of the universe; in its centre was the deep well or *mundus* whence, on certain days, the spirits of the dead would emerge to warm themselves at the fire-sides of the living. These dead were no longer buried but cremated, their ashes being placed in urns shaped like the huts they had lived in during life. A strange innovation this, not easy to explain. Maybe they thought that the fire, in separating the soul from the body, enabled it to descend more quickly to the world of shades.

After these prehistoric peoples came the Etruscans. Near Rome are the sites of three famous cities: Veii, which was besieged, like Troy, for ten years; Tarquinii,[1] whence came the Tarquins; Caere,[2] which Virgil calls Agylla. The towns have disappeared, but their tombs have endured. Strange and melancholy are the landscapes of Etruria. One enters Veii by way of the ravine of the Cremera, crossing it just where a cascade, falling between vertical walls of rock, is overshadowed by ancient, contorted trees. The place is completely solitary; this is the Veii which was already abandoned in the time of Propertius, when the only sound to be heard there was the shepherd's horn. At Caere, where stupendous circular tombs are arranged in avenues, death becomes awesome in its majesty. The necropolis of Tarquinii leaves the wide horizon free; yet, when dark clouds blow in from the sea, when the blue hills turn black and the storm bursts upon us, we understand the terror that thunder and lightning inspired in Etruria. Then the priests consulted their *Libri fulgurales* and made haste to appease the gods.

For us the Etruscans are a mystery. Originating, as it seems, in Lydia, they brought to Italy an unknown language; their inscriptions are in Greek characters but remain unintelligible.[3] We know this strange people chiefly from the paintings in their tombs, from

[[1] Known as Corneto from medieval times until 1922, when its ancient name was revived as Tarquinia.]

[[2] Cerveteri.]

[[3] All these statements, and some others made in the following paragraphs, need considerable qualification. See Pallottino, *The Etruscans*, Penguin Books, 1955, first published in Italian in 1943.]

which we gain the impression that they were both voluptuous and sad. The underground chambers of Tarquinii are sometimes adorned with banquets, dances and other festive scenes, sometimes with terrifying pictures of the other world. The demon Charon threatens the dead with his hammer, the vulturine Tuchulcha with his serpents. Apparently two unreconciled conceptions of death prevailed, for the Etruscans had adopted both burial and cremation. The dead laid in rock-cut chambers were held to go on living there, and so pictures of a blissful existence were placed before their eyes; but those whose ashes had been placed in urns fled away to the unknown, where formidable encounters might await them. In the *Books of the Acheron* of the Etruscan priests, as in those of ancient Egypt, one could doubtless learn how to overcome the hazards of the life beyond.

The religion of the Etruscans was a magical one, involving the use of incantations calculated to disarm the gods. In these matters the Etruscans owed much to the East, in particular that strange method of divination with the liver of sacrificed animals. At Piacenza a bronze liver was discovered, marked out into twelve sections corresponding to the twelve divisions of the sky. Similar livers have come to light in Chaldaea and Asia Minor.

Etruria borrowed her art from archaic Greece and especially from Ionia, as the fine Apollo of Veii in painted terracotta seems to witness. But the Etruscans do not show that wonderful youthful impulse, that confidence in their future, so characteristic of the Greeks. Etruria had no faith in herself, and came at an early period to accept her own doom as inevitable. The priests themselves used to announce that she would last but ten times the life-span of man. Sure enough, her end was approaching in Sulla's time when Rome overthrew the old 'hotbed' of Etruria for ever.

Yet Rome was infinitely indebted to the Etruscans, was indeed herself Etruscan (whatever the Romans may have said on the subject) for Etruria extended southwards in its days of greatness to beyond Capua. Roman religion bore the indelible mark of this influence, as did some Roman temples – that of Jupiter Capitolinus, for instance, with its three *cellae*. Etruscan also were the purple-bordered toga and the curule chair of the senators; so too the lictor's *fasces*, carried before the magistrates of the Republic.

Having once thrown off the dominion of Etruria, Rome fought against her, as she fought the Latins, the Sabines, the Aequi and the Volscians. It is surprising to find, so close to Rome, places like Gabii (Gavi), Fidenae (Castel Giubileo) and the Lake of Regillus (Regillo) [1]; while other Etruscan towns, Tibur (Tivoli), Velitrae (Velletri) and Praeneste (Palestrina) – which were all traditional enemies of Rome – are but little farther away. The legions gained their victories within a few hours' march of Rome. Early Roman history has for its setting the volcanic Alban hills with their beautiful if sombre crater-lakes, and the hither slopes of the Sabine mountains. This history is no more than an epic in which fact and fiction are inextricably merged, but the epic is a magnificent one. The Greek legends have a brilliant beauty, but those of Rome are incomparably splendid. Through the centuries they have moved many a fervent spirit: Shakespeare, Corneille, Bossuet, Jean-Jacques Rousseau, the

[[1] Drained in the 17th century.]

men of the Convention. They have taught the dignity of poverty, the love of one's country, the virtue of self-sacrifice. There was Cincinnatus, ploughing his five-acre field and wiping the sweat from his brow, when told that he had been appointed Dictator. There were the Decii, father and son, who both sacrificed their lives to save the army; Manlius, who had his son slain with an axe in the hour of victory because he had given battle against his orders. Again, we remember the town which went into mourning for the shame of the Caudine Forks, and sent those who had capitulated back to the Samnites. And there was the tribune's order to his soldiers: 'It is necessary to go that far, but it is not necessary to come back.' When legends have such grandeur they do testify to the greatness of the people that created them. His readings of Livy gave St. Augustine much food for thought. Deeply moved by such abnegation, by such steadfastness of character, he could not help writing that, if God made the Romans masters of the world, he did so as a reward for their virtues.

The embryonic Rome of the Palatine, the Capitol and the Quirinal grew in proportion to her victories. And once she had conquered the world, all the world was welcome there. All religious rites were celebrated in Rome, and the old gods of Egypt, who were particularly honoured, had no less than four temples dedicated to them. Of these the most magnificent was the temple of Isis, occupying the present site of the 'Minerva' and Sant'Ignazio. An avenue of lions, sphinxes and cynocephali (now preserved in the museums) led up to the great sculptured pylons of the temple and to the sanctuary of the goddess herself, and a spectator might well have fancied himself in Thebes or Memphis. The great gods of Asia had their temples too: the Magna Mater of Phrygia, whose head was a thunderbolt, was worshipped on the Palatine, the Syrian Jupiter (a war-god standing erect on a bull's back) on the Esquiline, the three gods of Palmyra on the Janiculum. Mithras, the Persian deity, received his devotees in dark subterranean shrines, near the Colosseum and under the baths of Caracalla. But, above all, Greek cults prevailed in Rome: those beautiful divinities gradually replaced the dreary and impersonal native gods of Latium. Greece had bestowed on Rome that most priceless of gifts – the gift of beauty. From Greece came an inexhaustible stream of statues for the sanctuaries, the fora and the villas of Rome; among them the masterpieces of Myron, Scopas and Praxiteles. From Greece too came the temple, the basilica, the theatre and the portico; also that perfect combination, calculated with the nicety of a verse of lyric poetry – the column, with its capital and base.

It would be quite wrong, however, to represent the art of the Romans as a mere copy of the Hellenistic; their architecture, for instance, shows various original features. Roman temples are raised on a high podium while Greek ones are approached by a few steps only. The temple of Castor in the forum proudly rises seven metres above the ground, and could only be approached by the steps leading up to its façade. The Parthenon, on the other hand, received its visitors all round and offered masterpieces for their enjoyment on all its four sides. The Greek theatre took advantage of a hill-side for its semicircular auditorium, while earth and sky, occasionally the sea, provided the setting for the drama. The Romans, declining any help from nature, raised the steps of their auditorium on a grandiose structure, in which the principle of the arch was associated with the architecture of the column. The theatre of Marcellus, restored in recent years, demonstrates the beauty of this original creation. The Colosseum is an immense oval amphitheatre, constructed with such consummate skill that seventy thousand spectators could take their places in it without confusion (1). Nothing is more characteristically Roman. For such a building Greece offered no model, for Greek humanism had no use for the bloodthirsty sports of the arena. There were some Romans, bred under the influence of Greek thought, who felt the same about gladiatorial combats as the Greeks themselves, so that Seneca, straight from the amphitheatre, could write: 'I know these men who die in the arena are criminals, but what crime have we committed that we should be condemned to witness such a scene?'

Nor was there anything in Greece to compare with those gigantic masses of brickwork like the Thermae of Caracalla and of Diocletian, or the Basilica of Constantine (5). Such structures have a different origin. When the Romans penetrated to the valleys of the Tigris and Euphrates they discovered the brick architecture of Babylon and Mesopotamia; seeing these stupendous walls and great wide vaults, they adopted them themselves and became the rivals of ancient Assyria. Nothing expresses the majesty of Rome more impressively than these great bare ruins, stripped of all their marble decoration – nothing, unless perhaps the long lines of aqueducts which brought rivers to Rome riding 'on triumphal arches' (11). True Roman architecture is an engineers' technique; it would have resembled what our architects attempt to produce today, had not the Greeks clothed it in beauty.

At Rome, antiquity is a ruin, but a grand ruin which appeals to all men – even the least cultivated. No one can remain indifferent to the Via del Impero [1] bordered by the various fora and closed at the far end by the Colosseum. But to the keen young classical scholar Rome gives many a thrill of emotion, for legend and history are always with him. In the forum, every step offers a new enchantment. Here is the pool of Juturna where the Romans thought they saw Castor and Pollux watering their horses after the battle of Lake Regillus. Those walls belong to the *Regia* which Caesar left on the morning of the ides of March, going to the Senate where his assassins were lying in wait. A semicircular recess cutting into one high platform shows the exact spot where Caesar's body was cremated, and the platform itself is that of the temple dedicated to him. On another rostrum Cicero's head was exposed. The neighbouring façade belonged to the Senate, and a few steps away is the dungeon, the *tullianum*, where Caesar left Vercingetorix to die.

These ruins of the forum make the stage of a tremendous drama – a drama that concerns humanity at large. The monuments of Rome are chapters in the history of the world: the triumphal arch of Titus records the capture of Jerusalem, that of Septimius Severus the conquest of the East, while Constantine's celebrates the triumph of Christianity (4). The more we know, the more Rome takes possession of us; as we wander in that city of dreams the

[[1] Now Via dei Fori Imperiali.]

modern scene disappears, while the distant past comes to life. Walking from the Lateran to the Villa Celimontana, we do not notice the gloomy modern hospitals but we conjure up in imagination the house of the Annia gens, where Marcus Aurelius was born; also that of the Valerii, where, along with a sculptured group of Eros and Psyche, we find a Christian lamp, reminding us that Melania, last of her ancient line, was a saint. Farther on, we can imagine the palaces of Symmachus and Nicomachus, mighty champions of dying paganism, who defended the old gods to the last.

Has Rome, then, nothing to offer but great ruins and great memories? Admittedly the finest of her monuments have disappeared. The Palatine, where the emperors' palaces – marvels of sumptuous art – used to stand, shows only fragments of walls, a few columns and slabs of marble. Of the temple of Jupiter Capitolinus there remains the podium only; the Circus Maximus, that giant ellipse, gave its shape to a valley but has left no other trace; Domitian's Odeon, numbered among the seven wonders of the city, has so completely disappeared that even its site remains unknown. The truth is – and it has been stated a hundred times – that Rome was not destroyed by the Barbarians but by the Romans; and it took them twelve hundred years to gain the upper hand in their struggle against the masterpieces of the classic age. A few monuments remained intact because the popes or the civic authorities took them under their protection; among these were the columns of Trajan and of Marcus Aurelius (109). Those armies of two thousand men ascending in spirals to the conqueror's statue at the top of each column astounded the imagination. But perhaps the real reasons for their preservation were, in the first case, that Trajan's soul was believed to have been saved through the prayers of St. Gregory; and, in the second, that a Christian miracle was supposed to figure among the reliefs.

The Pantheon, too, transformed into a church, was saved from destruction (8, 9). Its interior is the finest in Rome and one of the finest in the world. Here no effort is required of our imagination – there is nothing to reconstruct, we have but to admire. What is the secret of its beauty? We may trace it to the harmonious proportions and the attractiveness of the lighting. The diameter and the height of this magnificent rotunda are equal, determining what the ancients regarded as one of the forms of perfection; while the soft, clear light that floods the interior does not fall from windows (which the old temples never had) but from the great round hole at the summit of the dome. Though despoiled of its statues and of the gold ornaments from the coffered vaulting of its dome, the Pantheon remains an incomparable masterpiece. Its beauty enables us to visualise a multitude of lost monuments – temples, palaces, arcades, basilicas and patrician villas.

Nothing, perhaps, is more to be regretted than the disappearance of those splendid Roman villas whose gardens surrounded the town with the perennial verdure of their pines, laurels and evergreen oaks. So many wonderful things did they contain that man has not succeeded in destroying them all. The soil of Rome is sown with statues, and the lucky chance finds of centuries have given us many a splendid work, as for instance the Birth of Venus, the Dying Gaul and the children of Niobe. Such masterpieces witness to the high regard in which

Greek art was held by the owners of these sumptuous estates such as Maecenas, Lucullus, Sallust, Aelius Lamia and Acilius Glabrio. We should have no idea of these enchanting parks were it not that some remnants of Hadrian's villa, at the foot of the hills below Tivoli, have happily been preserved.[1] One doubts whether the imperial garden in all its magnificence can have been more delightful than the unkempt grasslands we see today, studded with wild flowers, among which the mysterious ruins rise. Their own rich colour, with the dark cypresses, the silvery olives and the blue mountains behind, make up so exquisite a harmony that we forget to wonder whether this or that belongs to the Poikile, the Academy or the Canopus – all re-created here according to the much-travelled Hadrian's fantasy. Despoiled through the centuries, these long porticoes, these apses and half-collapsed rotundas have yielded more than three hundred works of art to enrich the museums.

If Hadrian's villa allows us to picture the other patrician gardens around Rome, the ruins of Ostia Antica give us an excellent idea of plebeian dwellings.[2] At Rome the ordinary buildings in the popular quarters bore no resemblance to the charming homes of Pompeii where life must have passed so pleasantly. On the contrary, with their four or five storeys and their inner courts they differed little from Roman residential blocks today. Such were the houses of Ostia, inhabited by merchants, sailors and dockers. Excavations have revealed them, complete with their stairways and their balconies. We should dearly like to identify that house in Ostia where St. Augustine and his mother, who was soon to die, once sat talking at the open window which looked out on to the gardens. We read how mother and son, as they discussed the eternal life, roused themselves even to ecstasy. These are immortal pages of the *Confessions*, in which the sensitive human spirit finds a new message to ponder.

In the time of the emperors one would sometimes have seen funerals of some senator or consul passing along the Appian Way, with their weepers, their flute-players and those who wore the ancestral funerary masks. The funeral pyre was lit before one of those great tombs whose ruins still have so poetic an appeal. Other processions, solemn and silent, would be making their way towards the subterranean cemeteries excavated in the tufa at a little distance from the road; these were the funerals of the Christians. Without knowing each other, the past and the future of the world were marching along the same road. The Appian Way was one of those roads which the Christians held sacred: St. Paul had trodden its stones, and it was told that Christ himself, coming to meet St. Peter, had left his footprints upon it.

Most moving are the catacombs which border the Appia Antica to right and left (22). After walking through the fine cypress avenue leading to the catacombs of St. Calixtus, we

[[1] Since this was written further important excavations and some judicious restoration have notably increased the attraction and interest of the Villa. See the official guide, *Villa Adriana (Hadrian's Villa) near Tivoli*, by S. Aurigemma, English edition, 1955.]

[[2] Compare 3 and 9.]

drop down into the depths and there feel carried back to the earliest generations of Christianity. In one of the underground chapels we can recognise, on several marble slabs which close the narrow graves, the names of popes martyred in the 3rd century. What a contrast between the humble *loculi* of these men and the gigantic mausolea of Augustus and Hadrian! Yet the future belonged to these early martyrs and the spiritual world they knew was vaster than the empire of the Caesars. In the catacombs of St. Sebastian one can read, scratched in the plaster on the walls, invocations to St. Peter and St. Paul, whose bodies rested there for some years.

Nearly all the main highways have their catacombs. Three of them are associated with members of the ancient Roman aristocracy – names which take us back almost to the apostolic age. In the cemetery of Priscilla there is a subterranean chamber that belonged to the family of Acilius Glabrio, put to death by Domitian for having embraced the new faith. In the cemetery of Domitilla we read the names of the Flavians, some of whom were converted as early as the 1st century: the consul Flavius Clemens was condemned to death by Domitian (whose cousin he was) and his wife Domitilla exiled. Again, in Lucina's crypt in the catacombs of St. Calixtus the inscription of Pomponius Graecinus reminds us that Pomponia Graecina, wife of the conqueror of the Bretons, figures in the pages of Tacitus as an austere Christian. From the first the new religion, with its gentleness and its promise of immortality, achieved the miracle of overcoming patrician pride. The most ancient paintings of the catacombs are pervaded with this same gentle spirit, this faith in the eternal life, and few masterpieces of art are as touching as these modest, half-obliterated frescoes. Doves, sheep, a bowl of milk, a few flowers and trees, a young shepherd carrying a lamb on his shoulders, a woman praying in the antique manner, with outstretched arms – such are the subjects we find depicted among the tombs. In these tragic years, when the blood of the martyrs was flowing, Christian art expressed nothing but peace. This idyllic happiness belongs to another world, and God promises it to his faithful flock for all eternity, through his miracles. 'He will save us,' said the prayer for the dead, 'as he saved Noah and Jonah and the three young Hebrews in the fiery furnace; he will raise us up as he raised up Lazarus . . .' And these are the miracles which the artists have painted on the walls of the catacombs. Faith in the Eternal Life – such is the theme of the earliest Christian art. From the frescoes of the funerary chambers, from the inscriptions on the tombs themselves, this invincible hope shines forth.

In the age of the persecutions religious functions were held in ordinary houses, the largest room being turned into a church. One of these venerable sanctuaries still exists below the church of San Martino ai Monti. But after the Peace of the Church splendid basilicas arose. Old St. Peter's exists no longer and San Paolo fuori le Mura (St. Paul-outside-the-Walls), destroyed by fire more than a century ago, is, however magnificent, an almost entirely new church. Happily Santa Maria Maggiore and Santa Sabina have survived (28, 37). The moment we enter them we fall under the spell of antique genius, the genius which created the basilica – irresistible in its charm. The beauty of the columns, the restful lines, the perfect proportions, the pure light falling from high windows – all these things conspire to bring tranquillity to the spirit. Our Gothic cathedrals are all aspiration and prayer, exalting the heart to greater heights than their own high vaults; the Roman basilicas express the calm assurance of faith. In these buildings, conceived by the well-balanced genius of Greece, Christianity appears as the ultimate wisdom. In the serene atmosphere of the basilicas, mosaics add a touch of magnificence. This is where the East enriches, with its brilliant colours, the purity of Hellenic art. The Old and the New Testament shine down from the walls with strange, unworldly light.

The basilicas were built in a city still almost intact, where Christian art was beginning to be superimposed on pagan art – both beautiful in their different ways. It is difficult to picture the magnificence of Rome at the end of the 4th century; never had she been more splendid. But in the 5th century the Barbarians twice did violence to the city; in the 6th, the Goths besieged it and were themselves besieged there; the great ruin had begun. Gradually the temples fell into decay, their colonnades being carried away for churches and their marble facing for choir-enclosures and pulpits. Palaces collapsed and were never rebuilt. Bronze statues were melted down and marble statues burnt for lime. Desolation spread around the basilicas. Had it not been for the papacy and its great Christian associations, Rome might have disappeared like Memphis and Babylon. However, this poor fever-stricken, depopulated city, lost in a wilderness, remained glorious in the imagination of the medieval pilgrims. For them it was always *aurea Roma* – Rome the Golden. They fell on their knees when they first caught sight of the city from the Monte Mario. When they had prayed at the Apostles' tombs and at St. John Lateran, 'mother of all churches', what did they see as they wandered about the town they had longed for? They saw innumerable towers overlooking the ruins.

Some great feudal families had divided up among themselves the plain and the hills and, perfectly indifferent to the past, had turned the ancient monuments into fortresses. The Frangipani occupied the Palatine, the arches of Titus and Constantine and the Colosseum; the Pierleoni dominated the Tiber, by means of the Theatre of Marcellus and the towers on the island; the Colonna family had fortified the Mausoleum of Augustus, but their rivals, the Orsini, possessed Rome's most formidable bastion – the tomb of Hadrian (now the Castel Sant'Angelo). The Savelli were masters of the Aventine; the Caetani were astride the Appian Way, the tomb of Cecilia Metella, with added battlements, being the keep of their castle (6). Every noble family had its tower, proud symbol of its might.

Since the middle of the 12th century the Romans had erected their civic buildings and their bell-tower on the Capitol. The popes, who were continually in conflict with the Germanic emperors, were also obliged to struggle against Roman feudalism and the civic authorities of the town; indeed one pope, Lucius II, was killed leading an assault on the Capitol. Never was the papal office a heavier burden; never was more strength of character demanded of the popes.

What remains today from these tragic centuries? A few towers still stand up here and there among modern buildings, and there are two massive and imposing fortresses: the Torre delle Milizie, with its storeys narrowing upwards (13), and the truncated keep known as the Torre dei Conti. In spite of these considerable relics of the period, it is difficult now to visualise the warrior city of the Middle Ages; on the other hand, the holy city with its churches has come down to us. Many of these old sanctuaries, with their bell-towers, remain very much as the medieval pilgrims saw them (78, 80, etc.). Successive centuries added further churches of their own, but their type – surprisingly – remains unvaried. Whether these churches belong to the 7th century or the 13th, they always resemble the ancient basilicas. Throughout her history, Rome remained faithful to the classical tradition. Yet she had other models at hand. In the north of Latium Romanesque churches were built, but Rome seemed unaware of their existence. In the south there were Gothic ones, like those built by the Cistercians in the purest French tradition at Fossanova and Casamari, but Rome viewed them with the same indifference. The Dominicans of Florence built a rather gloomy Gothic church – Santa Maria sopra Minerva – in the city itself, but once again the Romans were not attracted. Nothing but the basilica accorded with their genius.

These Roman basilicas, in the 12th and 13th centuries, were sumptuously adorned. Figured mosaics, long abandoned, were used once more to enrich the apses. Another kind of mosaic, consisting of patterns in coloured marble flecked with gold, gave a novel charm to choir-enclosures and pulpits. All these works are collectively attributed – for the convenience of guides – to the Cosmati family.[1] The two cloisters of St. John Lateran and St. Paul-outside-the-Walls, whose little columns are encrusted with golden stars and polychrome marbles, delicate and precious as jewellery, are the masterpieces of 13th-century Rome (90–93).

The Middle Ages survive in Rome only in the form of churches, but the age of feudalism has lived on in the abandoned settlement of Ninfa and the old towns of Viterbo and Anagni, to which the popes so often retired. It lives on too in the Latian plains and mountains: how often do we meet a tall square tower out in the country, among the farms it defended (12). Sometimes a massive fortress stands on a height dominating the village. Sermoneta, with its high keep, its two drawbridges, its church-bell to announce the traveller's arrival, suggests an Arthurian castle (17). From the formidable towers of Bracciano we overlook a Galilean landscape – a lovely blue lake surrounded with vineyards and olive groves, where the fishermen's nets hang out to dry. The little hill-towns remain just as they were at the close of the Middle Ages, with their steep streets climbing up to the church or castle, their old houses and one or two palazzi, their heavy nail-studded doors. The air is pure, the outlook immense – over endless stony plains where the almond-trees blossom – and we feel the spiritu-

[[1] The same may be said of the splendid church pavements in polychrome marbles, also of the 12th and 13th centuries, which are described in Chapter 10. The art of the Roman *marmorari* was introduced into Britain, for Henry III summoned several of them to Westminster about 1270, to work on the shrine of Edward the Confessor and Henry's own tomb. See Edward Hutton, *The Cosmati*, 1950.]

ality of the high places, which are nearest heaven. It is not to be wondered at that mystics have been born in the hill-towns of Italy.

The Renaissance, which from the earliest years of the 15th century gave such charm to Florence, appeared much later in Rome. During the popes' residence at Avignon and during the dark years of the Great Schism the city seemed to be reverting to barbarism. When Martin V arrived there he found some of the old basilicas in a state of collapse, churches roofless, roads impassable; and wolves invaded the Vatican gardens at night. The popes had to be content with making repairs instead of building anything new. Good work of the 15th century is rare in Rome and does not strike the eye, but has to be looked for. Among the churches, and at the Vatican, there are a bronze door, some delightful frescoes, some stately tombs. The Palazzo della Cancelleria revealed to the Romans, in the last years of the 15th century, the virtues of Florentine architecture: simplicity, symmetry, studied proportions – all those new ideals of the Renaissance – were quietly manifest in this building. Still today the façade of the palazzo, irregularly darkened through weathering and somewhat blemished by subsequent additions, enables us to visualise its pristine beauty. The rhythmic ordering of the pilasters, the marble surrounds of the windows, the profile of the basement mouldings, all show a delicacy reminiscent of Greek art, while the two-storeyed arcades of the inner court have a truly Florentine grace. In these things Rome recognised her old ideal.

Rome's *beau siècle* was (in spite of the sack of the town in 1527) the 16th. For the first time in history men were fully conscious of the majesty of the ancient world, and Roman ruins came to be regarded as instructive. In Rome the genius of the greatest artists was still developing. Without Rome neither Bramante nor Michelangelo nor Raphael would have been what they were; Rome gave them the ambition and the courage to create a new world inspired by the world of the ancients, and to equal it.

Even the traveller with but a few hours to spend in Rome could, in this short time, admire the best that the Renaissance created there and at the same time understand how these great works came into being. Setting out from the Colosseum, he should notice the columns associated with each of its great piers, and the manner in which the orders become richer from storey to storey (Doric below, next Ionic, and Corinthian at the top) (1). Farther on he will meet the same applied columns, the same superposed orders, in the splendid court of the Palazzo Farnese. From the Colosseum he should pass on to the neighbouring basilica of Constantine (5). Gazing at those tremendous vaults, the visitor may conjure up in his mind that even bigger one which has collapsed, concluding that man never spanned the void with such audacity; yet what he sees at St. Peter's is vaster still. Proceeding by way of the Pantheon, he will be astonished at the magnificent proportions of this domed rotunda (8, 9); this again he will find repeated at St. Peter's, but raised up aloft on giant arches.

When our visitor enters St. Peter's he will understand Bramante's assertion 'I shall raise the dome of the Pantheon upon the vaults of Constantine's basilica'. This tremendous dream has been realised. At St. Peter's the antique world is brought to life again, and it was never so splendid. Antiquity would have recognised, in this vast building, its masterpiece. These vaults, almost equalling the giddy heights of the loftiest Gothic cathedrals, but far broader, do not express the urge towards the infinite, but rather security through strength. Under these vaults the pope appears in the majesty of the Caesars. There he receives the world. St. Peter's is not so much a church as the forum of Christendom. On the great feast-days it is an experience to see the vast multitude, gathered from all the corners of the earth, thronging nave and aisles and transept, acclaiming the Holy Father raised up on his *sedia*, while a burst of singing fills the air and the silver trumpets ring out from the heights. This unique interior matches the magnificence of the ceremonial enacted there, but the exterior of St. Peter's matches, in its majestic scale, the Eternal City itself (18). The superb cupola, rising splendidly in perfect curves above Michelangelo's apse, is higher than the seven hills; it comes into view long before one arrives in Rome and is the symbol of the city. Sometimes, when all Rome is in deep shadow, it rises in sunlit brilliance from the gloom, shining white like an apparition.

The traveller we are accompanying will still have an hour at his disposal to enjoy the two highest achievements of the Renaissance: the ceiling of the Sistine Chapel by Michelangelo and Raphael's Stanza della Segnatura.

From the paintings of the Sistine ceiling he will remember one great prevailing theme – man's age-long expectation. From age to age suffering humanity renews its hope and calls for the Redeemer; prophets and sybils, sublime in their sadness, their enthusiasm or their visionary dreaming, catch glimpses of him through the mist of times to come. Two frescoes, the creation of man and the creation of woman, will impress themselves deeply on our visitor's mind. Adam, beautiful as the hero who reclines in the pediment of the Parthenon, has not yet received the gift of the soul; the Lord as he passes by touches with his finger the finger of Adam and lights the divine spark within him. The man, wakened to thought, looks round at his creator in gratitude. Farther on we find him again, wrapped in profound slumber, while the Lord has approached to raise up Woman from his side. She is born in the attitude of prayer; inclined a little forward, she seems the embodiment of tenderness, of submission and of love; all womanly graces are united in her. God contemplates the supreme masterpiece of his creative thought gravely and sadly; in this Eve, so beautiful and as yet so pure, he foresees all the drama of the Fall and of the Redemption. Of all the poets and artists, Michelangelo is the only one who attained to the splendour of the Book of Genesis.

How will the young Raphael stand up to the presence, at such close quarters, of this inspired artist? He does so triumphantly. How this youth of twenty-five could carry within him a world so vast and so harmonious is indeed a mystery. In the Stanza della Segnatura he has captured all the genius of the Renaissance; and his pictures affirm that the poetry, the science and the philosophy of the ancients were, at least in some measure, divinely illumined. In his *School of Athens* he has brought together all the wise men and all the philosophers of

Greece under the imposing vaults of a temple, which is the temple of thought. In the middle is Plato (to whom he gave the features of Leonardo da Vinci in his old age), pointing with uplifted finger to the sky of ideas, while Aristotle, with his open hand, grasps the realities of this world.

Opposite, the *Disputation on the Holy Sacrament* reveals to us with perfect clarity those things which the ancients had but obscurely glimpsed. The skies open and the Trinity appears surrounded by the prophets, the apostles and the martyrs. On the earth below the Fathers and the Doctors of the Church, grouped around the altar and the Host, are studying, calm and confident in their conviction or impelled by love, the mystery of a God who gave himself to man. Interpreting the great popes of the Renaissance, Raphael sees in Greek thought a preparation for the Gospel, so reconciling Christianity with the philosophy of the ancient world. No grander work than this was ever conceived.

Thus, the traveller who made his way from the Colosseum to St. Peter's by way of Constantine's Basilica and the Pantheon, who visited the Sistine Chapel and the best of Raphael's *stanze*, has seen, in a day, the finest things in Rome. He will have learnt, at the same time, what the Renaissance was: it was Antiquity ennobled by the Christian faith.

In Renaissance times a new sort of church appeared in Rome which was to persist for two hundred years. The Gesù is the perfect example of the type. Its simplified interior has an aisleless nave bordered with chapels; it is provided with transepts and a large apse, and a cupola rises over the crossing. In order to combat Protestantism more effectively by word of mouth, Rome abandoned the colonnaded basilica in favour of the spacious vaulted hall where all could listen to the priest in his pulpit, as he refuted heresy and affirmed the faith. The Jesuits, champions of orthodoxy, built churches similar to the Gesù in every Catholic country. Rome, henceforth, knew no other type at all. But the simplicity of the interior plan was compensated by the magnificence of the decoration, carried out in gilt and coloured marble, while brilliant frescoes in the main vault gave the illusion, at times, that the church was open to the sky. The façades, at first sober and restful with plain pilasters, were enriched in the Baroque era with curved and broken pediments, with pediments of varying form fitted one inside the other, with columns now thrust forward, now drawn back, producing variegated effects of light and shade (19, 21). Movement becomes the guiding principle. Curves take the place of straight lines; string courses marking the storeys of the façade undulate over concave and convex surfaces. Bell-towers fall out of favour while cupolas, all inspired by St. Peter's, appear in their stead; Rome, henceforth, becomes a city of domes, as she had been a city of towers in the Middle Ages.

These 17th- and 18th-century churches are numberless. They include churches of the various catholic nations, of the religious orders, or corporations, of certain Italian cities. No two of their façades are quite the same and it is a pleasure to study their individual subtleties – all ingenious variations on the same theme. These churches which we meet in every street and every square give Rome its own peculiar character, and where we find no church, at least there will be an image of the Madonna at the street-corner. Memories of the saints surround us everywhere, for some of the greatest came to Rome and lived there. Innumerable church-bells answer each other among the roof-tops; the very air we breathe has a spiritual savour; Rome still remains a holy city.

While churches were increasingly embellished, the *palazzi*, however magnificent inside, retained a severe exterior. In Rome the heavy barring of their ground-floor windows was never given up. The beauty of their façades is due only to just proportions, to a rich cornice, to the imposing pillared entrance-doorway surmounted by an elegant, balustraded balcony.

Rome today is still the city of the 17th- and 18th-century popes, the city of Bernini and Borromini. A stroll in the old streets is a never-failing delight. Through an open doorway we catch a glimpse of some antique statue, or a graceful fountain playing, on the far side of an inner court-yard. On one façade we notice, in faded monochrome, painted scenes from the history of Rome. On another an image of the Madonna, supported by angels, has a little lamp burning continually before it. A neighbouring terrace wall is adorned with a handsome row of terracotta vessels full of growing flowers; above it a high and breezy loggia, for sitting out on summer evenings, stands silhouetted against the sky. Next we come upon a pontifical inscription in classical Latin, surmounted by the tiara and by St. Peter's Keys, bound with floating ribands. Inscriptions in Rome are always pleasing, and sometimes they are touching. Over the entrance to the Hospital of San Gallicano we read 'Benedict XIII to the abandoned ones, to those who are spurned by all'. In the cloister of San Giovanni Decollato (John the Baptist Beheaded), over the common grave of decapitated criminals, these words of pious compassion are inscribed: 'Lord, when thou shalt come in judgment, condemn them not.'

At every turn, the distant past is manifest. A round-arched doorway with rusticated voussoirs hardly differs from one in the Forum of Augustus. The yellow ochre and red ochre of the houses are the colours of Pompeii. Again as at Pompeii, the little windowless shops receive their light only through the door, and their scales are those of the Naples museum. The roofing tiles – arched tiles fitting down over flat ones with raised edges – closely resemble those which have been recovered under the Vesuvian ash.

The fountains of the city are almost as numerous as they were in the days of the nineteen aqueducts. These fountains, so brilliant by day, are no less beautiful for their music at night. Every one of them is distinguished for its fantasy or its grace, while some are even magnificent. The fountain of Paul V on the Janiculum is a triumphal arch of five openings through which five rivers flow. The Trevi fountain is Neptune's palace; the god is issuing from it to be carried away over the waters by his amphibious steeds. The two fountains in front of St. Peter's, near Bernini's great colonnades, have their tall jets dissolved into luminous vapour and wafted away by the wind.

Delightful as ever are the great villas, the creation of that highly cultivated aristocracy whose imagination was unfettered, whose taste impeccable. Rivalling the patricians of the

Imperial age, the great cardinals sought to combine the beauties of nature with the beauties of art; the Villa Borghese is at once a splendid park and a gallery of masterpieces. The Villa Medici, with its Palladian portico, its façade adorned with antique reliefs, its surrounding pine-trees and wide view of Rome, is one of those lovely spots where no base thoughts can afflict the mind. The Villa Celimontana offers not only the attraction of its high box hedges and ancient avenue of evergreen oaks but also an outlook over old Rome. Nothing in this extensive view recalls the present: giant ruins and old towers rise isolated among the wooded parks and gardens, which extend to the Scipios' tombs and the Aurelian wall.

Tivoli and Frascati have succeeded Tibur and Tusculum, and the villas of cardinals and aristocrats have replaced those of the Roman consuls. The Villa d'Este at Tivoli is simply a spacious summer residence overlooking its terraces and gardens which are laid out on the hill-side below. Here the waters of the Anio, artfully disciplined, are thrown up in innumerable jets, or fall gracefully into pools and basins surrounded with statuary. The Villa Aldobrandini at Frascati and its nymphaeum adorned with statues of the Olympic gods recalls the villas of antiquity. The Villa Falconieri, also at Frascati, is a picture of contentment and well-being. Here the members of the family, painted on the make-believe balcony of the great hall, lean over smilingly to welcome the visitor, and one of the rooms, freshened by its own fountain, has an open-air scene frescoed round the walls. In the gardens a small sheet of water, bordered with ancient cypresses, suggests a Persian landscape to the mind.[1]

To the north, on the slopes of the Monti Cimini, the country mansion of Caprarola was built by the Farnese in accordance with that taste for magnificence which was the hallmark of the family. This stately, five-sided palazzo is a work of Vignola's, but the somewhat unkempt garden, the rustic grottoes and fountains and the view of Monte Soratte transform its stateliness into something delightfully picturesque.

The Rome of today is no longer the Rome of Poussin and Claude Lorraine. This unique city used to captivate artists not only by its masterpieces of art but by an irresistible charm which took possession of the heart. When far away from Rome they felt as exiles feel. Nowhere else could they find the same mixture of poverty and splendour, of nature and art, of radiant light and melancholy. Rome has become one of the great European capitals, with its enormous ministries, its model hospitals, its stadia, its laboratories. Broad avenues have displaced old inhabited quarters and new quarters have come into being which double the extent of the old city. This modern Rome is still governed by tradition, by a sense of proportion and by good taste. Attractive villas painted in pale shades and tall houses from which the arch and column are not excluded perpetuate – while adapting them to present-day needs – the arts of earlier centuries. The town has become modern while remaining

[[1] This and the other villas of Frascati suffered fearful damage from war-time bombing (1943–44) but have now (1959) been to a large extent repaired.]

classical. It must be added, however, that our contemporary architecture has appeared in all its starkness in the last few years and is beginning to rob the town of that unity to which it owed such beauty and such dignity. The Vatican City too has erected, behind Michelangelo's apse, its great blocks, its seminaries and its Ionic railway-station. During five short years Rome has seen more change than in two centuries.[1]

Nor is the Roman campagna any longer the stupendous wilderness that Chateaubriand described. Suburbs sprawl along the ancient roads; airfields and reinforced-concrete factories have made their appearance; the grandstands of a race-course rise up near the tombs of the Via Latina; electric pylons – those trees of steel – make avenues across the countryside. The outline of the Alban hills is as beautiful as ever and, following the Appian Way, we can still recapture something of the loneliness, the silence and the poetry of the empty spaces. But elsewhere we find cultivated fields and, as time goes on, ever more and more houses. Perhaps the campagna will soon have returned to its aspect under the Empire, when it resembled a great garden dotted with villas. When that day comes, one of the beauties of the world will have vanished.

The great undertaking of the 1930s was the draining of the Pontine marshes. Canals have taken the place of the stagnant waters in which water-buffaloes used to wallow; crops have supplanted the *maquis*. The round shepherds' huts, just like those of the Volscians, are fast disappearing, while brightly coloured farmhouses spring up along the roads. When the sky is overcast these slow-flowing canals in the endless plain and the sea on the horizon awake memories of Holland. New towns have been born in these lands reclaimed from the marsh and the malaria – towns without a history, built in accordance with the latest architectural notions.

Thus everything renews itself in Rome and around Rome. Let us hope that the city of today will have enough respect for its past to leave something of its ancient character intact.

[[1] Mâle saw only the beginnings of Rome's accelerated expansion. Unreconcilable to the new architecture of the age, nostalgically devoted to old Rome, he would have been deeply distressed to witness the mad multiplication of tall blocks in the green spaces within and without the city during the years since World War II. The basic reason is easily stated: Rome's population has doubled between 1930 and 1958.]

CHAPTER ONE

The Catacombs of Domitilla and St. Petronilla's Chapels

[THE FIRST CENTURIES]

WHEN WE leave St. Paul's-outside-the-Walls and make for Saint Sebastian's church on the Appian Way we follow the ancient pilgrimage route known as the Road of the Seven Churches. It was used by pilgrims doing the round of the seven major basilicas of Rome. The modern town has already invaded the neighbourhood of St. Paul's but, following the old road, we are in open country again,[1] and it has a melancholy look, no matter how bright the sky. This is the region of the old Christian cemeteries. Soon we come to a modern building, classical in style, which marks the entrance to the catacombs of Domitilla, explored by G. B. De Rossi in the 1870s. Who was this Domitilla who gave her name to a Christian cemetery? She was none other than the grand-daughter of Vespasian, while her husband, the consul Clemens, was his nephew (and therefore cousin to his sons Titus and Domitian).

It had long been conjectured, on the basis of certain passages from Tacitus, Suetonius and Dio Cassius, that Christianity had made some headway among the great Roman families as early as the 1st century. But it was De Rossi who, as the result of his excavations in the various Roman catacombs, established the fact beyond doubt.

Tacitus relates that Pomponia Graecina (wife of the consul Aulus Plautius, conqueror of the Bretons) was suspected of belonging to some foreign sect because of her austerity, her sadness and the mourning clothes she wore. Now, De Rossi discovered a Greek inscription in the catacombs of Calixtus which included the name of Pomponius Graecinus, a member of her family. There was therefore every reason to suppose that Pomponia Graecina had been a Christian.

Dio Cassius and Suetonius tell us that Domitian put to death a member of the old Roman nobility, the consul Acilius Glabrio, for being guilty of atheism – that is to say, infidelity to the gods of Rome. And here again one of De Rossi's finds confirmed the story: he came

[[1] Since this chapter was written almost the whole of the Via delle Sette Chiese has lost its character through urban developments, and the section passing the catacombs of Domitilla is now (1959) threatened. The few hundred yards between the crossing of the Via Ardeatine and San Sebastiano remain rural.]

across the crypt of Acilius Glabrio's family in one of the oldest galleries of St. Priscilla's catacomb on the Via Salaria.

What exciting discoveries! We see that there were already Christians among the Roman patrician families but a few years after the death of Peter and Paul, while St. John was still alive. The Acilii Glabriones, descendants of this same Acilius Glabrio to whom a gilded statue was first set up in Rome after his victory over Antiochus at Thermopylae, and later referred to by Pertinax as 'the noblest of Romans', no longer burnt incense to their household gods. They had turned from the worship of the god of Rome, had given up building great tombs along the roads issuing from the city, and rested instead in subterranean crypts not far from the freedmen and the slaves. The Pomponii, disowning their ancestor, the sceptic Atticus, now had a faith, and something to hope for.

But it is still more extraordinary to see Christianity penetrating the imperial family itself. When St. Paul, in the epistles, greeted those 'that are of Caesar's household' he was probably addressing freedmen and slaves. Yet thirty years after his death Caesar's cousin, Flavius Clemens, was Christian, as was his wife Flavia Domitilla and his two sons, educated by Quintilian. Accused by Domitian of atheism, Flavius Clemens was condemned to death and Domitilla banished to the island of Pandataria (now Ventotene). So these Flavians who had rebuilt the temple of Jupiter Capitolinus and destroyed the Temple of Jerusalem, now rejected Jupiter and accepted the Word that came from Jerusalem. If only we could know through whom they received the new message! What persuasive power these luminous spirits must have wielded, to triumph over Roman tradition and Roman pride. The imagination seizes upon any possible clue to the secret of these early conversions. It may be a significant fact, for instance, that Flavius Sabinus, the uncle of Flavius Clemens, was Prefect of Rome at the time when Nero turned the Christians into living torches to light up his gardens. Flavius Sabinus was said to have a horror of blood, and one wonders if he may not have been drawn to the new religion by the courage of Nero's victims.

When these scions of the old Roman families attended service among the other worshippers, they listened with respect to words which would have made their ancestors' flesh creep. The priest would read from St. Paul's epistles, already sanctified by the approval of the Church, and thus admonish the Romans who had fought so furiously for office: 'Mind not high things, but condescend to men of low estate.' To those who used to treat their servants so harshly he would read: 'Masters, give unto your servants that which is just and equal; knowing that ye also have a Master in heaven.' To those proconsuls who had governed the subject peoples with such arrogance, convinced that the Romans were a higher form of life: 'there is neither Greek nor Jew . . . barbarian, Scythian, bond nor free: but Christ is all, and in all'.

This astonishing metamorphosis, undergone at that time by some souls of the élite, was one of the miracles of early Christianity; it happened slowly because for some time the Roman aristocracy was only aware of the new religion through uninformed rumour, sometimes not unmixed with calumny. Tacitus, contemporary of the first converts, wrote of Christianity as 'an execrable superstition'. Flavius Clemens and Acilius Glabrio knew better. We may suppose that they had vainly sought the assurance of immortality among the philosophers and the oracles, when the successors of the apostles showed them what they had been seeking in the person of Jesus Christ, who overcame death. They believed, and, in the words of Peter's second epistle, the day-star arose in their hearts.

Some of the Flavians were subject to a sort of religious disquiet which rendered them susceptible to all ideas emanating from Judea. Vespasian, before the siege of Jerusalem, had consulted the mysterious oracle of Mount Carmel.[1] Titus had lived among Jews; he had received the Jew Josephus, author of a history of his people, in the intimacy of his home; and he had loved a Jewess, the irresistible Berenice. It was believed that he had wished to save the temple of Jerusalem, which his soldiers destroyed against his orders. The Flavians could not have been ignorant either of the Jews' single God, or of their messianic hopes, and one can understand that some of them were ready to accept Christianity.

Among the converts of the Flavian family there was, besides Flavius Clemens and Domitilla, a girl named Petronilla described in an inscription as a martyr. Her name is a feminine diminutive of Petro and she was descended from Titus Flavius Petro, Vespasian's grandfather. This is why she was buried in the catacombs of Domitilla, which were those of her family.

In this antique cemetery of Domitilla the visitor first passes through a vestibule of the end of the 1st century, whence a passage leads down into the depths (22). Frescoes are visible which at first sight recall those of Pompeian houses, depicting little genii playing among the branches of a vine, and Psyche, with a butterfly's wings, picking flowers accompanied by Eros. Looking more attentively, however, one notices doves, sheep and bowls of milk – symbols of the new religion. The name of the Flavians has been found in inscriptions near by; one of them relates to a certain Flavius Sabinus who may have been the grandson of the prefect of Rome under Nero.

Soon we reach, among the network of galleries, a spacious basilica (24) built in the 4th century, after the age of persecutions.[2] It was dedicated to two soldier-martyrs, Nereus and Achilleus, whose tombs were venerated here. Another tomb attracted the prayers of the faithful – that of Petronilla, who is commemorated in a little chapel not far from the basilica. The chapel contains a curious fresco showing a young saint, identified by the inscription as *Petronella mart.*, leading into heaven another Christian named *Veneranda*; a few

[1] The Carmelites, who claimed that their origins went back to Elijah and the hermits of Mount Carmel, used to relate that Titus also went to the holy mountain to consult the head of their community. The future emperor had had a vision there: God showed his Son done to death by the Jews and told him that in destroying Jerusalem he would punish the faithless city for its crime. Gaspard Dughet, Possin's brother-in-law, represented this subject in Rome in one of the frescoes at San Martino ai Monti, the church of the Carmelites. This legend shows that the Carmelites felt there was a religious atmosphere associated with the Flavians.

[[2] The basilica is now approached direct by a stairway leading down from the entrance lobby.]

flowers represent Paradise – the garden of eternity (23). Veneranda has the outstretched arms of the *orans* or praying figure, which means, in the language of the earliest Christian art, that she is now but a soul released from the bonds of the body. Close by, in a round box, she has some scrolls – the sacred scripture which opened for her the way to heaven.

Petronella (always spelt Petronilla in the texts) was venerated in this underground basilica quite as much as Nereus and Achilleus, for the old pilgrims' guides associate her name with theirs. Unfortunately no information about Petronilla has come down to us from the earliest centuries and her real history is unknown. In the 6th century a legend was created for her. The author of this little romance, imagining that Petronilla was the feminine diminutive of Petrus, made the young saint a daughter of St. Peter. A Roman count called Flaccus, enchanted by her beauty, asks her to marry him, but the girl, who has vowed to consecrate her life to God, refuses. The count threatens to have her put to death as a Christian unless, within three days, she agrees to his proposal. Petronilla prays and fasts to gain strength in her resolve. At the end of the third day God, wishing to spare her the martyrdom which she has already accepted in her heart, calls her to himself. Count Flaccus can do no more than attend her funeral.

This tale, which is quite out of keeping with the Rome of the Caesars, or the age of the persecutions, was accepted as authentic. Thenceforth Petronilla was called St. Peter's daughter, and pilgrims were assured that the inscription they read on her tomb, *Aureliae Petronillae filiae dulcissimae*, had been cut by St. Peter himself.

The saint lay for several centuries in the catacombs of Domitilla. Pious visitors to Rome, guided by the 'itineraries', a few of which have been preserved, did not fail to descend to the chapel and to carry away a little oil from the lamps burning before her tomb. One of the famous ampullae of Monza contained some of this oil. On certain days the popes used to come and say mass in the subterranean basilica. It was there that St. Gregory the Great, seated on his marble throne in the apse, delivered one of his anguished sermons in which he spoke of the barbarians devastating Italy and approaching Rome, the defenceless city. 'Rome' said he on another occasion, with prophetic eloquence 'is an old bald eagle; once she flung herself at any prey, but now she has lost the feathers from her wings.' The great pope seems to be declaiming, among the tombs, the funeral oration of the Eternal City.

The sarcophagus of St. Petronilla remained in Domitilla's catacomb until the 8th century, when it was moved to St. Peter's. Strange to say, the transfer of St. Petronilla's relics is associated with one of the great events in the history of the papacy and the history of France.

In 753 Pope Stephen III was threatened by the Lombards. Their king, Astolph, wanted to complete the conquest of central Italy, take Rome and make it his capital. The pope, convinced that nothing could be expected from the eastern emperors, crossed the Alps and sought help and protection from Pepin the Short. The king sent his eldest son Charles, the future Charlemagne, to meet the pope, and afterwards received him himself with the deepest respect; it was then that a monarch was seen, for the first time in history, walking like an equerry beside the pope's horse. Pepin promised his support and he kept his promise. He led two victorious expeditions into Italy and took away part of Astolph's conquests, making them over as a gift to the pope. In order to ensure the independence of the papacy for the future, he created the Papal State, which was to last for more than a thousand years.

A 16th-century fresco in the Sala Regia at the Vatican shows Pepin advancing in triumph, clothed like a Roman emperor, but wearing the crown of the French king with its upstanding *fleurs de lis*. In front of him Astolph, with the simple iron crown of the Lombard kings on his head, walks in the abject attitude of the defeated. A young warrior carries a gold statuette on a tray: this is the personification of the Papal States, offered by the conqueror to the pope. Thus in the 16th century the papacy still expressed its gratitude to the Frankish king who had come so chivalrously to the rescue of the Church. But it had expressed this gratitude, in another way, ever since the 8th century.

Stephen III, while at Saint-Denis, had named Petronilla as Pepin the Short's patron saint and promised to transfer her relics from the catacombs to a chapel at St. Peter's, which would become the chapel of the kings of France. At first sight the choice of St. Petronilla seems extraordinary and the old chroniclers do not explain it. But we can guess the reason. In defending the pope and in giving him a realm, Pepin the Short had made himself the son of the Church, the son of St. Peter. In a letter which Stephen III had sent him (and which St. Peter himself was reputed to have written), the statement was put in St. Peter's mouth that Pepin and the two young princes, Charles and Carloman, were his 'adopted sons'. So it seemed natural that Petronilla, St. Peter's 'daughter', should become the patroness of the Frankish kings, who in a sense were now members of her family. A sister had, as it were, become the protectress of her brothers.

Pope Stephen III died too soon to keep his promise, but one of the first acts of his successor Paul I was to transport St. Petronilla's sarcophagus to St. Peter's. It was not placed in the church iself but in a neighbouring monument. To the left of the basilica there were two mausolea, built as their burial-place for the family of Theodosius; they were round, like the tombs of Hadrian and Augustus, but not of such colossal size. The family of Theodosius, which had given hope of a great future, left these two monuments almost empty. One of them, however, housed the tomb of the Empress Maria, wife of Honorius; and it was here that the sarcophagus of Petronilla was placed. The other mausoleum had also been converted into a chapel and was dedicated to St. Andrew. The fact that St. Andrew and St. Petronilla were thus brought near to each other enables us to guess what was in the pope's mind. Andrew was Peter's brother, and Petronilla was believed to be his daughter; so we see it was a sensitive and appropriate act to reunite, close to the apostle, those who had been dear to him in life. The two mausolea had been connected with each other and with the basilica by a covered passage-way so that pilgrims, after doing homage at St. Peter's tomb, could go and pray in the chapels of St. Andrew and St. Petronilla.

This spacious chapel of St. Petronilla was bare and austere, as befits a tomb, but the popes embellished it. Paul I gave it a set of frescoes, still extant in the 15th century, which related the history of Constantine. The idea behind these frescoes was an ingenious one: Pepin, defender and benefactor of the Church, was represented as a new Constantine. In decorating the chapel of the Frankish kings with the story of the first Christian emperor, the pope evidently wished to associate their names, and their glory.

But it was Leo III more than any other pope who enriched St. Petronilla's chapel. He wanted to make it worthy of Charlemagne, who found something new in it on each of his journeys to Rome. We catch glimpses of its magnificence through the obscure Latin of the *Liber Pontificalis*, the old history of the popes. The chapel was faced with marble, and six silver columns rose near the altar. Over the altar stood a ciborium with columns of gold and porphyry. A golden crown, set with precious stones, hung here: it symbolised the saint's triumph in the life to come. Stuffs of white, pink or purple silk, decorated with raised gold ornaments and scenes from the gospel, were draped turn about over the altar. But soon this splendid decoration came to be thought insufficient, and the entire altar was ensheathed in silver, gilded and encrusted with enamels. In this way the pope showed that he was not forgetting St. Petronilla's chapel, symbol of the alliance between the papacy and the kings of the Franks. Charlemagne did not fail to attend mass here whenever he came to Rome. The great emperor took immense pleasure in these journeys. In one of his letters he invited Alcuin to accompany him and 'to exchange the smoky roofs of Tours for the gilded roofs of Rome'.

This splendid adornment of St. Petronilla's chapel, on which the popes had lavished their best efforts, lasted no more than half a century. In August, 846, the Arabs from Sicily, landing at Ostia, marched up to Rome and, having easily overcome some improvised resistance, entered St. Peter's. In a few hours they stripped the basilica of the treasures accumulated there during five hundred years and, loaded with this rich booty, withdrew. Since the capture of Jerusalem Christendom had suffered no such cruel insult from the infidels. A wave of distress must have swept the West, and the medieval epics of a much later day still preserve the memory of this humiliation. Thoughts of a holy war were already becoming urgent in men's minds.

Pope Leo IV, with admirable constancy, laboured to repair the disaster. Having surrounded the Vatican with walls to render it impregnable, he started to redecorate the basilica. He replaced the silver facings of doors and altars, the golden crowns, the silver-encased icons, the hangings embroidered with pearls. The *Liber Pontificalis* refers continually to his largesse. These gifts were so many and so munificent that we may perhaps assume the participation in them of the Christian peoples.

St. Petronilla's chapel, with its gold ciborium and silver columns, had not been spared by the infidels. Nor was it possible to recover its former beauty. The pope was content to cover its walls with a dozen great hangings, while the altar, despoiled of its precious facing, was enveloped in a magnificent cloth, on which eagles alternated with crosses inscribed in circles of gold.

This is the last time that the papal history speaks of St. Petronilla's chapel; centuries of silence follow. But silence does not necessarily imply oblivion. The worship of the Roman martyr had become widespread in France, as is proved by the fact that her name was sometimes used in feudal families; in the 12th century, for instance, the abbesses of Fontevrault and of Aubeterre in Bourbonnais were both called Pétronille. This name was corrupted in the popular speech, becoming Perrine, Pernelle and Perronelle. It is probable that the French kings, though they no longer came to Rome, still remembered their protectress, and there is a most curious fact which points to this conclusion. At the time when Philip the Fair came into conflict with the papacy, the rumour spread abroad that St. Petronilla's body was no longer in Rome but had been brought to France. The precious relic was said to have been given by the queen to the Augustinian monastery of La Barre, near Château-Thierry. Thus the king who was to uproot the popes from Rome had apparently already seen fit to snatch away the saint who was the patron of the French dynasty. Petronilla had become a French saint, and it was soon possible to venerate her relics at Soissons and Compiègne.

For more than a century and a half after this we hear no more of St. Petronilla, but she was not forgotten, and her traditional cult was kept up in the royal family. Louis XI [1] had a great veneration for her, so much so that during the sickness of the dauphin, the future Charles VIII, he addressed his prayers to her. When his son recovered, the King wished to give the saint proof of his gratitude. He remembered that for seven hundred years St. Petronilla's chapel in Rome had been known as the chapel of the kings of France, and he determined to restore and beautify it. He therefore sent a considerable sum to the chapter of St. Peter's and at the same time established two chaplaincies to maintain services in the chapel.

Pope Sixtus IV was much touched by this mark of respect accorded by the French royal house to Rome, and wrote to Louis XI to thank him. He informed him, at the same time, that the sarcophagus containing the body of St. Petronilla, St. Peter's daughter, had been brought to light during the restoration. He added that the sarcophagus was adorned at its four corners with four dolphins (delphini or dauphins), which had thus foreshadowed, centuries before it came to pass, the devotion of the French dauphins to the saint. This was no more than a *jeu d'esprit*; but Louis XI learnt, from this letter, that St. Petronilla was still in Rome. Consequently, it had to be supposed that the Petronilla whose relics were worshipped in France was not the same person as the Roman virgin.

Charles VIII, who, as the royal family believed, owed his life to the saint's protection, revered her as much as his father had done. After entering Rome with his army he went, like Charlemagne before him, to attend mass at St. Peter's. Then he proceeded to St. Petronilla's chapel, where he touched for the king's evil [2] just as if he had been at Rheims.

[[1] Reigned 1461–1483.]

[[2] 'King's evil . . . Scrofula, which in England and France was formerly supposed to be curable by the king's (or queen's) touch . . . The practice of touching for the King's evil continued from the time of Edward the Confessor to the death of Queen Anne in 1714. The Office for the ceremony has not been printed in the Prayer-book since 1719'—*New English Dictionary*. The custom had existed in France at least since Merovingian times.]

Under Louis XII (1498–1515) the chapel was not neglected. A French cardinal, Jean de Bilhères Lagraulas,[1] to whom we cannot be too grateful, adorned it with a great work of art. There was then in Rome a young sculptor of twenty-three who had come from Florence and whose name was Michelangelo Buonarroti. He had already gained a certain reputation among connoisseurs from two or three statues of pagan gods he had executed, in which the art of the ancients seemed to live again. The cardinal, delighted with the precocious talent of this youth, gave him the commission for a *Pietà* to be placed in St. Petronilla's chapel. So it came about that Rome owes one of its masterpieces to a French cardinal. He wanted a Virgin similar to those he was used to in France. The austerely simple group of the Mother alone with her dead Son was certainly not unknown in Italy, but it had become elaborated there. To arrange the inanimate body of the Son on the Virgin's knees did not seem to the Italian painters and sculptors an easy problem, nor did the group in this form appeal to them. They therefore introduced additional figures: St. John to support the head of Jesus, Mary Magdalene to support the feet. Such are Perugino's *Pietà*, as well as those of Francia and Botticelli. Sometimes it is an angel that supports the upper part of Christ's body, as in the bas-relief by Giovanni della Robbia.

Michelangelo returned to the old tradition which the French artists preferred. There are many admirable examples in France, but not one has the stateliness, the architectural perfection, of Michelangelo's group, in which the Virgin and the Son form an ideal unity. Here beauty of sentiment is matched by beauty of form. The body of Christ has not the rigidity of a corpse, it retains the suppleness of life and seems to be awaiting the Resurrection. Mary, with her pure youthful features, embodies the dignity and the mystery of her virgin motherhood. Her veil throws no deep shadows on her brow, which is bathed in light. With downcast eyes and open hand she submits in gentle resignation to the divine Will. Michelangelo was taken to task for depicting a Virgin who seemed younger than her son; he answered that her purity gave her eternal youth.

Such was the great work of art with which Cardinal Bilhères Lagraulas enriched the chapel of St. Petronilla. But it did not stay there very long. In 1544, under Paul III, the works for the new St. Peter's necessitated the sacrifice of the old Theodosian mausolea. The chapel of the French kings was destroyed, but in destroying it a touching discovery was made. In a magnificent red granite sarcophagus from the valley of the Nile they found the remains of the Empress Maria, wife of Honorius and daughter of Stilicho. The body was wrapped in cloth of gold and surrounded with untold riches like a queen of Egypt. Close by the princess there were thirty vessels of gold, crystal or agate, some of them decorated with scenes in relief; along with these were a gold lamp and some little animals carved in precious stone. A miniature silver chest contained more than a hundred and fifty wonderful jewels: earrings, necklaces and rings set with pearls, sapphires or emeralds. On one gold lamella the names of the four archangels could be read – Michael, Gabriel, Raphael and Uriel; and on

[1] He had previously been called Jean Villiers de Lagroslaye; but Samaran, in the interesting study devoted to him, gave him his real name again.

another the name of the Empress Maria. There was no doubt about it; this really was the princess for whom Claudian had composed such a graceful nuptial poem. And these jewels were the very ones of which the poet speaks, brought from the depths of the sea by the Nereids, because Venus herself wanted to array the princess with them. But she hardly had time to enjoy these marvels, dying almost on the morrow of her wedding. In a century when ancient traditions still lived on in the deep places of the mind the young empress, though a Christian, was buried with all her treasures like a pagan of the early ages.

All this rich hoard has disappeared except for a golden locket preserved in the Trivulzio collection at Milan. Paul II had the jewels melted down and gave instructions that his tiara should be decorated with the gems (what strange indifference in a pope who was something of an artist and belonged to the Farnese family). However, this discovery endowed the long history of the Roman saint with new poetry, for the memory of the beautiful princess, who died so young, became associated with St. Petronilla's own romantic history.

The tomb of St. Petronilla, Michelangelo's *Pietà*, and the sepulchral slab of Cardinal de Bilhères Lagraulas, adorned with his effigy, were all accommodated in the new St. Peter's. The *Pietà* was raised on the altar of the first chapel in the right-hand aisle, the Cardinal's inscribed stone was relegated to the Grotte Vaticane (where it may still be seen), while the saint's tomb was placed in a chapel dedicated to her. The chapel is in the north transept [1] and it contains a mosaic reproduction of 'the funeral of St. Petronilla', Guercino's fine picture. It is a romantic work, in which light and shade contend. The young saint, lying dead, held up by hands rising from the darkness of the tomb, shows Count Flaccus her pale face and her brow wreathed in flowers for the last time, before disappearing for ever from human sight.

This chapel of St. Petronilla perpetuates the memory of the ancient alliance between the papacy and the kingdom of the Franks. Rome forgets nothing and every century seems to live on there. In 1889 Leo XIII had a lamp suspended above the altar, whose flame was never to go out and so would seem, in the words of the dedicatory inscription, to be praying ceaselessly for France.

Every year on her festival (May 31) a mass is said for France in St. Petronilla's chapel, and French residents in Rome are invited to attend. The ceremony is a simple one but not without beauty, while its setting, the creation of Bramante's and Michelangelo's genius, is overwhelming in its majesty.[2]

[[1] To the right of the main apse, as St. Peter's points west. It is not in the transept proper.]

[[2] The last paragraphs of this chapter have been slightly abbreviated, some details of little general interest being omitted.]

CHAPTER TWO

Where the Christians Met During the Great Persecutions

[THIRD CENTURY]

Remains at San Martino ai Monti, San Clemente, Santi Giovanni e Paolo and Santa Anastasia

DURING THE two and a half centuries of the persecutions, where was it that the Christians met for worship? According to some records and traditions they used to meet in certain private houses. According to others they were not afraid – in the East at least – to build real churches. Many of these were destroyed in Diocletian's time, but were rebuilt on a grander scale after Constantine's victory over Maxentius.

What enormous interest these earliest Christian sanctuaries would hold for us, where the faithful met for worship while awaiting torture and death! As far as was known, every one of them had disappeared, so that even to find their ruins seemed a vain hope. But now, almost simultaneously, three of these venerable churches have come to light again – one in Rome and two in the East.

The first was discovered on the confines of the Roman world, by the Euphrates. Here the fortified town of Dura-Europos stood on a promontory overlooking the river and the great plain of Mesopotamia. It was from this citadel that the twentieth cohort of Palmyran archers kept watch on the Parthians, those perennial enemies of Rome. The town, with its regular streets laid out originally by the Greeks, was situated on the edge of the Syrian desert; it was rich, standing as it did on the caravan route leading from the Persian Gulf to Palmyra and Antioch. Often as many as a thousand camels could be seen arriving from the south, laden with precious woods and gems from India, silks from China, perfumes from Arabia; an escort of horsemen protected these fabulous riches against the molestations of the nomads, camped in the wilderness in their black tents. The town maintained its prosperity as long as Rome was able to defend her frontiers; but when Persia revived and became a conquering power under the Sassanids, when Sapor invaded Syria and took the emperor Valerian prisoner, Dura had fulfilled her destiny, and the abandoned city was gradually smothered in sand by the desert winds. Some years ago the city was re-discovered under this sandy shroud. In 1923 the Palmyran archers were succeeded in Dura by French soldiers who, under the supervision of the eminent antiquaries Cumont and Rostovtzeff, began to uncover this new Pompeii. The first results, made public by Cumont in a fine volume,[1] were surprising. A temple dedicated to the gods of Palmyra was unearthed, adorned with frescoes of the 1st century A.D. which, in their hieratic immobility, foreshadow Byzantine mosaics. They also found a sanctuary of Artemis containing a Venus with the Tortoise reminiscent of a work by Phidias. Contracts written on parchment were found and deciphered, the cohort's military archives unrolled. A shield was recovered from the sand on which a soldier, transferred from the banks of the Danube, had recorded the stages of his journey. More recently a Jewish synagogue was brought to light in which the painters, forgetful of the Law, had represented some great scenes from the Bible.

The explorations continued to give excellent results and led to the remarkable and unexpected discovery of a Christian chapel, it too with frescoed decoration. Its date has been established. In 256, on the eve of Sapor's invasion, the walls of Dura were reinforced, on the inner side, by means of a massive *glacis*. The houses built against the walls were thus buried, and among them this Christian chapel was preserved. It belonged, therefore, to the heroic age of the persecutions. The thing so long desired was found at last.

This chapel does not in any way resemble a basilica; it is nothing more than a room made available to the faithful by a member of the Christian community. In general, these houses in Dura conformed to the old Greek plan, their rooms being lit from an inner court and having no windows opening on to the street. High windowless walls favoured the keeping of secrets, and secrecy had become necessary. Since the death of Septimius Severus the Christians had (except for the three years of Maximian's reign) enjoyed peace, but from the year 250 onwards the great persecutions under Decius and his successors renewed all their miseries.

Who were these Christians of Dura? Were they soldiers who had renounced Mithras for Christ, or merchants from Antioch, the first great Christian centre, or caravan-leaders evangelised by wandering apostles? We cannot tell; but what is certain is that these Christians were few, because the house and the 'chapel' are small. At one end of the latter a small canopy carried on columns possibly formed a shelter for the altar. A cycle of frescoes adorned the walls. Though clumsily executed, they are of passionate interest, being some of the very earliest Christian paintings we know. Next to Adam and Eve hiding their nakedness we see Christ carrying the lost sheep on his shoulders. Farther on, the Holy Women are making their way to the tomb carrying torches, for it is still darkest night and stars are shining in the sky. Then some miracles are depicted: the paralytic, healed by Christ, carrying away his bed; and Jesus walking on the water in the storm, stretching out his hand to St. Peter. We find also the Woman of Samaria at the well, and David, who has just slain Goliath.

What lessons did the faithful learn from these pictures? First of all they recalled the great

[[1] *Fouilles de Doura-Europos, 1922–1923.* Paris, 1926.]

truths of the new faith: the doctrine of the Fall, represented by Adam covering his nakedness; and the doctrine of the Redemption, represented by Christ carrying the lost sheep on his shoulders. Then they underlined what St. Paul had said about the Resurrection being the very basis of the new religion: 'If Christ be not risen, then is our preaching vain, and your faith is also vain.' Moreover, the frescoes showed how, through the grace of God, all things could be hoped for: he had made David's weakness triumph over the brute force of Goliath; he had held up Peter by the strength of his hand, lest he sink. Such images were calculated to sustain the heart. For centuries the scene of Christ walking on the waters and saving Peter in the storm remained, for the Church, the symbol of divine aid in times of trial. During the persecution of Decius these pages of Scripture assumed their full significance. On the border of one fresco – that of David and Goliath – two Christians of Dura wrote their names, with an invocation to God.

It has been maintained that the paintings could go back to the year 220, or even to 200, for the Holy Women wear the head-dress of the Syrian empresses of the beginning of the 3rd century. But the iconography of these frescoes is certainly not the creation of the humble artists of Dura; some of these figures, and some of their attitudes, occur again at a later date in the East and in Rome. There must therefore have been earlier originals and certain scriptural episodes already followed a fixed pattern. These facts open up new avenues of thought. We may guess that Christian art developed early in the eastern cities which the apostles had evangelised. But was it born there? Is it the creation of eastern genius, or the creation of Rome? This great question, still the subject of dispute among art-historians, presents itself today more insistently than ever. What was the origin of the models used by the painters of Dura? Did they come from Antioch, the nearest great Christian town? Perhaps the subsequent excavations undertaken by the French and Americans in that still mysterious city will eventually supply the answer. But, henceforth, one important truth can be taken for granted. We now know that, ever since the times of the persecutions, there existed not only the art of the catacombs, with its emphasis on immortality, but also, side by side with it, the art of the churches. This latter taught the truths of the faith, and kept up men's courage by assuring them of God's help.

Another church, roughly contemporary with the one at Dura, has been discovered in Rome in recent years. It was, to tell the truth, already in full view, but no one had realised its great antiquity, or understood its true character. The credit for having dated and explained it goes to a young chaplain of San Luigi dei Francesi, Father Vielliard.[1] The ruins in question, which are in part subterranean, can be seen close to the apse of San Martino ai Monti. These confusing remains were believed to be those of a church dating from the time of Pope St. Sylvester and the Peace of the Church. It was referred to in the texts under the name of *titulus Equitii*. Those old walls hung with the vegetation of ruins and those

[[1] See René Vielliard, *Les Origines du Titre de Saint-Martin au Monts à Rome*, Rome, 1931.]

sombre, crypt-like vaulted rooms made little appeal to the imagination. But their interest came back in full measure when it became known that they date, not from the century of the Peace, but from the age of the persecutions. Their walls, in fact, resemble those of the baths of Caracalla, since the bricks are of the same size and the mortar-beds the same thickness. The conclusion to be drawn is that they were built at the beginning of the 3rd century.

Father Vielliard came to the conclusion, as the result of a careful examination, that this church was simply a house containing a room used as a place of reunion by the faithful. Here, then, was one of the unpretentious churches of the era of the persecutions, coming to light again with all its poetic associations.

The *titulus Equitii* stood on the slopes of the Esquiline not far from the baths of Trajan, in an area where there may still have been remains of that great wild park where Nero – who according to Tacitus loved nothing but the extraordinary – wished to have his own forest and his own open fields in the middle of the city. The neighbouring garden of the Palazzo Brancaccio, with its great ruins, its fine trees and its delightful state of neglect, reminds one even today of Nero's park.[1] This house of Equitius differed widely from the houses of Pompeii and Herculaneum. It possessed neither *atrium* nor *tablinum* nor an interior colonnade. With its ground-floor windows, inner court and two storeys it resembled the plebeian houses of Rome and Ostia. There was nothing about it to attract attention. But, immediately after passing through the vestibule, one found oneself in a spacious vaulted hall divided by pillars into two aisles, and with room for some four hundred people. This hall is so well adapted to its purpose that it looks as if Equitius himself planned it when he had the house built. This was one of the sanctuaries in which the Christians of Rome used to meet at the time when Pope Fabian was martyred under Decius and when Pope Sixtus and his deacon Lawrence were condemned to death by Valerian (A.D. 258). The ancient hall was somewhat altered in the following centuries, but it was quite a simple matter to retrace its plan.[2]

So Rome has preserved, in the *titulus Equitii*, a church of the heroic age. The term *titulus*, followed by the name of the owner of the house, denoted those places of worship where the Christians assembled, for names of saints were not yet given to churches. If the *Liber Pontificalis* is to be trusted there were no less than twenty-five *tituli* in Rome at the time of the last persecutions. In recent years a few of them were explored methodically by a Catalan archaeologist whose eye missed little, Father Junyent. While he has not discovered any more assembly-halls of the faithful (for that of San Martino ai Monti is the only one yet known),

[1] Part of this garden, where the Rome of ruin and of solitude could still be found, has since been opened to the public and has lost its character.

[2] Unfortunately this venerable witness of the age of persecutions has recently been disfigured by clumsy restorations. [Doubt has been cast on the identification of these surviving 3rd-century buildings with the *titulus* and, assuming they were so used, on Vielliard's conclusion that they were specially built for the purpose. See Ward Perkins, 'Constantine and the Origins of the Christian Basilica', *Papers of the British School at Rome*, xxii, 1954.]

he has at least shown that there are still walls in existence of Roman houses which accommodated these primitive churches. Such were the *titulus Clementis* (San Clemente), the *titulus Byzantis* (Santi Giovanni e Paolo) and the *titulus Anastasiae* (Sant'Anastasia).[1]

At San Clemente the building in which the Christians met was separated only by a narrow lane from a pagan house where the Mithraic cult was practised, and the temple itself has been found. The rival religions were neighbours here, just as they were at the Vatican, near St. Peter's tomb. After the triumph of the Church the *titulus Clementis* was extended by an apse which encroached upon the house of Mithras, now deserted by its devotees.

At Santi Giovanni e Paolo on the Coelian the walls of the *titulus Byzantis* are visible on one side of the *clivus scauri*, that ancient Roman lane which has remained changeless in the city where all things change (27). The room used for worship, whose windows still exist, very probably occupied the combined first and second storeys of the building. The basilica which later took its place spared – by some miracle – the façade of the ancient house.[2]

Similarly there is an antique two-storeyed façade, belonging to the *titulus Anastasiae*, surviving from the times of the Severi on one side of the church of Sant'Anastasia. Here too it is probable that the two storeys were thrown together so that the assembly-room could be bigger.[3]

We see then that the archaeologists have been able to recover, and to hand back to Christian Rome, some eye-witnesses of her early history. Remains which for centuries were passed by with indifference must now once more be viewed with respect. Were these great halls of assembly decorated with frescoes like the little chapel at Dura-Europos? In the 17th century it was still possible to distinguish some Pompeian festoons, and dolphins spouting water into a fountain, at San Martino ai Monti. But were there not, apart from these purely decorative motifs, some solemn scenes in the place of honour, near the altar? There is reason to suppose that Christian art was already beginning to blossom forth on the walls of the *tituli* during the persecutions, and the evidence comes from certain unusual subjects found among the paintings in the catacombs. In one of the crypts of St. Domitilla's catacomb a fresco, probably of the 3rd century, shows Jesus Christ seated on a throne and accompanied, to right and left, by the apostles. It is surprising to come across this monu-

[1] E. Junyent, *Il Titolo di San Clemente in Roma*, 1932.

[[2] Any statements about the upper storeys of this building must be conjectural. But it is surprising that Mâle omits to mention the ground-floor rooms of the Christian *domus* which still survive, with much of their fresco-decoration and ample evidence of the cult of the martyrs, under the floor of the church. This early sanctuary, brought to light by Father Germanus of the Passionist community in 1887, was deliberately left intact (as far as this was possible) when the great basilica was constructed above it at the end of the 4th century. For further information see A. Prandi, *S.S. Giovanni e Paolo*, Marietti, Rome, 1958 (Italian and English editions). In this useful illustrated booklet a description will also be found of the restorations undertaken in 1948–52, which revealed most interesting features of the original basilica.]

[3] The latter *titulus* probably had a different name originally. Anastasia seems to have been the name of the Roman lady who had a basilica constructed in the hall.

mental work, so different in spirit from the usual paintings of the catacombs; it seems to anticipate the apse-mosaics of the basilicas, and one thinks, in particular, of Santa Pudenziana. It is probable, indeed, that this fresco in the catacombs of Domitilla is merely an imitation of those which once existed in the *tituli*. Such solemn subjects were more appropriate to the church than to the catacombs, where, as a rule, the subjects illustrated are the Lord's compassion and the promise of immortality.

When one finds in the catacombs (and at a later period on sarcophagi) Christ handing the scroll of the Law to St. Peter, one wonders whether such a scene could have been born anywhere but in those early Christian places of assembly that were used for baptisms. For it was there that the catechumen was initiated into the new doctrine and, like St. Peter, received the law.[1] So it is probable that, in Rome as in the East, there was a tradition of painting for the halls above ground, and another tradition for the catacombs, whose respective ranges of subject were not quite the same.

We have seen that neither the written records nor the oral tradition were at fault. The fact is now well established that, before the Peace of the Church, the Christians met together in houses which were made available to the community by certain of its own members. But these were modest dwelling-places, similar to those of the people and entirely different from the palatial colonnaded mansions of the patricians. It is therefore no longer possible to derive the Christian basilica – as certain scholars attempted to do some years ago – from antique houses of the Pompeian type. According to that ingenious theory, the colonnade of the basilica derived from the inner colonnade of the house where the community assembled; the *tablinum* where the master of the house sat became the apse where the priest sat, and the *alae* projecting on either side of the *tablinum* became the transepts. However, neither the house at Dura nor that at San Martino ai Monti show anything of the kind. The truth, amply demonstrated by Gabriel Leroux,[2] is that the Christian basilica was an imitation of those pagan basilicas in which the devotees of oriental cults used to meet. The sanctuary of Samothrace and the Baccheion of Athens are, though pre-Christian, real Christian basilicas. Constantine's architects had no need, therefore, to invent the two-aisled basilican church, adapting the old Roman house; it existed already, and they only had to copy it, while making it more magnificent and more worthy of the new religion.[3]

It will be seen what a crop of new ideas these exceptionally interesting discoveries have

[1] See on this subject the interesting article by Monsignor Kirsch in *Rivista di Archeologia Cristiana*, 1927.

[2] A young member of the French School at Athens, killed during the war of 1914–18.

[[3] Excellent discussions of the origin and later history of the Christian basilica may be found in the following: Ward Perkins, 'Constantine and the Origins of the Christian Basilica', *Papers of the British School at Rome*, xxii, 1954; Krautheimer, 'The Carolingian Revival of Early Christian Architecture', *Art Bulletin*, xxiv, 1942; Toynbee and Ward Perkins, *The Shrine of St. Peter*, 1956, Chapter 7 and Epilogue.]

offered to the historian. Let us summarise them briefly. In the age of the persecutions the Christians usually gathered together in ordinary houses, two of which – one at Dura and one in Rome – still exist today. These very simple houses, without colonnades, offered no model worthy of imitation, and they cannot have given rise to the Christian basilica after the Peace of the Church. In any case, basilicas similar to those in which the adherents of eastern cults assembled were already being built during the persecutions. Therefore, after the triumph of Christianity, Constantine's architects had no need to invent a new architectural form; all they had to do was to copy a model that had long been used in Hellenistic and Roman architecture. Christian painting appears in the early sanctuaries much sooner than was once believed. Side by side with the art of the catacombs, the object of which was to console, there was the art of the churches, intended to strengthen and to instruct. The discovery in the East of some of the earliest Christian paintings raises more urgently than ever the problem of the origins of Christian art.

CHAPTER THREE

Santa Sabina and the Problem of Eastern Influences in Rome

[EARLY FIFTH CENTURY]

Santa Sabina; San Giovanni a Porta Latina; Santa Maria in Cosmedin

IN THE first years of the 5th century A.D. the Aventine was one of the most splendid quarters of Rome. The old hill of the plebs had passed to the patricians. The Roman aristocracy, attracted by the beauty of the outlook, had built its mansions there. Sumptuous pagan dwellings rose alongside those of the Christians, and the temples of the gods were still standing next to some modest Christian churches. One of the richest houses on the hill was that of Marcella, a fervent Christian who had once welcomed St. Jerome. Among her friends had been some of the great ladies of Rome who were converts to Christianity: Paula and her daughters Eustochium and Blesilla, Paulina, wife of the proconsul Pammachius, Lea and Fabiola. But now her friends were dead, or had withdrawn to Bethlehem to be near St. Jerome, and she was living alone with her adopted daughter Principia, devoting herself to prayer and contemplation.

When visiting Santa Sabina on the Aventine, and looking at the two solemn female figures in the mosaic which personify respectively the converted Jews and the converted pagans, I always think of Principia and Marcella (32). This is only a fancy, for the mosaic dates from twenty-five years after their death, but how else should we visualise these rigid Christians? Dressed in dark clothes, with head covered and a cross embroidered on their *pallium*, Gospel in hand, sad-eyed, they are the perfect image of those Roman ladies of the latter years, who had made a Thebaid of their palaces. Strange years, when Claudian celebrated Ceres and Proserpina for the last time; when Symmachus, failing to have the statue of Victory returned to the Senate, set one up in his own palace. Old Rome, still inviolate, was enjoying her last days of felicity. The Aventine retained all its charm, and its baths, known as the thermae of Decius, which abounded in works of art, remained the most elegant in Rome.

During the night of August 24, 410, after a rather long siege, the Goths under Alaric suddenly entered Rome by the Porta Salaria uttering wild cries. A violent storm broke out at this instant; peals of thunder mingled with the shouts of the barbarians; the temples were struck by lightning and the statues of the old gods overturned. Fires started by Alaric's soldiers were fanned by the fury of the wind – and it seemed that this city, to which the oracles promised eternity, had seen its last day. The Aventine in particular suffered sorely. Its sumptuous houses were pillaged and some destroyed in the fire, for excavations on their sites have often revealed calcined marbles. Marcella and her daughter, after being despoiled of all they possessed, were able to escape to San Paolo fuori le Mura, which had become a place of refuge. They did not long survive the emotions of those three terrible days – three days, because Alaric limited the pillage, as he had promised, to that length of time, and then withdrew.

The Roman world was stupefied by the unheard-of news of the sack of Rome. The pagans took for granted that Dea Roma, who held a spear in one hand and the statue of Victory in the other, had been forsaken by her fellow gods and they attributed the catastrophe to the impiety of recent generations who had turned away from their altars. Augustine replied to them in the *City of God*, showing that there was a city of the soul more exalted than Rome, and which the barbarians could not approach.

The Romans made efforts to repair the ruin, but some great houses never rose again – their owners had fled as far as Africa and as far as Palestine, where St. Jerome received them. However, life gradually resumed its accustomed course and people imagined that Rome was as great as ever. There is nothing more touching than the verses composed by the Gaul Rutilius Namatianus seven years after the disaster. He speaks of Rome, which he has just left, with the affection of a son; he places the crown of laurels on the white hair of his old, wounded mother, and promises her eternal life afresh. At the moment when her empire is about to collapse he offers thanks to Rome for having given a single fatherland to all peoples, and for having extended the City to the farthest limits of the world.

Alaric's sack of Rome had not discouraged the Christians. Like St. Augustine, they thought the real Rome was not the Rome of stone, brick and marble, but the Rome of men's souls. Like St. Augustine himself, they were working in the city of God.

A few years after the catastrophe of A.D. 410 an Illyrian priest named Peter built, on the Aventine, the beautiful church of Santa Sabina, which has remained almost intact for fifteen centuries (28–31). This is one of the most precious of monuments, for Santa Sabina, with Santa Maria Maggiore, is our perfect model of the early Christian basilica. St. Peter's, St. John Lateran and San Paolo fuori le Mura have all been reconstructed.[1] Santa Sabina calls up for us the times of St. Augustine, just as Vézelay recalls the century of the crusades, and the Sainte Chapelle the age of St. Louis. These type-buildings are the milestones of history.

Why did the priest Peter choose this particular spot on the Aventine as the site for his church? It was long held that he built it on the actual ruins of the temple of Juno Regina, which, people thought, Alaric's Goths had destroyed a few years before. It was the old temple to which Camillus brought the Juno of Veii in triumph after the capture of the town, like a prisoner with whom one would wish to ingratiate oneself. Augustus had rebuilt the

[1] [San Paolo, however, was at least rebuilt on exactly the same plan after the tragic fire of 1823, and engravings showing it before the event are available (74).]

old sanctuary more magnificently. Until recent years it was maintained that the beautiful Corinthian columns of Santa Sabina were derived from the temple of Juno; however, excavations have proved that the church was not built on the site of a temple, but on the site of a Roman house of the 2nd or 3rd century A.D. The mosaic pavement of a room was soon exposed at a depth of two metres; as for the temple of Juno, no trace of it was found, and it is still uncertain exactly where it stood.

The remains of the house were explored and everything seems to indicate that it was a meeting-place of the Christians of the Aventine during the persecutions. The name *titulus Sabinae* long applied to the church was a reminder that the house had been made available to the community by a Christian woman called Sabina. By the beginning of the 5th century the number of the faithful had greatly increased and the room hitherto used as a chapel must have become much too small; it was then that Peter built his church on the same site as the house. There is nothing surprising about this, for some of the most venerable sanctuaries in Rome arose in the same way. A careful study of the foundations of San Clemente, Sant'Anastasia, Santi Giovanni e Paolo and San Martino ai Monti has shown that all these old churches were built over the meeting-places of the early Christian community (see Chapter Two). In using existing sites there was a double advantage: new land did not have to be bought; and a place already consecrated by the tragic or moving events of the heroic age was preserved. Therefore, it was on top of a pre-existing house and not on the site of a pagan temple that Peter of Illyria raised the new church. He had, says the inscription in the mosaic, 'a great fortune of which he kept nothing for himself'; so he wanted his church to be beautiful and of perfect proportions.

As the result of recent restorations Santa Sabina has recovered its original character. Going inside, we become instantly aware of that unique and slightly mysterious charm of the old Latin basilicas. How is it that such simple buildings can be so appealing?

Their secret is that they sprang from the harmonious genius of Greece. It is no longer believed that the Christian basilica derived from the forms of the antique house in which the faithful assembled. It now seems that triumphant Christianity borrowed, from Hellenistic sources, the buildings used as places of initiation; the Baccheion of Athens and the sanctuary of Samothrace, with their double colonnades and their apse, are already, to all intents and purposes, Christian basilicas. Hellenic genius expresses itself, above all, in balance and proportion. Greek architects always remained devoted disciples of Pythagoras and never ceased to believe in the virtue of numbers. One must read Vitruvius, as illumined by the mind of Choisy, to understand what number meant to the Greeks. Vitruvius was one of their pupils and his treatise summarises the books, now lost, of the great architects of the Hellenistic age. Now, according to Vitruvius, geometry and number are the very essence of architecture. In the basilica which he built at Fano, a circle could be inscribed in the nave – in other words, its width and height were equal. These are the proportions of the Pantheon in Rome, with its enchanting harmonies; and, within a little, they are also the proportions of Santa Maria Maggiore.

The first thing that impresses the visitor in the Latin basilicas is the great width of the nave. The north-Europeans are particularly sensitive to this feature, owing to their Gothic churches being (for the sake of greater height) so narrow. In Rome the visitor from Gothic lands finds, instead of the urge and aspiration expressed in his native churches, an atmosphere of serenity and peace. The fact is that Christianity was received, in Rome, into a building created by the genius of antiquity, which is the genius of moderation and proportion. That is what first astonishes the man of the North, whose churches are like hymns or prayers.

The proportions of Santa Sabina are not exactly those which Vitruvius adopted in the basilica of Fano. Its width is very striking, but is nevertheless exceeded by the height. An open timbered roof further increased the effect of height; but in 1936 a flat wooden ceiling was placed in the same position as the original one (than which, however, it was certainly less magnificent). Thus the exact proportions of the original 5th-century nave were restored (comp. 28 and 29).

Inside, the basilica gives an immediate impression of antique dignity. This impression is due not only to its studied proportions but also to the beauty of the columns. They are in Parian marble, and of the Corinthian order. They do not at all resemble those rows of dissimilar columns, taken from collapsed temples and arcades, which the later architects of basilicas were content to use. All equal and all perfect, they belong to a time when art was still faithful to its laws. Did they come from a temple or from some rich mansion destroyed by the Goths under Alaric? We do not know. It seems impossible that they should have been made for the church, for could columns so pure in taste have been carved in Rome about A.D. 425? They show, indeed, true classical proportions: the height of the column is nine and a half times its diameter at the base (the ratio given by Vitruvius), while the intercolumnar spaces are five times the diameter – again according to the rules, which are not, however, inflexible. It is true that the Corinthian capitals do not show exactly the proportions they would have had in Vitruvius' time (the beginning of the reign of Augustus). At that time the height of the capital was equal to the diameter of the column at its base. At Santa Sabina, on the other hand, it exceeds that measure by about one-seventh; later on, it was to exceed it by one-third. So the height of the capital increases regularly with time. The columns at Santa Sabina, therefore, do not belong to the end of the empire, but to an intermediate period, still quite close to the classical age.

These twenty-four Corinthian columns with their fluting and cabling, carved from the purest Greek marble, lend a quality of antique perfection to the interior of Santa Sabina. The column is one of the masterpieces of Hellenic genius. The perfectly adjusted proportions, into which the same unit of length (namely, the radius of the column) always enters; the slight swelling of the shaft which bridges the gap between geometry and life; the magnificence of the capital in which the artist interprets the monumental beauty of the acanthus leaf (39, 40); the delicacy of the concave and convex mouldings of the base, recalling the subtle cadence of the lyric poet's short and long syllables – all these refinements of taste and intelligence make the Greek column one of the marvels of architecture. It is touching to see all this perfection offered in the service of the Gospel. These columns suggest so many lovely priestesses of the old gods, converted to the new religion.

There is something symbolic about the presence of Greece in the Christian basilica. It was to the Greeks that the Fathers of the first centuries owed their alphabet and their thought. How they would have warmed to Homer and Plato, whose writings were the delight of their adolescence. Some of the Fathers, like St. Justin and St. Clement of Alexandria, loved them to the point of claiming that Greek genius was, in some degree, divinely inspired. The Word, they believed, had not turned aside from the Greeks. St. Justin, whose faith is not in question (for he died a martyr), links with the followers of Christ both Socrates and Heraclitus and all those who, in his own words, 'lived according to the Word'. St. Basil, who was brought up by the Athenian philosophers and grammarians, invites young people to seek among the works of the great Greek writers for outstanding examples of virtue. At the time when Santa Sabina was built St. Augustine was still alive; and how often, when reading St. Augustine, are we reminded of Plato! Thus do the pagan columns of Santa Sabina lead us on towards the Christian altar.

The works of recent years have restored to Santa Sabina the bright light which was one of its original beauties. The naves of the old Roman churches were flooded with light, for they had as many windows as bays. The Counter-Reformation considered that twilight was more appropriate for prayer and meditation. In the times of Sixtus V and later it was the custom to wall up the windows of basilicas; at Santa Maria Maggiore half of them were done away with, but at Santa Sabina only six survived out of twenty-six. The serenity of these churches, born of the spirit of antiquity, disappeared; instead, they were invaded by the shadows, and the joy of the Redemption seemed to be supplanted by the soul's anguished struggle for salvation.

The twenty-six windows now opening again, as they once did, into the nave of Santa Sabina, have brought back the light, which penetrates through transparent sheets of selenite mounted in elaborately perforated panels. These panels, lacking the elegant simplicity of the early *transennae*, are a little surprising. The perforations consist of superimposed circles, lozenges and squares, of a complexity rather out of keeping with the pure lines of the interior. This was no fault of the restorer's, who faithfully reproduced the panels found when the windows, walled up in the 16th century, were re-opened. But they do not belong to the 5th century; they date rather from the time of Pope Leo III, the contemporary of Charlemagne, or his successor, Eugenius II (824–827), both of whom, as we know from the *Liber Pontificalis*, took an active interest in Santa Sabina. Without a doubt these *transennae* belong to the Carolingian age, for one of the windows of Santa Prassede, built between 817 and 824 by Pope Paschal I, has preserved exactly similar subdivisions. So one can hardly criticise the restoration undertaken by Muñoz, for what should he have put into the windows in place of these pierced panels? In retaining them, and in re-erecting, at the same time, the *schola cantorum*, decorated with Carolingian interlacing, he has given us the church as it was in the 9th century. In view of the impossibility of recovering Peter of Illyria's basilica in its original purity, it was wise to accept the march of history and to let time's handiwork be seen. Equally legitimate was the retention of the chapels of St. Hyacinth and St. Catherine of Siena, to perpetuate the great Dominican associations of Santa Sabina. One of the beauties of the Roman basilicas is that the passing centuries have left their mark upon them.

The restorations at Santa Sabina have not only opened up the windows of the nave but also those in the façade and the apse. Apse-windows are uncommon in Rome, where the dark apse was always preferred. Constantine's St. Peter had no such windows, judging by a painting of the old basilica in the Vatican. Churches of the 5th century like San Vitale and Santi Giovanni e Paolo had none either. In Carolingian times and, much later, in the 16th and 17th centuries, many Roman apses were plunged in darkness. This obscurity seemed to lend an air of religious mystery to the altar. In the East it was quite otherwise. From the first centuries onwards, from Salonica to Syria and Asia Minor, one continually encounters old churches whose apses are pierced by windows and whose interiors are full of light. This follows from the fact that, in the Greek world, churches were orientated from an early period. As far back as the 4th century the Apostolic Constitutions, drawn up in the East, require that the sanctuary should point eastwards. These sanctuaries, turned towards the source of light, were felt to have a symbolic significance. It was natural to provide the apse with windows, so that the sun's first rays, image of the light of the Eternal, might fall upon the priest at the altar.

In Rome, on the other hand, the churches face any and every point of the compass. Many of them occupied the sites of houses used by the primitive Christian Community; others were built inside pagan monuments.[1] In any case, the Roman clergy do not seem to have attached as much importance to orientation as the Greek or Syrian clergy. The sun does not rise, but sets behind the apse of St. Peter's in Rome.

In having apsidal windows Santa Sabina therefore resembles an eastern church.[2] Should one conclude from this that there was an actual eastern influence? One is much tempted to do so, especially when reviewing some of the other old Roman churches which have windows in their apses. This feature was to be observed, for instance, at Sant'Agata dei Goti, a 5th-century church built by the Arian Ricimer. The whole of this church, with its capitals surmounted by pulvins,[3] and its earthenware jars in the vaulting, is closely linked with the art of Ravenna and the Eastern Empire. San Giovanni a Porta Latina retains an apse pierced by three windows. But the apsidal region of this curious building (which dates back to the 6th century) has, as a whole, a markedly eastern character. The main apse is

[[1] E.g., San Lorenzo in Miranda in the temple of Antoninus and Faustina (2); San Nicola in Carcere; Sant'Urbano (7).]

[2] Santa Sabina, built as it is on a Roman house, is not perfectly orientated; its apse does not point exactly east, but somewhat north of east.

[[3] Pulvins or impost-blocks – the large blocks which often surmount Byzantine capitals and usually extent the area available for the springing of arches. They are often called *dosserets* in the literature, but this word is ambiguous, being more often applied, in French usage, to semi-columns and pilasters.]

flanked, as in the Syrian churches, by two minor apses, forming the two chapels known in the East as *prothesis* and *diaconicon*. Moreover, these three apses, instead of retaining their semicircular form externally, become polygonal, each with three facets; and this too is an eastern arrangement. It must not be forgotten that San Giovanni a Porta Latina was built at the time when Theodoric, the master of Rome, made his capital at Ravenna, which was a centre of eastern influence.[1]

An apse with windows and flanked by minor apses occurs again in Carolingian times at Santa Maria in Cosmedin. But this was the church of the Greeks, who were settled in the neighbourhood of the Aventine. It followed eastern traditions so closely that there were women's galleries above the aisles. Traces of them can still be seen.

These examples induce us to believe that Santa Sabina, built by the priest Peter of Illyrian origin – from a country, that is, in touch with the art of eastern Christendom – betrays in its illumined apse an eastern influence.

Should we go farther and conclude that the nave arcades of Santa Sabina are yet another sign of eastern influence? This has been maintained, for the following reasons. The combination of the arch and the column, that graceful innovation which was to come into its own in the future, was a late invention of the Hellenistic East. Classical Greece knew nothing of it; in its great days columns carried an architrave, and this horizontal line gave buildings a character of majestic calm. The arcade on columns was thought not to appear until the eve of Christianity's triumph, the earliest known example of it being provided by Diocletian's palace at Spalato,[2] a work of entirely eastern inspiration. In this union of the arch and the column there was something light and elegant which was to enchant the world of antiquity and first enchanted the East. Rome, always so bound by tradition, seemed less ready to welcome the new invention. Her earliest basilicas remained faithful to the architrave. This was true of old St. Peter's and, it was thought, of St. John Lateran, which was rebuilt several times in the course of centuries; true also of Santa Maria Maggiore and San Lorenzo fuori le Mura. If the arcade prevailed at San Paolo fuori le Mura the explanation given was that this basilica, first built by Constantine, was reconstructed by Theodosius, who was accustomed to the arcaded churches of the eastern empire. Rome had so strong a predilection for the architrave that she returned to it several times during the Middle Ages.

It was therefore not unnatural to conclude that Santa Sabina, the work of an Illyrian, gave evidence in its arcaded nave of an eastern influence in Rome. Such was, in fact, the doctrine to which a certain number of antiquarians subscribed; but recent discoveries have necessitated its revision in more ways than one.

When the forum of Lepcis Magna, in Tripolitania, was uncovered, porticoes were

[1] See Krautheimer in *American Journal of Archaeology*, 1936.

[2] Now Split.

discovered whose columns carried arcades, not architraves.[1] Now this forum of Lepcis Magna, a work of Septimius Severus, dates from the end of the 2nd century, and is therefore more than a hundred years older than Diocletian's palace at Spalato. But such arcades were certainly still older, as is proved, for instance, by the example at Pompeii, to which art-historians have as yet paid little attention. It has become evident that the arcade on columns was known in the Roman world much earlier than used to be thought. There may have been more than one monument of this type in Rome, and the apparent novelty at Santa Sabina was probably no novelty at all. Another recent discovery points the same way. In exploring the ground under St. John Lateran the excavators found fragmentary remains of 4th-century arcades, and it was concluded that the Constantinian basilica, contrary to expectation, had had arcades instead of architraves.[2]

Nowadays, therefore, it seems difficult to maintain that the architect of Santa Sabina borrowed his arcades from the East; he could have found his model as readily in Rome. Nonetheless, the ultimate eastern origin of the columned arcade remains highly probable. In Rome, a terracotta relief in the Capitoline museum shows a landscape on the Nile, with crocodiles and ibises, seen through a portico whose columns carry arches. The date of the work is uncertain, but it proves that Hellenised Egypt knew this elegant combination of arch and column, and suggests even that it may have been invented there. Pompeii, where the same architectural form appears as early as the 1st century, is in many respects to be regarded as an artistic colony of Alexandria, and relations between Alexandria and Lepcis Magna must also have been frequent.[3]

It is uncertain, therefore, whether or not the use of the arch at Santa Sabina is due to eastern influence. But the East is in evidence elsewhere. Santa Sabina has a door in cedar-wood, contemporary with the church, and here there seems to be no doubt about this influence from the East (33–36). The door is adorned with bas-reliefs in which has been discerned the intention to show parallels between the Old and New Testaments. However, the displacement of some panels and the loss of several others have thrown some doubt on the correspondences. At least two artists executed the reliefs; the work of one has the heaviness characteristic of the last sculptured sarcophagi, while the other retains traces of the freedom and the feeling for the picturesque of Hellenistic art.

Eastern influence can be detected in several significant features. One of these bas-reliefs shows a church framed between two towers (34). At the time, in Italy, nothing like this existed, and it was only in the region of Antioch that churches could be met with dominated by two symmetrical towers.[4] The sculptors of Santa Sabina's doors were familiar not only

[1] On this subject see an article by Giovannoni in *Palladio*, Part 1, 1937.

[2] See Josi's article in *Rivista di Archeologia Cristiana*, 1934, p. 335.

[[3] See an interesting discussion of Lepcis Magna, in the light of his subsequent excavations, by J. B. Ward Perkins in *Proceedings of the British Academy*, Vol. XXXVII, 1951.]

[4] In front of the door of this church with twin towers there is a standing figure accompanied by an angel. Before him, onlookers with their hands raised seem to be expressing astonishment. This

with Syria, but also with Palestine, and they knew the legends of those lands. One of them has represented, below Elijah, who is being carried up into heaven, some young men armed with axes (33). They appear terrified, and one of them throws himself to the ground, covering his face. Now, we know from Antonino of Piacenza, a 6th-century pilgrim, that travellers were shown, at the foot of Mount Hermon, the place where Elijah was carried up to heaven and 'where the sons of the prophets lost their axes'.[1] This legend is one of those numerous oral traditions in which pious visitors to the Holy Land took delight. Their itineraries abound in them. This curious incident, adorning the door of Santa Sabina, implies familiarity with the East. And we may well conjecture that the artists who depicted a two-towered Syrian church and a legend of the Palestinian highways were themselves easterners.

To these arguments others might be added. The scene of the burning bush, for instance, conforms to a model occurring in Greek illumination: Moses, young and beardless, takes off his shoes at God's command (36). But God himself does not appear in the flame, nor does he speak to Moses; it is an angel, standing beside the burning bush, who speaks to him. The scene is visualised in the same manner in a miniature from the Sermons of St. Gregory Nazianzen at the Bibliothèque Nationale, Paris. This famous manuscript only goes back to the 9th century, but it often reproduces very early originals. Undoubtedly, there were illustrated manuscripts of the Bible at an early date in the Greek world in which the burning-bush scene appears in this form; both the panel at Santa Sabina and the miniature from St. Gregory's book are reminiscences of it.

Another highly characteristic scene occupies one of the panels of the door. It represents Christ in heaven, standing in an aureole. On the earth below a woman, no doubt the personification of the Church, appears in the attitude of the *orans*; St. Peter and St. Paul stand on her right and left and hold a star above her head (35).

Some years ago the discovery was made at Bobbio [2] of some *ampullae* of the 6th century very similar to the famous ampullae of Monza.[3] They used to contain a little oil from the lamps burning in the sanctuaries of the Holy Land, and the reliefs stamped upon them reproduced, as is generally agreed today, mosaics from these sanctuaries. One of these ampullae bears a scene surprisingly analogous to the panel from Santa Sabina. Jesus Christ,

scene has been interpreted in various ways. Some have seen in it St. Peter's departure for Jerusalem; others a Christian emperor acclaimed by the people; others again Kind David. For my own part, I am convinced that the artist wished to illustrate the beginning of St. Luke's Gospel. Zacharias has been struck dumb because he has seen an angel in the sanctuary who announced to him that he would have a son, to be called John. The crowd is awaiting Zacharias outside the temple, astonished because he is staying there so long. In the words of the Gospel: 'when he came out, he could not speak unto them; and they perceived that he had seen a vision in the temple'. The angel's presence, standing beside Zacharias, recalls the vision.

[1] *Itinera Terrae Sanctae*, ed. Tobler, Vol. I, p. 122.

[[2] In the Appenines between Genoa and Piacenza; chiefly noted for its associations with the Irishman St. Columbanus.]

[3] See Celi in *Civiltà Cattolica*, 1923, and Cecchelli in *Rivista di Archaeologia Cristiana*, 1927.

seated in an aureole, appears in heaven; on the earth stands a woman in the attitude of prayer; there is a star above her head and two figures stand on her right and left. The resemblance to the panel at Santa Sabina would be complete if the two figures represented SS. Peter and Paul; but they have here been replaced by St. John the Baptist and his father Zacharias. In the East the Church is flanked by the precursors of Christ; at Santa Sabina by the two pillars of the Roman Church, SS. Peter and Paul. The eastern model has therefore been amended for the adornment of a Roman church. The model itself, in all probability, was a mosaic from some church in Palestine.

Thus a reflection of eastern light falls on Santa Sabina. The fact was that the attraction of the East had become irresistible. Jerusalem, with its great memories and magnificent monuments; Palestine, where churches had arisen to mark every holy place; Egypt, where the cells of the Desert Fathers were venerated; Asia Minor, with Antioch and Ephesus, where the traces of the apostles were sought out; all these consecrated lands and these cities where one felt nearer to God attracted the pilgrims of all the world. As St. Jerome said, the whole universe hastened to Jerusalem. Paula and her daughter Eustochium wrote from the East to Marcella entreating her to leave her palace on the Aventine to come and join them. They would go together, promised the letter, to weep at the Holy Sepulchre; they would contemplate a Jordan purified by Christ's Baptism; they would see Cana and also Nazareth 'whose name means *flower*, and which is the flower of Galilee'. Marcella did not come, but thousands of others undertook the journey. A number left records of it, as did the mysterious Aetheria, whose artless description has such a lively interest. The East was not only the land of great memories; it was at that time the most creative part of the ancient world, and it teemed with life. The new architecture and new forms of decorative art were being elaborated there. Rome herself, whose brilliance was on the wane, could not remain unaffected by eastern influence. Hence the particular interest of finding, at Santa Sabina, traces of the East with all its high prestige. For it is abundantly true that the attraction of Rome's most celebrated churches does not reside merely in their beauty, but also in their power to evoke the history they have lived through.

The outside of Santa Sabina is of extreme simplicity, the brickwork being wholly unadorned. The façade, partly hidden by a portico, lacks any monumental quality. The Christian basilica was as austere externally as the pagan temple was magnificent; the former seemed an image of Christianity itself, reserving all its beauties for the interior. These walls, gaunt though they be, become splendidly transformed in the light of the setting sun, which imparts a tinge of purple to the bricks of Rome. The tiles of its roof are another adornment to Santa Sabina. Ancient tradition is here preserved in its purity: the concave tiles cover the joints of the flat ones, forming ridge and furrow of light and shade. The exquisite pale tones of the baked earth are set off here and there by a touch of gold left behind by the summer sun. In this harmonious association of the flat and the curved tile we recognise the gracious genius of the Mediterranean peoples. Legend attributes their invention to Kinyras, that priest of Aphrodite of whom Pindar speaks; and a happy invention it is, that makes a work of art of the humblest roof. A simple brickwork apse covered with these hollow tiles becomes a masterpiece to enchant the eye (74). But the secret of this charming combination, preserved in Rome almost to our own day, is now lost. The modern terrace has triumphed over all ancient roofing. Only some lovers of the past still wish to have their villas roofed in hollow tiles, but these, being no longer manufactured, have to be bought up when an old house is demolished.

Such is this church of Santa Sabina, in which we find the basilica of the first centuries in its purity. It is true that most of its mosaics and its facing of polychrome marble are wanting, but the essentials remain – the beautiful colonnades, the happy proportions and those fine calm lines which bring a sense of peace.

Having once experienced the charm of Santa Sabina, one is not surprised that Rome remained so long wedded to the basilica. Still today these old basilicas are one of the delights of Rome; we recognise in them that pathetic moment of history when vanquished paganism came and offered to Christianity the best thing it possessed.

CHAPTER FOUR

Santa Maria Maggiore and the Puzzle of its Dating

[FIFTH CENTURY]

I

THE VISITOR who enters the nave of Santa Maria Maggiore feels himself transported to the ancient world (37). Is it a Christian church, or is it the Athenian Stoa where the philosophers gave lessons in wisdom? Those fine Ionic columns surmounted by an architrave, those long horizontal lines, those wide spaces, all give a sense of serenity and peace. In spite of the additions of the last few centuries, in spite of the big arches broken through the colonnades on either side by Sixtus V and Paul V – disturbing as a false note in a melody – we feel permeated in this stately interior by the quiet calm of classical antiquity. This is why it has been claimed that Santa Maria Maggiore is no other than a pagan basilica of the 2nd century A.D., adapted for Christian use two centuries later (about 352) by Pope Liberius. A curious discovery seemed to confirm this view: it was noticed, while examining the roofing, that a large number of tiles bore manufacturers' stamps of the 2nd century.[1]

I admit I was once much attracted by a hypothesis which accorded so well with the classic beauty of the basilica, and I even applied myself to strengthening it through a study of the proportions of the building. I had before me the plates devoted to Santa Maria Maggiore by Letarouilly, in his *Edifices de la Rome Moderne*, one of those fine works born of their authors' devotion to the Eternal City. Letarouilly measured every part of the basilica with minute care, and one can trust him implicitly. Now, examining his figures, I recognised in them almost the exact proportions laid down by Vitruvius. The width of the nave is about equal to its height, so that the interior could, like that of the basilica at Fano erected by Vitruvius, have a circle inscribed in it. Again, true to Vitruvian principles, the width of the aisles equals the height of the columns. These beautiful Ionic columns in Parian marble measure nine and a half times their diameter, while the distance between columns (measured from axis to axis) is four times the diameter.[2] These are the very measurements of what Vitruvius called the Ionic 'eustyle' – a pleasing system of proportions originally devised by the Greek architect Hermogenes at the end of the 3rd century B.C. Finally, the entablature with its architrave and cornice measures, within a little, one-fifth of the height of the column,

[1] P. Crostarosa, *Nuovo Bollettino di Archeologia Cristiana*, 1896.

[2] The variations amount to a few centimetres only.

which is yet another Vitruvian rule. These calculations inclined me to the view that the archaeologists who saw a pagan building in Santa Maria Maggiore might perhaps be right.

Pope Liberius did not, in that case, have a basilica constructed on the Esquiline, near the market of Livia, as the *Liber Pontificalis* says; [1] he must have been content, as another document from the *Gesta Liberii* seems to affirm, with adding an apse to an already existing building.[2] Besides this he would have given this pagan basilica a Christian character by decorating both sides of the nave with mosaics. These mosaics, devoted to the stories of Abraham, Jacob, Moses and Joshua, still exist today, and G. B. De Rossi himself attributes them to Pope Liberius.

According to this reasoning, we should not take literally the passage in the *Liber Pontificalis* from the life of Pope Sixtus III (432–440), where it says that he 'built, near Livia's market, the basilica of St. Mary, which formerly bore the name of Pope Liberius'. Doubtless the alleged building would have been a mere restoration. Sixtus III would simply have consolidated the ancient basilica, which had been damaged some time before in a riot, and enriched it, at the same time, with a new mosaic – that of the chancel-arch – where his name is inscribed.

Therefore neither Liberius nor Sixtus III would be the builders of Santa Maria Maggiore, but an unknown pagan architect of the 2nd century. Thus would be explained the wholly antique character of this fine nave, whose lines and proportions move us so deeply today, for they breathe the spirit of Vitruvius – that is to say of the Greek architects, his masters.

Presented in this fashion, the history of Santa Maria Maggiore is satisfying to the mind, and one can well understand that more than one archaeologist has been carried away by it. But is this plausible story really true? That is the problem which a Roman scholar, Monsignor Biasiotti, set himself.[3] There was only one way of solving it – by studying the walls of the basilica so as to establish, if possible, their date. This is what Monsignor Biasiotti accomplished with scrupulous care, examining the walls at all levels, sounding their depths, having the mortars analysed and digging down even to the foundations.

He soon saw that the masonry of these brick walls could not belong to the first four centuries. At the beginning of the Imperial era the bricks are very regular and separated by a very thin layer of mortar: the thickness of this mortar-bed increases so much with time that in the 4th century it almost equals the thickness of the bricks themselves. At Santa Maria Maggiore the mortar often exceeds the bricks in thickness. And nothing could be more haphazard than the masonry: the bricks are all of different lengths, thicknesses and colours. Without a doubt, they are materials borrowed from pre-existing buildings. On many of these bricks one finds marks of the hammer used to free them from old mortar. The core of the wall, investigated by trial soundings, seemed to consist of fragments of bricks and tiles. We have moved far from the fine brickwork of the 2nd century, far even

[1] *Liber Pontificalis* ed. Duchesne, Vol. I, p. 208: *Hic fecit basilicam nomini suo juxta macellum Libiae.*

[2] Ibid., p. 210, note 20: *In ejus tempore fabricata est absis in urbe Roma, in regione quinta.* The fifth region is that of Santa Maria Maggiore.

[3] *Bollettino d'Arte*, 1915.

from that of the century of Constantine. Evidently the basilica of Santa Maria Maggiore was built of débris; the bricks of the walls as well as the roofing-tiles are all products of demolition.

Curiously enough, the architrave which surmounts the beautiful columns of the nave is not of marble, as the columns are, but of brick, disguised under a layer of stucco. Nothing of this sort would have been done in the time of the Antonines, or even of the Severi. So we must reject the seductive but certainly mistaken idea that Santa Maria Maggiore could be a pagan basilica: vastly more trouble would have been taken over a building of the 2nd century. Equally, we must reject the supposition that Santa Maria Maggiore is a building erected by Liberius in the 4th century and restored by Sixtus III in the 5th. The wall-structure is the same throughout – everywhere one finds borrowed material, bricks of assorted shapes and sizes, thick beds of mortar. These walls, revealing so clearly the decadence of the art of building, cannot be of the 4th century; they date from the sad years that followed the capture of Rome by Alaric. The passage from the *Liber Pontificalis* devoted to Santa Maria Maggiore must, after all, be taken quite literally: Sixtus III, towards A.D. 432, built a new church which he dedicated to the Virgin Mary. Moreover, a contemporary inscription said as much in the pope's own words: *Virgo Maria, tibi, Xystus, nova tecta dicavi.*[1, 2]

If this is so, there is nothing at Santa Maria Maggiore which could go back to the century of Pope Liberius, and the mosaics of the nave, devoted to the Old Testament, must belong to the time of Sixtus III just as much as the famous mosaics of the sanctuary arch.

But a recent discovery has caused an unexpected difficulty to arise. With a view to restoration, these mosaic pictures from the Old Testament were detached whole, one after another[3]; it was then observed that they were not in their original positions but came from elsewhere. In fact, each of these pictures forms a single block and carries on the reverse side, like a mould, the impression of the wall in which it was formerly embedded. It was a brick wall with very thick mortar-beds, indicating an age of decadence. Where did these mosaics come from, which were placed so high in Santa Maria Maggiore that one can hardly see them? We do not know. Could they have been torn from the basilica of Liberius? But that basilica, built at least seventy years before, must have been better built and could not have presented such thick mortar-beds. Apart from this, these nave-mosaics of Santa Maria Maggiore differ in no respect, as far as technique is concerned, from those of the sanctuary-arch in which the name of Sixtus III is inscribed. In both series the enamel cubes have the

[1] In a pamphlet entitled *La Basilica di Liberio sull'Esquilino*, 1935, M. Biasiotti has shown that the Basilica of Liberius, situated near Livia's market, was at a considerable distance from Santa Maria Maggiore, which rose on the foundations of Roman houses levelled to the ground, and was created entirely by Sixtus III.

[[2] Though his conclusion is generally accepted, the author has exaggerated the difference between 4th- and 5th-century building methods. The spoils of older buildings were already being re-used in Constantine's time.]

[3] This skilful restoration is the work of Sig. Biagio Biagetti.

same chemical composition, the same dimensions and the same colours. The costumes also present striking analogies: in each series certain people wear the same short boots with parallel bands, and the daughter of Pharaoh in the nave is clothed, like the Virgin of the sanctuary-arch, in the rich costume worn by the empresses of the Eastern Empire. We do notice, it is true, some iconographic differences: the angels of the nave are wingless, whereas those of the sanctuary-arch are winged. But that only proves that the mosaics of the nave reproduced an ancient series of Bible-illustrations in which the angels had this archaic aspect,[1] while the mosaics of the sanctuary-arch, whose iconography is (as we shall see) so characteristic, appear to be an original work. It therefore seems likely that the nave mosaics, brought from some unknown monument at an unknown date,[2] are roughly contemporary with those of the sanctuary-arch. But what we can regard as certain is that the basilica of Santa Maria Maggiore and the mosaics adorning its great arch are the creation of Pope Sixtus III.

II

The Council of Ephesus, at which the Virgin Mary was proclaimed 'Mother of God', took place in 431. It was during the following years, perhaps from 432 onwards, that Sixtus III began work on the basilica of Santa Maria Maggiore. One cannot doubt that a close relationship existed between Santa Maria Maggiore and the Council of Ephesus. G. B. De Rossi was the first to understand that the Pope wished to celebrate the Virgin's victory by raising up a church in her honour. He went still farther, for he put forward the theory that the mosaics of the sanctuary-arch, inspired by the pope, expressed that supernatural splendour of the Virgin which had been solemnly recognised by the Council. This

[1] The three wingless angels received by Abraham at Santa Maria Maggiore are comparable to the three wingless angels served by the Patriarch at San Vitale in Ravenna: the two almost identical scenes derive from a common original. We suspect in the mosaic-cycle of Santa Maria Maggiore the imitation of one of those manuscript Bibles, illuminated in the East, where the story was illustrated with extreme fidelity even down to its insignificant details. We no longer possess these illustrations, but here and there we find fragments of them. Thus the Octateuch of Constantinople shows us a Joshua staying the sun similar to the Joshua of the mosaic in Santa Maria Maggiore. These Bible-pictures, which served the mosaic-makers as a model, did not amount to a plain narrative, but one already penetrated by theology. At Santa Maria Maggiore, in the scene of the three angels received by Abraham, the figure of the central angel is surrounded by a complete aureole which the other two angels lack. Difficulties have been experienced in accounting for this aureole, yet there is no real doubt about the explanation. At an early date the three angels were considered to symbolise the Trinity. Abraham saw all three of them but worshipped only one, whom he called Lord; '*tres vidit unum adoravit*' is repeated continually by the Doctors. The angel surrounded by the aureole is therefore the image of the One God.

[2] We know that Pope Leo the Great (440–461) restored the churches destroyed by Genseric in 455. It has been supposed that it was he who had the mosaics from a church destroyed by the Vandals transported to the nave of Santa Maria Maggiore. This is an ingenious hypothesis, which, however, there is nothing to support.

reasoning has found general acceptance. Not all the scholars, however, have found it completely convincing, and objections have been raised. It has been noted that the Virgin occupies only a secondary position in these mosaics and that the Child appears, on the contrary, to be the principal subject portrayed. The scenes represented are indeed those of the Childhood of Jesus, following the canonical as well as the apocryphal gospels.

I am too fully convinced of the influence of the great religious disputes on Christian art, and have seen too many examples of this, to doubt G. B. De Rossi for a moment. His proofs, I admit, are not always convincing, but his instinct has not deceived him here. His one shortcoming was his failure to study more closely the doctrine of Nestorius, which enables us to understand the true meaning of these mosaics.

The desire to explain the union of the divine and human natures in the person of Jesus Christ has provoked the principal eastern heresies. Nestorius is the last of a whole succession of theologians who, in order to make this union intelligible, started from human nature. For them Christ was born man and became God; at a certain moment in his life he attained that perfection which justified his union with God and enabled him to become God's Son. In this conception there was something of Hellenic thought. Cerinthus, Paul of Samosata, Diodorus of Tarsus, Theodore of Mopsuestia, regarded Jesus Christ as a kind of Greek hero who raised himself, through virtue, to divinity. For some of these heretics the Baptism marked the moment when this union of the two natures occurred. The Holy Spirit had hovered over Christ's head and the Father had uttered these words: 'This is my beloved Son, in whom I am well pleased.' From that moment, Jesus Christ had been the Son of God.

These were the ideas of Nestorius, Patriarch of Constantinople, but he revealed them to his listeners only with a certain prudence. His sermons were already beginning to cause astonishment, but he raised a scandal the day he declared that the Virgin was not to be called Mother of God (Theotokos) but only Mother of Christ (Christotokos) – for according to him Christ owed only his humanity to the Virgin Mary. What he dared not preach he revealed in private conversation. He could not believe, he said, in a God two months old, a God three months old; he would never worship a child brought up on its mother's milk, and fleeing to Egypt to save its life. These words were reported to the Council. His conclusion was that during his childhood, Christ was not yet God.

Such a doctrine did not raise Christ much above the prophets, for they too had received, at a certain moment, the spirit of God. The Redemption lost all its meaning, since God had not really become incarnate in the Virgin's womb, to save and to die for humanity. At its very first session the Council of Ephesus deposed Nestorius and condemned his doctrine. It proclaimed that the Virgin was not merely the Mother of Christ but the Mother of God as well and that the only name appropriate to her was Theotokos – a decision which filled with joy the city of Ephesus, where the Virgin, according to tradition, had once lived. The Council continued in session for some time, but had done what was expected of it right at the beginning in condemning Nestorius and in raising the Virgin above all created beings. It was from this moment that the cult of Mary, the Mother of God, began to develop; her festivals were instituted one after another, first in the East, then in the West, and churches were dedicated to her in every part of the Christian world. This brief summary will make the mosaics of the sanctuary-arch in Santa Maria Maggiore more easily intelligible (38).

The Virgin is here invested with a grandeur as yet unexampled in Christian art. For the first time she is shown wearing the costume of the empresses of the East. In all scenes where she figures she wears a diadem on her brow, ear-rings of precious stones, a necklace of pearls, a jewelled buckle in her belt. The Annunciation has a majesty hitherto unknown and not to be seen again. The Virgin, seated on a throne like a Byzantine empress, holds the scroll of the apocryphal Gospels; the Angel of the Annunciation, like a winged Victory, flies above her head, and the dove glides over her in the sky; four other angels, standing solemnly on either side of the throne, form a guard of honour for the Sovereign Lady. Here is assuredly the Theotokos, exalted above all earthly creatures, even above the angels, by the Council of Ephesus.

But the Child, as soon as he appears, is glorified yet more than his Mother. The Adoration of the Magi has a unique character, foreshadowed by no previous, imitated by no subsequent work. It is extraordinary that the Child should not be represented sitting on his Mother's knee, and that he is not a few days, but some years old. More majestic than a king's son, he is seated alone on a great throne decorated with precious stones, with attendant figures at a respectful distance. The Virgin, notwithstanding her imperial robes, is seated modestly to the right hand of the throne; a mysterious woman in dark draperies to its left.[1] The Child has not only the nimbus but bears a small golden cross above the forehead, and the Star shines in the sky over his head; behind the throne are four standing angels. The Magi, who come forward in Persian attire, have no difficulty in recognising God himself in the person of this Child, radiant with majesty. Do we not feel here the desire to wipe out the impious words of Nestorius by reminding the faithful that this Child was born the Son of God?

The Presentation in the Temple is a further proof of his divinity. The Child who, according to Nestorius, did not yet partake of the divine nature, is welcomed as the Saviour of the World by the aged Simeon, who leans forward respectfully before him. The prophetess Anna points to him in whom she has recognised the Messiah, while the presence of an angel endows the scene with an other-worldly atmosphere.

But nothing is more significant than the representation, after the massacre of the Innocents, of the Holy Family's arrival in Egypt. Here, the mosaic returns a direct answer to the blasphemies of Nestorius, and does not hesitate to seek that answer in the Apocryphal Gospels. This Child, in whom the heretic would not see more than a human creature fleeing from death, is received, in Egypt, not as a king, but as a God. The Book of Pseudo-Matthew tells, in fact, that when the Child arrived in Egypt at the city of Sotinen, all the

[1] Does this woman represent the Church of the Circumcision, thus balancing the Virgin, personifying the Church of the Gentiles? Ingenious but unconvincing reasons have been given for the supposition. The Virgin could not represent the Gentile Church, since, for the Doctors, she personifies the Universal Church.

idols fell from their pedestals. It thus happened that Affrodisius, governor of the town, came and worshipped him. In the mosaic we see Affrodisius, dressed as a dignitary of the imperial court, advancing with his retinue. Among them we notice one who represents human wisdom – a long-bearded philosopher leaning on his stick. The Child, standing between two angels with the little golden cross on his head, solemn, motionless, inspires a religious awe in these strangers. They feel they are in the presence of the true God; to him they bring the homage of their faith.

We cannot, it seems to me, avoid the conclusion that these scenes of the Childhood, which are in some ways so unusual, have a deep significance. It is the divinity, intimately united with the humanity of the Virgin's Son which they set out to demonstrate, and it is to the heresy of Nestorius that they reply. Mary herself is celebrated in these mosaics, as the grand scene of the Annunciation proves, but she is celebrated above all in the person of her Son. Since he, in infancy, was already God, and the two natures were united in him from the beginning, the Virgin truly merits this name, which places her above all mortals: Theotokos, Mother of God.

So I think we can assert without fear of error that the mosaics of the sanctuary-arch of Santa Maria Maggiore, as well as the church itself which includes them, are born of the decision of the Council of Ephesus. Among all churches raised to the Virgin Mary, this one is unique.

III

One problem, however, still remains to be solved. How should we explain the contrast, in Santa Maria Maggiore, between these walls so carelessly constructed – walls already to be described as barbarian – and this interior where the pure classic tradition seems to live again? So happily proportioned is it that Letarouilly felt obliged to measure it down to the smallest details, so as to furnish to architects an example of a perfect work. And are not the Vitruvian rules indeed employed here, with only the slightest variations?

Some unpublished documents kept in the Biblioteca Vallicelliana at Rome provide the answer. From them we learn, with some surprise, that the original nave of Santa Maria Maggiore was not exactly like the one we see today. What happened was that between 1741 and 1750 some extensive rebuilding was undertaken here on the instructions of Benedict XIV. He put in charge of the work a talented architect of Florentine origin, Ferdinando Fuga. After having built the new façade of the church, inspired by that of St. John Lateran (without, however, repeating the Palladian dignity achieved by Alessandro Galilei), Fuga began to restore the interior of the basilica. An Oratorian, Father Bianchini, watched the progress of the work and recorded it in a manuscript now preserved at the Vallicelliana.[1] From this we discover that the columns, perfect as they are today, were not at that time quite equal, either in height or in thickness. To enable them to reach the same level they had been

[1] Vol. 75.

placed from the beginning on bases of varying height. Until the mid-18th century, therefore, the interior of Santa Maria Maggiore resembled that of many other Roman basilicas, where somewhat heterogeneous columns succeed in giving, with the help of some subtle contrivances, an impression of unity. Whence, then, these identical columns, these perfectly similar bases, these happy proportions? We learn from the same manuscript that this perfect regularity is Fuga's doing. Father Bianchini records, without betraying the slightest surprise, that the architect pared down those columns which were too stout, and shortened those that were too long. At the same time all the capitals were replaced. He re-made the bases too, but these – after the operation performed on the columns – could all be made the same size. The credit, therefore, for the harmonious proportions of the colonnade, noted with such respect by Letarouilly, goes rather to the 18th-century than to the 5th-century architect. Fuga was familiar with Vitruvius and, we can be sure, consulted him. Thus, if the rhythmic sequence of the columns in Santa Maria Maggiore so closely approaches the Vitruvian 'eustyle', it is because Fuga so wished it. We see how untenable the theory has become which, because of its happily proportioned colonnades, tried to make of Santa Maria Maggiore a 2nd-century building.

The beauty of Santa Maria Maggiore is therefore due, in some measure, to Fuga. It is true that he found a nave and aisles of splendid breadth, perpetuating antique traditions; but he had the skill to give those irregular colonnades a most delicate rhythm. He deserves the credit (deserved by few in his time) for having achieved a fine restoration by correcting the faults of the old building. If only Borromini had been as discreet at St. John Lateran, and restored instead of rebuilding! But the creative centuries have not usually respected the past. The architects of those fruitful times are too easily carried away by their own creative force, too naïvely convinced of their superiority to the builders of earlier generations, to accept any restraints on their work: they rebuild. Fuga makes a welcome exception. Yet he too was a creator and of his works (the Palazzo Corsini, the church of Santa Maria della Morte, the Consulta on the Quirinal hill) some have dignity, and others charm. The more credit to him, then, for entering into the thought of the old architect of Santa Maria Maggiore, and carrying that thought to the point of perfection.

Of all Roman churches Santa Maria Maggiore is the one that best reflects the passage of time. Many centuries have left their imprint upon it. In the 13th century Torriti embellished the apse with the grand mosaic of the Coronation of the Virgin; in the 14th Rusuti told the story of the miracle of the snow in other mosaics, now hidden by the façade. In the 15th century Cardinal d'Estouteville, while rebuilding the choir at Mont Saint-Michel in Normandy, and while building Sant'Agostino in Rome, also decorated the ciborium of Santa Maria Maggiore with its graceful bas-reliefs by Mino del Regno. Alexander VI put his coat-of-arms in the coffered ceiling of the basilica, gilded with the first gold brought from America. In the 16th century Michelangelo, if we are to believe Vasari, designed the Sforza chapel, so solemn in style. Sixtus V had the Chapel of the Sacraments, with its grandiose dome, built by the architect Fontana. In the 17th century Paul V repeated, on the left-hand side of the church, what Sixtus V had done on the right. He made his chapel more magnificent still, covered it with frescoes intended to refute Protestant iconoclasm and placed, under the Virgin's feet, a crescent moon on which the mountains revealed by Galileo's telescope are shown for the first time. Rainaldi was responsible for the noble and restrained exterior of the apse, which Bernini had dreamt of surrounding with a colonnade.

Finally, in the 18th century, Fuga built the façade (110) and gave the inside of the church its harmonious lines. With magical skill he endowed this interior with a beauty so purely classic that it could be attributed – for a fleeting instant – to the century of the Antonines.

CHAPTER FIVE

Links with the Holy Land and with Dalmatia

[FIFTH AND SEVENTH CENTURIES]

Santo Stefano Rotondo; San Venanzio at the Lateran Baptistery

SANTO STEFANO ROTONDO, a great circular church with double concentric colonnades inside, resembles no other church in Rome (42–45). It does not stand on the ancient foundations of the 'macellum Neronis', as was once thought, and whose plan it was believed to reproduce; it dates, on the contrary – apart from a few later modifications – to the time of Pope Simplicius, who reigned from 468 to 483. It was built during those fifteen or twenty sad and poverty-stricken years after the sack of Rome by the Vandals, at the very moment when the last of the Roman emperors, Romulus Augustulus, lost his throne to a barbarian (476).

The church is of great size, but since the circular aisle is covered by a timber roof, it is very simple and does not resolve any difficult structural problem. The columns are, naturally, borrowed from antique monuments, but many of the capitals carry a pulvin above the abacus – a clear sign of eastern influence.[1]

How was it that Stephen the Protomartyr, whose relics (discovered in 415) were beginning to be scattered throughout the Christian world, came to be honoured in Rome by such an unusual monument? Some antiquarians used to believe that the Roman church reproduced one erected some years before by the Empress Eudoxia, over the tomb of St. Stephen at Jerusalem. They thought this had been a round church, like other memorial churches in the Holy Land. This seemed an ingenious hypothesis, but some years ago Eudoxia's church of St. Stephen was brought to light by excavation: it is a simple basilica and not a rotunda.

Nevertheless, it is very true that a circular building with interior colonnade is reminiscent of the East. Santo Stefano Rotondo can only be compared with the group of circular or polygonal churches in Jerusalem: the Holy Sepulchre, the church of the Ascension on the Mount of Olives and the church (now destroyed) built in honour of the Virgin in the Vale of Joshaphat and imitated at Nicaea. The East has always favoured colonnaded rotundas:

[1] The pulvin or block on top of the capital appears in Syria in the Praetorium of Mousmich as far back as the 2nd century A.D. [These pulvins surmount the capitals of the outer circle, now mainly walled up, but not those of the inner circle.]

such was the Marneion of Gaza in the Emperor Hadrian's time, and such – long afterwards – was the octagonal 'Mosque of Omar', the work of Byzantine architects.

At first sight, Santo Stefano Rotondo seems to resemble the church of the Holy Sepulchre most closely. Certainly there are differences, for the Roman church comprises an extra circuit of columns and a Greek cross is inscribed in it,[1] but there are also striking resemblances. An archaeologist has measured the principal dimensions of Santo Stefano Rotondo and compared them with those of the Holy Sepulchre.[2] The figures speak for themselves. The inner colonnade of Santo Stefano has a radius of 12·06 metres; that of the Holy Sepulchre 12·02 metres. The circumference of Santo Stefano, measured with a line, comes to 75·76 metres, that of the Holy Sepulchre 75·80. Figures for the height are: Santo Stefano 20·9 metres; the Holy Sepulchre 20 metres. The church of the Holy Sepulchre has been restored several times, but the principal dimensions have been preserved through the centuries. Evidently Pope Simplicius had requested these measurements from Jerusalem with a view to reproducing in Rome the holiest church of Christendom. The Holy Sepulchre exercised so considerable an influence on art between the century of Constantine and the Middle Ages that we need not be surprised to see it imitated in Rome in the 5th century.

Built in difficult times, the church of Santo Stefano Rotondo was originally almost completely bare. In the following century John I and Felix IV embellished its interior with precious marbles and with incrustations of costly material, including mother-of-pearl. This rich adornment has long since disappeared. It has been replaced by some fearful frescoes, depicting the most hideous tortures from the times of the persecutions. The Jesuits had them painted in the 16th century, in the dark years of religious strife, to teach their pupils that the forces of evil are eternal and to prepare them for martyrdom.[3]

Santo Stefano Rotondo is filled with tragic memories. It recalls at once the persecutions of the early centuries, the collapse of the Roman Empire and the widespread conflicts of the Reformation.

There is, moreover, an unpretentious mosaic in one of the chapels, and this too commemorates one of the great catastrophes of history (46). It represents two victims of Diocletian's persecution, SS. Primus and Felician, standing on either side of a large golden cross which is decorated with precious stones and surmounted by a half-figure of Christ enclosed in an aureole. Now we know that Pope Theodore, between 642 and 649 (the dates of his pontificate), had the remains of two martyrs [4] transported from the catacombs of the Via Nomentana to Santo Stefano Rotondo – the first example of the translation of relics within

[1] This second (outer) ring of columns is walled up and is thus not apparent to the visitor, who cannot quite realise, today, what the original plan was.

[2] Krautheimer in *Rivista di Archeologia Cristiana*, 1935, pp. 51 ff.

[3] I have spoken of them at greater length in *L'Art Religieux après le Concile de Trente*, pp. 111 ff.

[4] *Liber Pontificalis*, ed. Duchesne, Vol. I, p. 332.

the bounds of the city. It was in their honour that he had the mosaic made in which they figure. It is true that the work does not bear his name, but the inscription which accompanies it cannot be complete. An ancient collection give us another inscription, which would seem to be the sequel to the first. It reads: 'Piety inspired the heart of Pope Theodore, who wished to decorate this sanctuary. He applied all his zeal to honouring the bodies of the saints by this fine decoration (*hoc cultu*), nor did he forget the remains of his father.'[1] So the tomb of Theodore's father stood near the mosaic. G. B. De Rossi thought that *hoc cultu* referred to all the ornament of the church as embellished by Theodore;[2] my own feeling is that *hoc cultu* refers the spectator to the mosaic before him.

At first sight it seems that Theodore's work is just a simple homage rendered to two martyrs. But a curious detail attracts the art-historian's attention: the great golden cross is surmounted by the head and shoulders of Christ, and exactly resembles those seen on the ampullae of Monza – a fact which had struck both Father Garucci and G. B. De Rossi long before. The Monza ampullae contained oil taken from the lamps of churches in the Holy Land. Pilgrims brought back the phial as a souvenir and used the oil as a medicament. They all appear to date from the end of the 6th century. These metal ampullae, of eastern origin, are decorated with evangelical scenes, and great interest has been taken in them since it was realised that they reproduced the mosaics from churches in Jerusalem and the Holy Land. Now several of these ampullae show the Cross of Christ standing empty between those of the two crucified thieves but surmounted by his head and shoulders. The fact is that in Constantine's time, if the Cross was represented at all Christ was not yet shown upon it. At that time Christian art had a triumphal character: it did not celebrate Christ's sufferings, but his victory. The monuments erected by the emperor on the Hill of Calvary were called 'trophies'. This is why one of the mosaics of Jerusalem, reproduced on the Monza ampullae, shows Christ as the vanquisher of death, dominating the empty Cross: a grand conception, in which we recognise something of the heroic genius of the ancients.[3]

There was another cross at Jerusalem – a real cross, and a very famous one. It stood between the Anastasis (church of the Resurrection) and the Martyrium. It crowned a small eminence which was the actual summit of Golgotha. This tall cross was of gold, and precious stones were set in it. It was protected by a sort of canopy, and this had a cupola which, as a passage in the Pilgrimage of Aetheria gives us to understand, was decorated in gold and mosaic.[4] It had been very plausibly conjectured that here too the bust of Christ would have

[1] *Exquirens pietas tectum decorare sacratum*
Pastoris summi Theodoris corda direxit
Qui studio magno sanctorum corpora cultu
Hoc dedicavit, non patris neglecta reliquit.

[2] See G. B. De Rossi, *Mosaici cristiani delle chiese di Roma*, 1899.

[3] It was probably a mosaic from the Martyrium. What seems to prove it is that a Monza ampulla shows the two crucified thieves on their crosses, alongside the bust of Christ dominating his Cross. Now it was in the Martyrium that the three crosses re-discovered by St. Helena were preserved. Hence this crucifixion, in which the thieves figure.

[4] Geyer, *Itinera Hierosolym.*, p. 76: 'Nam quid dicam de ornatu fabricae ipsius quam Constantinus, sub praesentia matris suae ornavit auro, musivo et marmore pretioso tam Ecclesiam majorem quam Anastasim, vel *ad Crucem*, vel cetera Ioca sancta in

been seen above the cross. Some years ago the conjecture gained still further support from the discovery, at Bobbio, of ampullae similar to those of Monza, but sometimes presenting new subjects. And one of these shows us an isolated cross dominated by the bust of Christ.[1]

There are good reasons, therefore, for believing that the mosaic in Santo Stefano Rotondo reproduces the golden cross of Jerusalem which stood between the Anastasis and the Martyrium. This will be still more readily agreed when we realise that Pope Theodore had close links with Jerusalem; his father was a native of the place, and Theodore himself was probably born there.[2] This is a weighty argument which Garucci [3] has already made the most of; but there is still more to be said on the subject.

During the thirty years preceding Theodore's pontificate, Jerusalem had been the scene of the most tragic events. In 614 Chosroes, King of Persia, had invaded Syria and gained possession of Jerusalem. It was one of the great catastrophes of history. Constantine's magnificent buildings, the Anastasis, the Martyrium, the cross of Golgotha and its canopy were all burnt, the town pillaged, part of the population massacred and part taken away into slavery, as in the times of the Assyrians. The conqueror carried off the True Cross, enclosed in its sheath, as the symbol of his triumph. The whole of Judaea was devastated; Chosroes spared only the church of Bethlehem, because he saw a mosaic on its façade which depicted the Magi wearing Persian costume. One can imagine the consternation throughout the Christian world and the despair of the contemporary Pope, Boniface IV; but in these sad centuries, if history still had a voice in the East [4] she was speechless in the West. The *Liber Pontificalis* has not a single line on the capture of Jerusalem. Western Christendom, dumbfounded, maintains an almost unbroken silence. Where the eloquence of the prophets themselves was called for, we have but an uninspired sentence from the *Chronicle* of Isodore of Seville: 'In the fifth year of the reign of Heraclius the Slavs conquered Greece from the Romans and the Persians took possession of Syria, Egypt and a large number of provinces.' [5]

The Emperor Heraclius spent eight years preparing his revenge. Beginning in 622, he undertook three campaigns against the Persians and their allies the Avars: on each occasion he gained resounding victories. At last, in 628, Chosroes having been killed, defeated Persia asked for peace. She obtained it by relinguishing all her conquests and by returning into the conqueror's hands the True Cross, still enclosed in its sheath.

Jerusalem.' To this passage we must add another by Theodosius, a 7th-century pilgrim who tells us that there was a ciborium over the cross with a golden mosaic: 'Et ipsa crux est de auro et gemmis ornata et coelum desuper aureum.'

[1] G. Celi, S. J., *Cimeli Bobbiensi*, 1923, p. 25, fig. 8.

[2] This is how M. Duchesne interprets the passage from the *Liber Pontificalis.* It has to be punctuated thus: 'Theodorus, natione graecus, ex patre Theodoro episcopo, de civitate Jerusalem' (*Lib. Pontif.* I, p. 33). Theodore does not figure on the list of bishops of Jerusalem; 'episcopo' cannot therefore be read together with 'civitate Jerusalem'. 'De civitate Jerusalem' indicates the origin either of the father or the son, and probably of both.

[3] Garucci, Vol. IV, p. 89.

[4] See the Greek chronicle known by the name of *Chronicon Pascale*. Ed. de Bonn, 1832, p. 704.

[5] *Patrologia Latina*, Vol. LXXXIII, col. 1056.

Having triumphed at Constantinople, the emperor resolved to return the Cross to Jerusalem. The town was rising again from its ruins; the Abbot Modestus, helped by the Patriarch of Alexandria, was rebuilding the ruined churches while preserving the main lines of Constantine's originals. The rotunda of the Anastasis rose again, also the basilica of the Martyrium and the cross on Golgotha – but they were far less magnificent than before. The Golgotha cross was no longer gold but silver. On March 21, Heraclius was received at Jerusalem with enthusiasm. The emperor was saddened at the sight of the ruins, but admired the great works of restoration undertaken by Modestus. He thanked him for his zeal, and then returned the True Cross to the church of the Martyrium.

It did not long remain there. Three years later a fresh invasion threatened Palestine: that of the Arabs. Heraclius, alarmed at this unforeseen danger, returned (according to the Greek historians) to Jerusalem, and carried away the wood of the Cross to Constantinople. It was a fortunate inspiration, for in 638, after a prolonged siege, Khalif Omar entered Jerusalem as conqueror. Thus Christendom lost its holy city, for which long centuries of servitude were beginning. Omar, poor and sober like the desert Arab he was, astonished the Christians by his austerity. He was seen, wearing the cloak of the nomads, riding a camel which carried a bag of rice and a bag of flour on one side, a water-skin on the other. Full of respect for the sacred city, he first prayed on the steps of the Martyrium, then conversed with the Patriarch Sophronius. Omar consented to leave him the churches, but the crosses which crowned them had to go. The silver cross of Golgotha could be saved, because it did not stand out against the sky: Modestus had built a covered enclosure for it. This cross certainly survived, for pilgrims of subsequent centuries still spoke of it in the records of their journeys.

Theodore, who was not yet pope, must have learnt with profound emotion of these tragic events. Perhaps he was involved in them, for we are ignorant of his life before 642 and do not know at what date he left Jerusalem, where he probably passed his early years. It is certain, in any case, that he knew of the destruction of the sacred monuments by the Persians, of their restoration by Modestus and finally of Khalif Omar's victory and the humiliation of the Cross. The *Liber Pontificalis*, the dreary biography of the popes of these times, contains not a word to hint at the sad state of Theodore and his predecessors. Nevertheless, the papacy was wounded to the heart and for more than four centuries its secret thought was to reconquer the tomb of the Saviour and that summit of Golgotha where the Cross had been set up.

It is Constantine's cross from Golgotha, the gold cross with its adornment of precious stones, that we recognise in the mosaic in Santo Stefano Rotondo. The pope, who could have seen it in his youth, had it represented here as a melancholy souvenir of past times. Gazing upon this cross, those who had made the pilgrimage to Jerusalem would find all their old memories called up, their old emotions renewed and intensified. For many a poetic fancy surrounded it. It was said to rise in the very centre of the Earth, and as the Earth was the centre of all creation, the cross marked the mid-point of the Universe itself:

the sun and the planets revolved around it. Dante knew something of this tradition, still surviving in his time.[1]

The cross was sunk into the earth at the very place where Adam had been buried, so that the blood of Christ, running down upon the father of all men, had purified humanity at large. Near the foot of the cross had stood the altar on which Abraham had resolved to sacrifice Isaac, thus prophesying to the world the willingness of the Father to sacrifice his Son for the salvation of mankind. Such were the thoughts which the cross in Santo Stefano Rotondo called to mind.

Should it surprise us to find one of the tragic events of history recorded in a mosaic? Not at all, for this is not the only example. A few years before, Pope John IV (640–642) had a mosaic made at the Lateran Baptistery, and here again we find the record of a disaster. The Balkans were at that time being ravaged by the Slavs; in Dalmatia the local inhabitants, fleeing before them, retreated behind the walls of Diocletian's palace at Spalato, or sought refuge among the islands of the Adriatic. Pope John IV, who was of Dalmatian origin, moved by the misfortunes of his compatriots, sent a faithful retainer to buy back those who were reduced to slavery and to rescue the remains of the early martyrs threatened by the barbarians. To receive these holy relics he added the chapel of St. Venantius (San Venanzio) to the baptistery of St. John Lateran, and adorned it with a mosaic which still exists (47). In this mosaic, alongside the Virgin, St. John the Baptist and St. Peter, we see those who spilt their blood for the faith in Dalmatia, at the time of the persecutions. There are St. Venantius, St. Domnio, St. Anastasius the Fuller; besides Paulinus, Telius, Asterius, Septimius, Antiochianus, Gaianus and finally Maurus, Bishop of Parenzo. At the beginning of the century M. Bulic, the well-known Dalmatian archaeologist, excavating the old Christian cemetery of Salona, discovered the funerary inscriptions and the empty sarcophagi of some of these martyrs. Thus it was proved that their remains had indeed been transported to Rome.

But for the Slav invasion and the ruination of Dalmatia, the mosaic in the chapel of St. Venantius would not exist. It is also true that without a few lines of the *Liber Pontificalis*, rather more explicit than usual, we could not understand its true significance. We might suppose that John IV the Dalmatian simply had a particular reverence for the saints of his homeland; but we could not guess that his mosaic recorded the most tragic years in the history of Dalmatia.

The works of art of ancient times conceal mysteries which at times we cannot hope to penetrate. Great historic events – those which shook the innermost soul of man – have, it is true, often left their traces, and we may sometimes glimpse them. The *Liber Pontificalis* tells us nothing of the mosaic in Santo Stefano Rotondo, but some significant details – the shape of the cross, the pope's place of origin, the recent capture of Jerusalem – enable us to conclude that this strange work commemorates the days of deepest mourning of the Christian world. Profound grief is here intermingled with great hopes for the future. The pope

[[1] See *Purgatorio*, Canto II, 1–6.]

had the two martyrs (Primus and Felician) shown standing on either side of the cross on Golgotha; by this iconographic novelty he wished no doubt to suggest that fresh martyrs would come forward to shed their blood for the Cross, now threatened by the infidels.

These dark and dismal memories give the church of Santo Stefano Rotondo an atmosphere of unwonted melancholy which its lonely and abandoned state[1] only serve to emphasise. Thoughts whirl among the labyrinthine columns, straying from catastrophe to catastrophe, from the horror of the persecutions to the collapse of the Roman Empire, from the capture of Jerusalem by Omar to the massacres of the religious wars. Santo Stefano Rotondo would be a depressing place indeed, if a church full of Christian hope could be so.

[[1] It was threatened with collapse in recent years and is still (1959) closed to the public.]

CHAPTER SIX

Art in Rome During a Hundred Years of Iconoclasm

[EIGHTH AND NINTH CENTURIES]

Santa Maria Antiqua; Santa Maria in Domnica; Santa Prassede; Santa Cecilia; San Marco

I

EVER SINCE Pope Gregory II ascended the throne in 715, his pontificate had been a succession of heartbreaking anxieties. The Moslems – the 'sons of Hagar' or 'Hagarites' as they called them in Rome, after traversing Asia Minor with a powerful army, and the Aegean with a fleet of eighteen hundred vessels, had laid siege to Constantinople. This was indeed a momentous and critical moment in history. The fall of Constantinople would have sealed the fate of Christianity in the East. But the emperor, Leo III the Isaurian, worthy successor to Miltiades and Themistocles, repulsed the Arabs in 718 and, once again, Hellenic civilisation was saved.

In the West, a formidable threat remained. The pope had seen the Moslems make short work of Spain, seizing almost the whole country from the Christians in but a few years. Now, with consternation, he saw them invading Gaul. In Narbonne, city of St. Sebastian, there were mosques already, and the infidels were marching on Toulouse, the city of St. Saturninus, bishop and martyr. Would they really conquer Gaul, desecrating St. Hilary's tomb at Poitiers, and St. Martin's at Tours? Were the Christian communities in Europe about to collapse, as had those of North Africa, of Syria and Palestine? It must have been a great joy to the pope when he learnt, in 721, that Eudo, Count of Aquitaine, had inflicted a crushing defeat on the Moslems and halted, at least for some time, their onward march.

Gregory II had some consolations, even in these melancholy times. St. Boniface had just left, with the pope's blessing, to evangelise the wildest of the Germanic tribes. What the Arabs were taking away from Christendom in the south, the valiant missionary was to recover from the north. But the popes of these tragic centuries could hardly hope that their joys would last. They were like Charlemagne in the *Chanson de Roland*: 'when the great emperor, lying on his bed at Aix-la-Chapelle, thinks he will be able to rest from his labours, an angel appears and orders him to take up arms once more in the service of the Lord'.

In 726 there was grave news for Gregory II. Leo III the Isaurian, the great defender of

Christendom, the saviour of Constantinople, had just issued an edict forbidding the veneration of images, whether of God, of the Virgin or of saints and angels. And not only so; he also ordered the destruction of the images, and had set the example by having the statue of Christ, which stood above his palace door, pulled down and smashed. The people rose in protest and blood had flowed. Such was the beginning of a conflict which, with intervals of comparative calm, was to last more than a century.

II

How could such hatred of art burst forth in a city crowded with masterpieces? Admirable works of the Greek sculptors still adorned the public squares of Constantinople, and the Jupiter of Phidias had been visible for many years in the Palace of Lansus. The Byzantines had inherited from the Greeks their love of beauty. They too had created a whole world of wonders; they had filled their churches with frescoes and mosaics, whose praises the poets had sung.

How is one to understand this crime against the spirit? Today, we can see fairly clearly the causes of the great revolution. The image had become, in the East, something quite other than a work of art. People had come to the point of believing that a little of the virtue of the saints, of the Virgin, even of Christ, had passed into the images themselves. Greece retained a Platonic habit of thought; she went on imagining that great heavenly principles came down to earth and imprinted themselves on material things; they believed that the image possessed a mystic power, that it *was* a 'mystery'. Power emanated from images, miracles could be worked by them and were required of them. They could quell tempests and heal the sick, and some scrapings of paint from an icon could be used as medicine. Through the image, the general public seemed to be returning to paganism. There was a conspicuous contrast between these popular superstitions and the monotheism of the Arabs, pure and uncontaminated as the desert. The Moslems, pressing upon the Byzantine world and observing it, felt only contempt for these Christians who had reverted to idolatry. The iconoclastic emperors, natives of Asia, brought up in proximity to the Arabs, had been struck most forcibly by the contrast and soon felt the necessity of reform; but with the clumsiness of men of battle, they destroyed instead of correcting. Motives of profit also played their part in these struggles. The monasteries, where frescoes, miniatures and icons were painted, seemed to the emperors too numerous and too rich. While forbidding the worship of images, they suppressed the monasteries and confiscated their property. The monks, who were at once painters of icons and champions of orthodoxy, were the chief victims of the persecution.

This dispute about the images was one of the great events of history. The whole future of religious art hung in the balance. Had the popes given way, we can scarcely imagine what would have become of the pent-up artistic sense of the Mediterranean peoples. Perhaps there would have been churches adorned with arabesques and inscriptions, like mosques; but we should never have had the splendid Romanesque tympana, nor the myriad statues of the Gothic cathedrals, nor the frescoes of Giotto and Fra Angelico. What years of wretchedness!

We must reflect that no dogma was involved in the dispute and that only a matter of discipline came in question. The popes might have been convinced by the arguments of the innovators, who showed them the danger of a return towards paganism through image-worship. They knew that several of the early Doctors – Clement of Alexandria, Eusebius, Epiphanius – had shown themselves hostile to figured images and that in Spain they had been forbidden by the Council of Elvira. Since the destinies of Christianity were not bound up with those of art, they could have sacrificed the images to put an end to this life-and-death struggle, with its violent persecutions, banishments and spilling of blood which were the prelude to the separation of the churches. But the popes proved themselves as intelligent as they were courageous; they refused to do this violence to the human spirit, and by this refusal they saved Christian art. They did in the 8th and 9th centuries what they did again in the 16th, when the Protestants were burning pictures and breaking up statues: now, as again later, they came to the defence of civilisation.

Gregory II, then, refused to submit to the Emperor's edict and the greater part of Italy rose in his support. The rebels learnt with indignation of pictures being destroyed, frescoes and mosaics hidden under coatings of plaster, and of artists being persecuted, imprisoned and done to death. They announced that they would elect a new emperor, take him to Constantinople and throw out Leo the Isaurian. The pope made every effort to calm the angry spirits; he hoped to lead his sovereign to a more enlightened understanding, and restore him to good sense, by persuasive means. He wrote him two letters which have not come down to us, for those attributed to him are not authentic. No doubt Gregory II had to repeat what Gregory the Great had once written to Serenus, the iconoclastic bishop of Marseilles, for it could not well be better said: 'In forbidding the worship of images you are worthy of praise; in destroying them, worthy of blame. It is one thing to worship images; it is another thing to learn, from the images, whom we should worship.'

Gregory II had been too optimistic in his reliance on reason, and he died without seeing the persecution relent. His successor, Gregory III, a Syrian Greek, felt that he could temporise no longer and that the moment for action had arrived. After writing two letters to the emperor without, however, succeeding in having them delivered, he convened a synod, at which there were present not only bishops and deacons but also citizens of Rome accompanied by their consuls. It was here decided that those who profaned the images of the Saviour, the Virgin, the apostles and the saints should be deprived of the Body and Blood of Christ and cast out from the community of the Church. Leo the Isaurian replied by sending a powerful fleet to the Adriatic which was to break the resistance of the pope and of Italy. But this invincible armada was dispersed and destroyed in a tempest.

When one reads the life of Gregory III in the *Liber Pontificalis*, one is struck by the great energy he devoted to the decoration of churches. It is a most noteworthy fact that at Rome, in the first centuries of the Middle Ages, art was never more flourishing or more fruitful than during the struggle against the iconoclasts. The 7th century, as well as the end of the 9th century and most of the 10th, seem unproductive compared with the years from about 730 to 840; one cannot but suppose that the persecution which brought about the destruction of images in Constantinople caused them to multiply in Rome. As happened later, in the times of Protestantism, the papacy affirmed that which the heretics denied. In the 8th and 9th centuries the churches of Rome were filled with works of art, as happened once more at the end of the 16th and in the 17th century.

Only a small number of these ancient works of art has survived, but we still have written evidence of them. Gregory III began erecting, at the very beginning of his pontificate, two magnificent monuments, one on either side of the Apostle's tomb at St. Peter's. They had columns of onyx surmounted by a silver-encrusted architrave. Upon these architraves he caused to be engraved, on one side, the image of the Saviour with the apostles; on the other side, the Mother of God accompanied by the Holy Virgins. He gave the place of honour to those things which Leo the Isaurian was destroying throughout his empire.

Not far from the Apostle's tomb he built a chapel to express his devotion to all the saints of Christendom. Here he collected together many relics of the apostles and martyrs, and then made a college of priests and monks responsible for reciting daily prayers in their honour. One can still see, in the Grotte Vaticane, the now mutilated marble tablets on which he had the terms of his foundation inscribed, that posterity might preserve its memory. A splendid picture of the Virgin, comparable to the most magnificent in the East, adorned this chapel. It was a painted icon upon which the pope had the Virgin's diadem encrusted with gold, the necklace likewise with gold, the ear-rings with precious stones. With these emblems of respect he replied to the insults heaped upon the Virgin and the saints by the emperor.

In Santa Maria Maggiore, most ancient and venerated of the Virgin Mary's churches, he set up another icon of the Mother of God carrying the Child, it too clothed in gold and precious stones. It stood near the Crib of the Nativity, that holy relic which had probably been brought from Bethlehem at the moment of the Arab invasion.

At the same time he had various churches and chapels built or restored, and covered them with frescoes: San Crisogono, San Callisto, Santa Maria in Aquiro, Sant'Andrea. He had the external colonnades of St. Peter's painted. We could always assume that the saints were gloriously celebrated in art in all these churches, though in the past this was only conjecture, for Gregory's great works seemed to have disappeared without leaving a trace. But, not many years ago, excavations carried out under San Crisogono in Trastevere revealed, at a depth of seven metres, the remains of an 8th-century church with a big apse. Here and there were fragments of frescoes, the oldest of which must have been made by Gregory III's artist's.[1] These mutilated paintings, on the point of final disappearance, exhibit saints only –

[1] The frescoes which recount the histories of St. Benedict and St. Sylvester are subsequent. They were painted towards the beginning of the 11th century by the Benedictines then established at San Crisogono.

standing full length between columns, or as busts in circular medallions. Two of their names are still legible: *Sanctus Felicissimus* and *Sanctus Agapitus*. They were two once celebrated Roman martyrs put to death under Valerian, on the same day as the heroic pope St. Sixtus. There is a very dignified female saint, her head veiled, and wearing the beautiful robe of the Byzantine princesses, but no inscription gives a clue to her identity. These poor remains of the great artistic cycles undertaken by Gregory III testify to his desire to do honour, at Rome, to the saints who were persecuted in the East.

III

During the reign of Constantine V Copronymus,[1] son and successor of Leo the Isaurian, the persecution, far from dying down, was intensified. Constantine Copronymus seems to us a precursor of the 16th-century reformers; moreover, the Protestants placed him among the spiritual ancestors of Luther and Calvin. Not only did he forbid making images of the Virgin, but her name was no longer to be invoked. He spoke of her with insulting sarcasm, and the historians have preserved one of these utterances. He had only contempt for the cult of the saints and had their relics thrown into the sea. Thanks to him, the dispute became still more extended and the popes had to defend at once the images and the relics. The monks never had a more formidable enemy: he drove them from their monasteries, forced them to break their vows and to marry; those who resisted were imprisoned and martyred. Blood flowed more than once in his reign. Disdaining the warnings and the condemnation of the popes in Rome, he appointed himself pope, convoked a Council at Hiera in 754 and caused more than three hundred bishops to condemn 'the criminal art of painting'. The anathema was hurled at whomsoever should depict Christ, the Virgin or the Saints. From then on the fury of destruction was redoubled. In the church of Blachernae (Constantinople) some beautiful frescoes devoted to the Virgin and the miracles of Christ were demolished and replaced by landscapes and flights of birds.

During this long reign of thirty-five years the popes who succeeded each other in Rome – Zacharius, Stephen III, Paul I, Stephen IV, Adrian I – proved themselves unflinching and invincible. Most meritorious of all was the resistance of Zacharius and Stephen III, for they found themselves abandoned defenceless by the emperor while the Lombards were threatening Rome, which they wished to make their capital. What would have become of a papacy reduced to servitude? It was then that Stephen III, convinced that nothing more was to be expected from Constantinople, called the Franks to his rescue. He crossed the Alps in mid-winter to implore the aid of Pepin the Short. The French king, who called up his troops only, as he said, 'for the love of St. Peter and the remission of his sins', defeated the Lombards twice, and then created the Papal State, making the pope a secular ruler (756).

In spite of these great events, the popes did not forget their championship of the images.

[1] Ruled A.D. 740–775.

They all remained faithful to the cause. The texts provide evidence of this, as does a church, adorned with frescoes, discovered in Rome at the beginning of the century.

Some scattered passages in the *Liber Pontificalis* prove that the popes had constantly borne the profanities of Constantine Copronymus in mind. They took every opportunity to reply to them by exalting the images and the relics. Pope Stephen III was the first to arrange a great procession, which became for centuries one of the traditions of Rome. He carried from St. John Lateran to Santa Maria Maggiore a mysterious portrait of Christ, said to have been painted by St. Luke but completed by the angels. It was the famous image 'made without hands', kept for twelve hundred years in the *Sancta Sanctorum* at the Lateran.[1] According to the legend, it had been saved from the fury of the iconoclasts by Germanos, Patriarch of Constantinople, who put it in a boat and left it to the mercy of the sea. Impelled by a favourable wind, it reached the mouth of the Tiber and sailed upstream to Rome, where the pope, miraculously forewarned, received it. It was about the same time, and in the same manner, that the famous wooden crucifix or *Volto Santo* of Lucca – the workmanship of Joseph of Arimathea and the angels – was supposed to have arrived. Such epic tales were born of imaginations stirred by the great persecution. Evidently Stephen III, in exalting the image at the Lateran, wished to express his respect for all images. He proved it again when he had a golden effigy of the Virgin made for Santa Maria Maggiore. It may either have been a bas-relief in *repoussé* or an icon partly concealed under incrustations of gold.

While Constantine Copronymus destroyed the relics of the saints and the very churches which contained them, the popes treated the relics in their possession with the very utmost respect. Zacharius, having discovered the head of St. George in a forgotten reliquary, announced this news to the town; then, followed by the entire population singing hymns of triumph, he carried the precious relic to the church of San Giorgio in Velabro (then called San Giorgio *ad velum aureum*).

But it was in Paul the First's time that relic-worship reached its climax. The Roman cemeteries, where the bodies of the martyrs rested, were no longer kept up. Already five hundred years old and pillaged by the Lombards, the catacombs were beginning to fall in. Paul I took from them the relics most endangered and transported them in solemn procession to the churches of the city. It was then that he removed Petronilla, 'daughter of St. Peter', from the catacombs of Domitilla, to lay her near the Apostle's tomb. He did more than usual honour to the remains of two celebrated popes: St. Stephen (who was said to have been beheaded on his own bishop's throne in the catacombs) and St. Sylvester, witness of Christianity's triumph. He placed their relics in his own house, converted into a church and monastery. The city was continually traversed by these pious processions, which had come to replace the triumphs of antiquity. For the exiles from the East – numerous at that time in Italy – there was indeed a contrast between the respectful ceremonial seen in Rome and the desecrations of Constantinople.

[1] The image of Christ has almost completely disappeared and the one now visible covers up the original. It is painted on cloth and dates from the time of Innocent III.

These saints, whose relics inspired such veneration, were celebrated also in art. On the popes' instructions artists decorated the churches with frescoes, mosaics and bas-reliefs. Zacharius had a sanctuary of St. Cecilia on the Via Tiburtina adorned with paintings. The rotunda where St. Petronilla's body rested was covered with frescoes by Paul I; but the two chapels he dedicated to the Virgin in St. Peter's were even more magnificent, for they were furnished with mosaics. The church in which he re-interred the bodies of SS. Stephen and Sylvester likewise had mosaic-decoration. Stephen III had icons set up in St. Peter's, on the architraves surrounding the altars of St. Peter and St. Andrew; others were placed around the altar of St. Paul at San Paolo fuori le Mura.

The *Liber Pontificalis*, in which these facts are mentioned, is far from being complete. In fact, it hardly says a word about the church of Santa Maria Antiqua, splendidly decorated by the popes of the iconoclastic epoch and re-discovered some years ago.

It was one of the major discoveries of recent years. Until 1900 there existed in the Forum, at the foot of the Palatine, a church known as Santa Maria Liberatrice which had been restored in the 18th century. It had formerly been called *Sancta Maria de Inferno* or *Sancta Maria Libera Nos a Poenis Inferni*. It was mainly of interest for its name, which recalled a medieval legend. This Virgin of the Forum gave protection against hell, an entrance to which was believed to open close by. Indeed, pilgrims were shown a spot, near the church, where a nameless hero of other days had fallen headlong into the abyss – a last reminiscence of the story of Curtius, who gave himself up to the gods of the underworld. Near this sinister place, under the temple of Vesta, a redoubtable monster was hidden – the dragon subdued by St. Sylvester. These poetic reminiscences did not avail to save the church from destruction. But there were no further regrets when an ancient sanctuary, covered with paintings, began to come to light in its place. It was a Roman structure turned into a church in about the 6th century and called *Sancta Maria Antiqua* in the old texts. The frescoes, fairly well preserved at the time of the discovery (when reproductions were made), have since faded, and some have completely disappeared. The majority of them, except for a few which are a little older, date from the times of Zacharias, Paul I and Adrian I, who are represented with the square halo used for persons still alive. So these frescoes are almost all contemporary with the iconoclastic emperors – hence their extraordinary interest.[1] Considered in this light, they reveal to us some of the pre-occupations of men's minds at the time.

Let us enter the left-hand chapel. Under a Christ on the Cross, clothed in the long Syrian robe, we read the name of Zacharius against a dark-complexioned, black-bearded Oriental figure. This pope, with his pitiful looks and unnaturally large eyes, resembles the Egyptian Greeks painted by the artists of Antinoe.[2] It is certainly a portrait, for the head is surrounded

[1] The church was abandoned not many years after the iconoclastic dispute. Pope Leo IV, between 847 and 855, built a new one beside the Via Sacra. It was first called Sancta Maria Antiqua like the church it replaced, and later on Sancta Maria Nova (now Santa Francesca Romana).

[[2] His features have since completely disappeared.]

by the square halo of the living, the round halo being reserved for those already in heaven. The portrait of Pope Zacharius and, not far off, that of Theodotus (a personage of the pontifical court mentioned in contemporary texts) give us the date of the frescoes in this chapel. They belong to the period of Constantine Copronymus and they seem to reply to him. They exalt the Virgin Mary, who sits majestically on her throne, and they celebrate also two saints of the Eastern Church – St. Quiricus and St. Julitta (48, 49). Thus Christ, the Virgin and the saints, whose images were being destroyed in Constantinople, are celebrated here, and in particular SS. Quiricus and Julitta receive marks of respect hitherto unexampled, at least in art. We are shown, in a series of frescoes, the judgment and the execution of the mother and her young son – a tale full of marvels borrowed almost in its entirety from the apocryphal Acts. It is the earliest western example of a martyrdom described, by artists, in all its details. Another feature catches our attention: Theodotus has had himself represented at the feet of the two saints in an attitude as yet almost unknown in art. Kneeling in a humble posture of supplication, a candle in each hand, he prays before the two saintly figures. Confident in his faith, he hopes that his faults will be forgiven him through the intercession of the martyrs, for St. Quiricus, according to his *Acts*, had uttered this prayer as he died: 'O Lord, if one burdened with sin enters the tabernacle of my passion and repents with his whole heart, accord him thy forgiveness.' It is common enough, in the Middle Ages, to find the donor portrayed on his knees and sometimes prostrate before the saint to whom he prays; but it is curious that one of the earliest examples of this attitude should go back to the epoch of the iconoclasts. We must not forget that in Roman mosaics prior to the 8th century donors are not shown kneeling but standing alongside the saints, and distinguished from them only by the square form of their haloes. We see, therefore, that the persecution led to new forms of respect being adopted.

One of the most interesting frescoes at Santa Maria Antiqua shows a long file of saints unfolding on either side of Christ enthroned. The saints of the Roman Church stand to his right, those of the Eastern Church to his left. Both series are identifiable by Greek inscriptions. The Roman saints are, first of all, the great popes – St. Clement, St. Sylvester, St. Leo, St. Gregory. They are modest as priests, bare-headed, without other mark of their dignity than the woollen *pallium*, decorated with a cross. Following them come two Roman martyrs, St. Valentine and St. Alexander, the one venerated by pilgrims on the Via Flaminia, the other on the Via Nomentana. Four eastern saints mingle with these Latins, but the devotion accorded them in Rome for many years had naturalised them there. Two of these were the Greek martyrs SS. Sergius and Bacchus, honoured both in the Forum, close to the Temple of Concord, and at the foot of the Claudian Aqueduct near the Lateran. The others were two monks from Palestine, St. Sabbas and St. Euthymius, devotees of the ascetic life, honoured in the eastern monastery on the Aventine.

The Greek Church was represented on Christ's left hand by the great theologians of Syria, Cappadocia and Egypt: St. John Chrysostom, St. Gregory Nazianzen, St. Basil, St. Peter of Alexandria, St. Cyril, St. Epiphanius, St. Athanasius. These were accompanied by

St. Nicholas, whose relics still rested at Myra, and by St. Erasmus, who had come from Antioch to die in Campania. In this fresco, painted under the eyes of the pope, Rome united in the same loving embrace her own saints and those of the East. Of set purpose she honoured those whose images were being destroyed in Constantinople; and she affirmed that the two Churches were but one. The thoughts it expresses make this a moving work; it is an imposing one too in its solemn, hieratic dignity. This is eastern art in all its purity, completely alien to the liberty of classical Greece, deeply rooted in the ancient arts of Syria, as revealed to us by excavations. Greece brings the divine near to man; the East holds it aloof from him. The saints of Santa Maria Antiqua, with their distant gaze, their solemn stillness as of another world, belong to eternity. The popes and Doctors of the Church carry a book, the martyrs a crown and a small cross, attributes which sum up, and were the very purpose of, their lives. Only St. Clement carried the anchor, which was tied to his neck when they threw him into the sea, and it is the first instance of an instrument of execution becoming, in the martyr's hands, an emblem of victory – an idea much imitated in the following centuries. At Santa Maria Antiqua we seem to meet the Middle Ages in their infancy.

These frescoes, completely clothing the walls of Santa Maria Antiqua, tell stories from the Bible, show the Virgin on her throne for the veneration of pilgrims, glorify the Doctors and martyrs, both of the East and the West, depict donors on their knees before sacred images. They constitute, in fact, a retort on the part of the papacy to the iconoclasm of the emperors. SS. Quiricus and Julitta, SS. Sergius and Bacchus, the Forty Martyrs of Sebaste, St. Abacyrus, who all figure here, had their churches in Constantinople, where their effigies were being destroyed. For the expatriate Greeks in Rome this respect shown for the saints of their country meant both consolation for the present and hope for the future.

In the 7th century these immigrant Greeks, who had arrived at the time of the Arab invasions, were already numerous in Rome; but during the iconoclastic persecution their numbers multiplied. At that time they had seven monasteries, and in the 9th century (when the struggle broke out again in the East) there were nine or possibly even ten. Rome, with her Syrian popes, her eastern quarter of Santa Maria in Cosmedin, her festivals borrowed from the Byzantine Church, was a city half-Hellenised. It was for these foreigners that Pope Zacharias had the *Dialogues* of St. Gregory translated into Greek.

Thus it is more than likely that the frescoes of Santa Maria Antiqua, often accompanied by Greek inscriptions, are the work of eastern monks driven out by the persecution. If there was collaboration on the part of the Latins – as some Latin inscriptions lead one to suppose – they can only have conformed, for these are the unchanging scenes of an ancient eastern tradition. The crucified Christ with his long robe is paralleled in the Syriac manuscript at Florence. The standing Virgin, holding the Child surrounded by an aureole, offers a very close analogy to another Syriac manuscript, that of the Bibliothèque Nationale at Paris. The frescoes discovered some years ago in Cappadocia, which Father Jerphanion made known in a handsome work,[1] present striking similarities to those of Santa Maria Antiqua: the attitudes

[[1] G. de Jerphanion, *Les Eglises Rupestres de la Cappadoce*, Paris, 1925–42.]

and the features of the Saints are the same. Moreover, at Rome as in Cappadocia, the Virgin appears seated on a throne which has a graceful back in the form of a lyre. So these exiled monks had introduced into Italy the style and iconography of eastern painting.

IV

The persecution had already lasted in the East for sixty years when the Empress Irene, shortly after succeeding to the throne, re-established the worship of images. From 787 to 813, from Irene to the accession of Leo V the Armenian, peace seemed to reign at Constantinople, in Greece and in Asia Minor. But an imperial decree was not enough to calm men's minds: the opponents of images had not suddenly reversed their beliefs, many high church dignitaries were still faithful to the doctrine now condemned and almost the entire army remained iconoclastic. It was a victorious soldier, Leo the Armenian, who once again proscribed the images and revived the persecution. It lasted on for thirty years, through the reigns of three emperors, and was at times as violent as under Constantine Copronymus. Churches were despoiled for the second time, frescoes obliterated, pictures burnt, and the sacred vessels, with their ornamental reliefs, destroyed. Monks who refused to obey the emperor's orders were imprisoned, flogged or tortured. They were subjected to ghastly eastern tortures, their eyes being put out, their noses mutilated, while some had insulting verses, written by the emperor himself, seared on their foreheads with red-hot irons. The monk and painter Lazarus had his hands burnt away. Others were sewn up in sacks and thrown into the Bosphorus.

News of these events, arriving in Rome with the fugitives, meant renewed tribulation for the popes. Paschal I was deeply moved by the distress in the East. The monk Theodore, abbot of the monastery of Studion and heroic champion of the images at Constantinople, wrote to the pope requesting him – the father of the faithful – to come to the rescue of those who were defending the outraged truth. The pope immediately sent a letter to Leo the Armenian, but the emperor had the messenger beaten and then shut up in a tomb by way of a prison. Again there was an exodus of monks to Italy, especially to southern Italy which became – as in earlier times – completely Greek. Paschal received many of the fugitives in Rome and built a monastery for them near Santa Prassede.

It would be surprising indeed if the arts of Paschal I's time did not bear traces of these soul-rousing struggles. By an extraordinary chance the three churches built in Rome by him between 817 and 824 have in fact survived, and they retain their mosaics almost intact. The three are: Santa Maria in Domnica, Santa Prassede and Santa Cecilia, well-known churches which certainly enchant the traveller, who, however, would be far more deeply moved if he reflected on those years of conflict during which they were built.

Santa Maria in Domnica, an ancient church on the Coelian Hill, was falling into ruin when Paschal reconstructed it. It has changed little since, for the embellishments added in the 16th century by Leo X were unobtrusive. As he enters and sees the broad nave of the Latin basilica, the visitor from beyond the Alps enjoys a sense of deep satisfaction. These proportions are wholly different from those of our tall and narrow Gothic churches, but they are in keeping with the classical tradition. Created by Greek genius, the basilica expresses repose, while the Gothic church – that typical product of Christianity – is the embodiment of aspiration. It is probable that Pope Paschal, in rebuilding Santa Maria in Domnica, left its proportions unchanged and the columns in their original position. However, he modified the region of the sanctuary, for each aisle terminates, not in a flat wall, but in a small apse – a Syrian arrangement no doubt familiar to the exiled Greeks.

Eastern influence is still more clearly evident in the great mosaic of the apse (54). Its date is not in doubt, since it bears the monogram of Paschal I and a little poem, in gold letters on a deep blue background, celebrates the pope's work. The subject of this mosaic was quite new to Rome and highly significant, because the Virgin here occupies the place of honour in an apse for the very first time. She sits majestically on her throne, while the Child sits on her lap exactly in the middle, and looking directly forward. White-robed angels with golden wings form a guard of honour on either side, and their haloes, one above another, give the impression of an army in deep formation. Pope Paschal, recognisable from the square halo of the living, kneels before the Virgin and grasps her foot with both hands in the humble attitude of a suppliant. Thus the Virgin, once again outraged in Constantinople, is here exalted. She is the Queen of Heaven, surrounded by an angelic host; precious stones are shining on her throne and, all around her, the celestial pastures are bright with flowers. In her presence the pope is more humble even than Theodotus at Santa Maria Antiqua. One can hardly fail to recognise an expiatory intention in this work: hieratic though it may be at first sight, it expresses such passionate feeling. This longing to make the Virgin forget – through the power of love – the insults of the heretics, can be met with elsewhere. Just about the same time, in Molise, Abbot Epiphanius had himself painted in the chapel of San Lorenzo on the Volturno; he too is shown prostrate before the Mother of God, whose feet he is about to kiss.

More than one detail of this mosaic at Santa Maria in Domnica betrays the workmanship of the exiled Greeks. One feels that they were heart and soul behind the pope and happy in their task of portraying the Holy Virgin – now proscribed, just as they were themselves. The Virgin of Santa Maria in Domnica is, in fact, purely Byzantine and recalls in several respects that of Saint Sophia at Salonica. This mosaic in the apse of Saint Sophia belongs, there is every reason to believe, to the time of Empress Irene, who decorated the church between the two persecutions; it is therefore only a few years older than the mosaic in Rome. These two figures of the Virgin have the same posture, and the same costume. But they share, in particular, another detail: both hold in the hand a sort of light cloth with a fringed border.[1] Is it, as has been claimed, the celebrant's maniple, conferring thus on the Virgin Mary a priestly character? It is simpler to interpret it as the elegant *mappa* carried, in the

[1] In the Church of the Dormition at Nicaea there is a mosaic, probably of the 9th century, which shows the Virgin holding the same fringed cloth.

mosaic at Ravenna, by one of Theodora's ladies-in-waiting. The *mappa* gave the finishing touch to the toilette of the Byzantine princesses, and the Virgin on her throne had to be arrayed in all the magnificence of a queen.

The charming device of the superimposed haloes, making of the attendant angels an infinite multitude, is derived from eastern art. It may be seen in a miniature from the famous homilies of St. Gregory Nazianzen in the Bibliothèque Nationale at Paris – a work of the same century as the Roman mosaic. It was so familiar to the eastern artists that we even find it in the subterranean churches of Cappadocia, decorated by the Basilian monks. Classical Greece had known true perspective and the vanishing line; the Christian East reverted to the artless drawing of Assyria, in which persons are placed one above another, and the middle distance rises up instead of receding. What an astonishing triumph of the old Asiatic spirit over Greek science! But we must admit that at Santa Maria in Domnica this return to the child-like art of past ages was a fortunate error. The effect is singularly poetic, and every artistic traveller carries the memory of it away with him when he leaves Rome.

The Virgin in Majesty and her retinue of angels occupy the conch of the apse. On the wall above them (outside the apse) a mosaic frieze, representing Christ among the apostles, runs across the end of the church. Here again the East is in evidence. For the first time in Rome we find Christ seated on a rainbow, surrounded by a halo of light; but he had been so represented long before, in the mosaic recently discovered in the monastery of Hosios David at Salonica. Eastern art, seeking inspiration to express the divine majesty, had drawn on those verses from Ezekiel where the prophet compares the rainbow with the light of heaven. The apostles advance towards Christ bearing the sacred books in their hands, which are veiled with napkins. Their rapid march forward allows the skirts of their tunics to float out behind them; and their folds, which the wind has not deranged, are most finely drawn. At the very first glance one recognises a technique familiar to the Byzantine miniaturists, and which still survives in the French bas-reliefs of the 12th century.

And so, in this mosaic of Santa Maria in Domnica, no matter which detail engages our attention, we see the impact of eastern art every time. Rome had once had, and perhaps still had, her own mosaic-makers, but it is clear that in the days of iconoclasm they took their cue from the Greek refugee artists who had settled in Italy.

V

The basilica of Santa Prassede which Pope Paschal built on the Esquiline would give as pronounced an impression of early date as Santa Maria in Domnica, had it not undergone modification at some unknown period. At intervals along the colonnades of the nave the columns have been replaced by piers, and these carry transverse arches which support the main span of the roof and consolidate the whole building. An alternating rhythm – familiar in Lombardy but strange to Rome – supplanted the unbroken regularity of the colonnade.

In its original form, Santa Prassede was the purest of classical basilicas, more classic even than Santa Maria in Domnica because the columns supported, not arches, but an architrave. We feel that the pope, in rebuilding this church alongside a more ancient one, borrowed from the old basilica not only its columns and its architrave but also its proportions, and its spirit. The columns, which passed from church to church, seem to have been derived originally from those fine arcades which bordered the streets of Rome in the latter years of the ancient world, and which the new age allowed to fall into ruin.

Santa Maria in Domnica was raised in honour of the Virgin, Santa Prassede in honour of the saints – those saints whose relics Constantine Copronymus had destroyed, and whose images Leo the Armenian had obliterated. There can be no doubt whatever that Paschal I wanted to reply to the heresy of the iconoclasts by rendering particular honour to the martyrs and confessors. In fact, he gave orders that the catacombs should be searched for such relics of popes and martyrs as still remained there, and he had them solemnly transported to Santa Prassede. The saints were escorted by the people and clergy of Rome. A long inscription, cut in marble and preserved in the church, names the popes, bishops, deacons, virgins and martyrs whose remains were withdrawn at this time from the abandoned underground passages. Many saints had to remain anonymous because, as the inscription says, 'their names were known to God alone'. The pope had prepared a crypt below the altar to receive the relics. This may well be one of the most ancient crypts in Rome. Until that time the basilicas only had a *Confessio*, placed just below the altar, and this was no more than a narrow vault into which the faithful did not penetrate. They had to be content to pray before the little opening or *fenestella* through which they could see the martyr's tomb; sometimes, they could let down a piece of cloth to touch the sarcophagus, and so be charged with beneficent power. The crypt, on the other hand, was a subterranean church complete with stairways for entry and exit, passages, nave and tombs which could be touched with the hand. Crypts had their own altar where a mass was celebrated in honour of the saints on the date of their death – which the Church called 'the day of their birth'. It is natural that the crypt should appear in Rome at the time of the iconoclastic persecution.[1] It was born of the deep respect which the saints inspired and of the ever-increasing cult of relics. We still see in the crypt of Santa Prassede the sarcophagi in which the remains of the confessors and martyrs were enclosed; we see also, against the wall, the ancient altar which the Cosmati, four centuries later, covered with exquisite mosaic-work. The gloom, the silence, the mystery of these crypts were reminiscent of the catacombs and inspired in worshippers the same religious emotion.

The crypt of Santa Prassede could not contain all the relics brought from the catacombs, and in any case the pope had to allot a certain number of them to the chapels which he built along the sides of the church, notably to the beautiful chapel of San Zeno. Others were

[1] If the crypt of Santa Maria in Cosmedin really dated back to Pope Adrian I it would be anterior to that of Santa Prassede, but the probability is that they both date from the iconoclastic persecution. The same can be said of the crypt of Santo Stefano degli Abissini.

deposited in the oratory of the monastery attached to the Basilica, and here it was the duty of Greek monks to sing the praises of the saints day and night in their own language.

But it was necessary, at a time when all images were condemned by a part of the Christian world, to celebrate through art as well as through the liturgy that multitude of the Blessed, which seemed to fill the church. Their presence had to be made manifest to the eye. So the pope had the apse and the sanctuary-arch adorned with stately mosaics, where the saints appear in their glory.

The apse-mosaic shows Saint Praxedes herself and her sister Pudentiana (along with another saint, probably Zeno) being received into heaven (51). These two daughters of the Senator Pudens had not been martyred, but they had collected the blood of the martyrs and had buried their mortal remains. Saints Peter and Paul, each with a hand on the shoulders of the two saintly women, present them to Christ, who, attired in gold, seems to be descending from heaven by a stairway of purple clouds. Under this deep blue sky, in this palm-shaded paradise, one living man has found a place: it is Pope Paschal, identified by his square halo and the church he carries in his hand. It is remarkable that Paschal, prostrate at the Virgin's feet in Santa Maria in Domnica, should here be standing erect before Christ and the saints. The explanation is that the pattern given to the artist demanded this attitude on the part of the votary. The pattern in question was the magnificent mosaic of Santi Cosma e Damiano by the Forum (50): every detail of it is imitated in so far as it was possible to imitate a work of the 6th century in the 9th. Nothing has been forgotten. Below are the same twelve sheep approaching the Mystic Lamb standing on a hill; above, the same elders of the Apocalypse holding out their crowns towards the Lamb, now lying on the throne between the Seven Candlesticks and the Four Beasts. The pope had chosen his model well, for the arrival of the saints in heaven after their victory could not be represented more majestically. We may visualise Paschal as a wistful admirer of the great works of art of the past, of the basilicas lost among the ruins. To him it seemed that one could only imitate, without ever hoping to equal them. Rome has always turned back to her past with a nostalgic affection, and in that past she has found some of her grandest inspirations. It is easy to understand how, faithful to her tradition, she remained almost impervious to the Romanesque and the Gothic. Pope Paschal built basilicas modelled on those of the ancients, because he was acutely conscious of their beauty. Moreover, he liked to retain, if possible, some souvenir of the vanished past. In front of Santa Maria in Domnica he placed a pagan votive offering, the famous marble boat re-made by Leo X; in the atrium of Santa Cecilia he left, as its most precious ornament, the splendid antique vase which can still be seen there; and at Santa Prassede he placed another such vase over the doorway of St. Zeno's chapel, which itself is composed of antique fragments. The pope regarded these objects, spared by the ravages of time, as reminders of a great past, and he viewed them rather as family relics.

Paschal I was not content with copying the mosaic of Santi Cosma e Damiano, but had another executed in honour of the confessors and martyrs whose bones lay in the crypt.

This mosaic covers the sanctuary-arch and represents the Heavenly Jerusalem of the Apocalypse, the city of the elect built with precious stones. In the middle stands Christ flanked by two angels; to the sides come the Virgin, John the Baptist, Saint Praxedes and the eleven apostles; Moses and Elijah stand on Christ's right and left hand as on Mount Tabor. Before the walls, built of precious stones, the procession is being received by angels, and St. Peter holds the keys of the Celestial City. These saints advancing towards the Heavenly Jerusalem – popes, confessors, virgins and martyrs – are precisely those whose remains were preserved at Santa Prassede. They come forward carrying golden crowns in their veiled hands. But they are not alone: below them we see the host of the elect clothed in white and carrying palms – a mighty host in which the faithful, coming to pray at Santa Prassede, hoped themselves to find a place on the great day of reckoning. These multitudes are waiting to enter the Holy City at the moment when God shall come, when he, in the sublime phrase from the Revelation which has wrung so many hearts, 'shall wipe away all tears from their eyes'.

There could be no theme more tremendous; nor could there be one more inaccessible to the art of the 9th century. This infantile town, these lined-up saints, these crowds with their heads one above another, could only have been signs or signals to provoke thought and set the imagination in motion. Byzantine art has usually such grandeur, such majesty in its figures and compositions evolved through the centuries, that one might well wonder if the naïve Jerusalem of Santa Prassede were not created by Paschal's native artists. I thought so for a long time, but have had to give in to the evidence. At the Bibliothèque Nationale in Paris there is a Greek manuscript of the same century as the Santa Prassede mosaic, in which the Heavenly Jerusalem is represented in the same manner.[1] We see Christ, standing between two angels, overlooking an enclosure made of precious stones, where the saints appear crowded together. The analogy is so close that one must admit the existence of eastern models for this scene, which were known to the exiled Greeks in Rome.

This Heavenly Jerusalem is their work, but one recognises their hand also in the apse-mosaic, copied from Santi Cosma e Damiano, which we have just been considering. A new technique appears here. While figures of the 6th century preserve something of antique fullness and flexibility, those of the 9th show the immobility of eastern art; the haloes accentuate their hieratic character and the golden, bejewelled robes of the two young saints turn them into princesses of Constantinople. At Santi Cosma e Damiano the clearly-defined shadows still give the illusion of reality, and we feel that, in the 6th century, some traditions of Hellenistic art were still alive. In the 9th century these traditions are forgotten. At Santa Prassede – and, for that matter, in all Pope Paschal's mosaics – almost all sense of depth has gone and we are left with a coloured pattern, a decorative arabesque. The artist abstracts himself from real life and creates these figures, which throw no shadow, and are subject to no law of nature; yet these distant figures work all the more powerfully on the imagination, for they seem to carry us away to the supernatural world.

These same mosaic-workers were certainly responsible also for San Zeno's chapel, which

[1] The MS. bears the number 923. The miniature gives only the central part of the composition.

the pope built into the right-hand aisle of Santa Prassede. To be sure of this we need only compare the apostles' costumes in the two sets of mosaics – white cloaks banded here and there in brown. Nothing could be more reminiscent of the East than this little sanctuary, with its gilded surfaces shining softly in the faint candle-light. Everything here makes us think of Salonica and Ravenna, and of Asia beyond. From the four corners four angels standing on azure spheres curve upwards with the groining of the vault and raise above their heads the half-figure of Christ enclosed in a corona of triumph (52). It is a splendid design, first seen in a tomb at Palmyra and repeated in the Byzantine mosaics at Ravenna.[1] The round medallions of apostles and saints resemble those on the walls of St. Demetrius at Salonica. We can make out, in the half-light of San Zeno's chapel, several striking features of Byzantine iconography. The Transfiguration (of which only a portion remains) is conceived like a similar scene from the life of St. Gregory Nazianzen, from the Greek manuscript in the Bibliothèque Nationale. Jesus, Moses and Elijah, instead of being separated, are enveloped in the same aureole. On another wall of the chapel the Virgin and John the Baptist, placed facing each other symmetrically with gestures of entreaty, reproduce the 'deësis' of eastern artists, in which the Mother of God and the Forerunner together intercede for man. Close by, Peter and Paul appear on either side of an empty throne (53). Nothing could be more solemn and mysterious than this imposing throne, on which someone must come and take his seat. It is the throne which awaits the Supreme Judge when he comes to judge the world on the Last Day. This great conception derives from a sermon by the Syrian St. Ephraim, which had wide currency in the East from the 4th century onwards. He describes the Last Judgment in such precise detail that the passage became famous and inspired all the eastern artists. It is he who describes the throne prepared for Christ's coming.

All these artistic motives connect the chapel of San Zeno with the East. If we consider, further, that the saints stand out against a golden background, and that SS. Praxedes, Pudentiana and Agnes are clothed like Byzantine empresses, it will seem natural to attribute the whole composition to the Greeks. The Romans felt there was some rare quality in this little gold-encrusted chapel, for they called it 'the garden of Paradise' – *Hortus Paradisi*. It is legitimate, therefore, to believe that the whole of the work undertaken by the pope at Santa Prassede was carried out by the exiled Greek monks, assisted by native artists.

VI

One day when Pope Paschal had gone to pray at Santa Cecilia in Trastevere he was much struck by its dilapidated appearance. It was always his concern to do honour to the saints, so he resolved to reconstruct the church. In the 9th century the oldest basilicas in Rome had already stood for five hundred years and several of them threatened to collapse. To the men of that generation the age of Constantine, surrounded as it was with legends, already seemed very remote.

[[1] In the chapel of the Episcopal Palace and, in a slightly different form, at San Vitale.]

The walls, apse and main dimensions of the church built by Paschal I are preserved, but the bad taste of restorers in recent centuries, added to their contempt for the past, has altogether deprived it, internally, of its character (102). Up to the 18th century Santa Cecilia retained a remarkable feature: there were galleries over the aisles. Today these galleries are no more, but when, some years ago, a talented architect prepared plans for a restoration, hoping to restore to the church its ancient beauty, they were not forgotten. There are weighty reasons for believing that they went back to Pope Paschal's reconstruction. Such galleries are one of the characteristics of eastern basilicas. For a long time Rome knew nothing of them, but they appeared there at the time when the government of the Byzantine Exarchs, and the immigration of the Greeks, brought with them the language, the liturgy and the art of the Eastern Empire. They appear at the end of the 6th century at San Lorenzo fuori le Mura (30), in the 7th century at Sant'Agnese, in the 8th at Santa Maria in Cosmedin, in the 9th at Santa Cecilia.[1] In this fine basilica, which Paschal had rebuilt in honour of the celebrated Virgin Martyr, one essential was lacking – the saint's relics. This was a matter of grave concern to the pope. One Sunday morning at dawn, as he was celebrating in St. Peter's the eve of the Apostle's festival, his eyes closed for a moment and he saw a vision. A young girl with the aspect of an angel appeared to him; she told him that she was St. Cecilia, that her body had not been carried away by the Lombards (as he had feared), but that, by searching, he could find it, and deposit it in the church he had raised in her honour. The pope, full of confidence in his vision, set about the search straight away and was not slow to discover the tomb among the catacombs of the Appian Way. St. Cecilia was found lying there still dressed in a golden gown. At the same time he found St. Valerian (to whom Cecilia was married), near whom blood-stained clothes were lying, and then the bodies of their friends SS. Tiburtius and Maximus, who were martyred at the same time. Finally, he found the remains of two popes of the persecutions – Urban and Lucius. Paschal, filled with joy, transferred these much-desired relics to the church of Santa Cecilia.[2]

To do honour to the saints whose remains he had just discovered, the pope built a monastery where their praises were sung day by day. Then he celebrated them in the great mosaic of the basilica. The theme of Santa Prassede – created originally by the artists of SS. Cosma e Damiano – was here taken up once again, but less successfully. The saints, standing side by side, retain their solemnity, but are no longer united by a common sentiment. Peter and Paul, presenting SS. Cecilia and Valerian to Christ, no longer touch their shoulders with a tender and familiar gesture.[3] Curiously enough, it is St. Cecilia who puts her hand on the shoulder of Pope Paschal, shown with the square halo of the living, to introduce him to heaven. At Santa Prassede the pope, standing a little apart, only timidly joins the august

[[1] Also at the Santi Quattro Coronati (60).]

[2] Some 12th-century frescoes which told this story were long visible in the portico of the basilica, but only one of them has survived. It has been removed to the inside of the church and represents the young saint appearing to the pope in his vision.

[3] The figure at one end of the row is St. Agatha, to whom the monastery attached to Santa Cecilia was dedicated.

assembly. Here, such is his confidence in the saints' intercession that he enters into eternal life under St. Cecilia's protection. These isolated figures seem a little more stark and rigid even than those at Santa Prassede; the colours themselves are duller. In short, the mosaic of Santa Cecilia is the product of a different workshop. We must remember that Pope Paschal, who reigned for only seven years, decorated almost simultaneously three great basilicas and two chapels – those of San Zeno at Santa Prassede and of SS. Processus and Martinian at St. Peter's.[1] These tremendous undertakings necessitated more than one mosaic workshop. Perhaps some Roman workers joined the Greeks, but Greek influence predominated. At Santa Cecilia there is one revealing detail: Christ no longer raises his hand in a grand welcoming gesture, but gives his blessing in the Greek manner. In the Greek benediction the two first fingers are raised and the thumb crosses to the third finger; in the Latin benediction the thumb and first two fingers are raised, the third and fourth fingers turned down. The Greeks, say the old liturgical authorities, form the initial letters of the name of Jesus Christ; the Latins express the mystery of the Three Persons of the Trinity and the two natures of Christ. The two gestures are therefore quite different, and wherever the thumb and third finger meet, eastern influence is clear. On the wall above the apse at Santa Cecilia there was a mosaic frieze now destroyed, but of which Ciampini made a drawing. It represented female saints wearing the beautiful costume of the Byzantine empresses. Among the palm-trees of the heavenly garden they were advancing towards the Virgin carrying crowns in their veiled hands: an eastern motive, of which Sant'Apollinare Nuovo at Ravenna offers an early example.

Such are the three fine basilicas in which Paschal I so magnificently expressed his devotion to images and his veneration for the saints.

VII

The death of Leo the Armenian, that implacable iconoclast, did not bring the persecution to an end. His two successors, Michael II and Theophilus, continued to proscribe Christian art, and Theophilus showed himself, at times, as violent as his most impassioned predecessors. His reign coincides with that of Pope Gregory IV, another defender and diffuser of images.

One of Gregory IV's great undertakings was the reconstruction of San Marco, which had been built on the Campus Martius, not far from the Capitol, in the 4th century. The visitor entering this old church today only finds a 17th-century interior and ornamentation in stucco. There is nothing to carry him back to Carolingian times until he notices the gleaming gold of Gregory's mosaic in the apse. Like those of Santa Prassede and Santa Cecilia, it imitates the beautiful mosaic of SS. Cosma e Damiano, but the imitation is becoming less and less faithful. Isolated, motionless figures stand side by side to right and left of Christ.

[1] The chapel of SS. Processus and Martinian, the four groins of whose vault rose from four corner-columns, must have been very similar to the chapel of San Zeno.

Only St. Mark the Evangelist puts his hand on the shoulder of Gregory IV, with his rectangular halo of the living, to present him to Christ. The saints here assembled are those whose relics the church possessed: three martyrs (Agapitus, Felicissimus, Agnes), Mark the Pope and Mark the Evangelist.

This work, more hieratic even than the mosaic in Santa Cecilia, again bears the unmistakable imprint of eastern art. Christ blesses in the Greek manner and his ascetic features are lined with sorrow: it is the Byzantine Pantocrator afflicted by the sins of the world. His feet do not rest upon the earth but on a little floating platform. In the same way each of the saints stands on a sort of pedestal. This device enhances the solemnity of the figures, but removes them yet farther from life. The idea has been attributed to Gregory's artists, but in reality it had long since been familiar to the Greeks. At Sant'Apollinare in Classe, Ravenna, St. Michael and St. Gabriel, dressed as dignitaries of the Byzantine court, are already shown raised up in this way. Byzantine ivories, as well as manuscripts, offer further examples. Emperors and empresses stand on pedestals which seems to raise them above humanity, while Christ, raised up yet higher, extends his hands over their heads. The old mosaic of Santi Cosma e Damiano, which is still the prototype, has thus been more and more transformed by artists imbued with the spirit of eastern art. For movement they substituted immobility, which to their mind better expressed the changelessness of eternal life; and the blue background which recalled the sky was set aside in favour of a gold ground suggesting the light of eternity that would never wane.

Gregory IV created other works of which nothing remains. He decorated the triclinium of the Lateran with a great mosaic, and the portico of St. Peter's, on either side of the silver doors, with another mosaic sequence. On his orders, the portico of San Giorgio in Velabro was decorated with frescoes. Probably all these frescoes and mosaics celebrated the saints, for whom Pope Gregory professed an ardent devotion. Feeling that the bodies of St. Calixtus, St. Cornelius and St. Calepodius, buried under Santa Maria in Trastevere, were not receiving the honour due to them, he raised the level of the sanctuary and deposited the relics in a crypt constructed beneath it.

It would seem that the violence of the iconoclastic emperors had the effect of positively promoting the cult of the saints and their relics – not only in Rome but all over the West. In fact, it was in the second half of the 8th and in the early 9th century that the French churches and monasteries sent to Rome asking for the bodies of confessors and martyrs for their crypts. France was following the example of the popes who removed these saintly remains from the catacombs, that they might be better honoured. In 751 the abbot of Saint-Denis, with the consent of Pope Zacharius, carried away from the catacombs the relics of St. Vitus (known in France as St. Guy). In 756 the Bishop of Metz took from Rome the bodies of St. Nabor, St. Nazarius and St. Gorgonius – the same Gorgonius whose panegyric was to be written, many centuries after, by Bossuet. In 826, during Leo the Armenian's persecution, the relics of St. Sebastian were taken from Rome to Saint-Médard de Soissons and the great Roman saint (who was said to have been born at Narbonne) became a French one. In 840 a monk of Hautvillers, near Reims, carried home the body of St. Helena, taken from her supposed tomb on the Via Labicana. So St. Helena became a saint of Champagne, and a statue of her appeared in due course in Reims cathedral, as well as a bas-relief showing the discovery of the True Cross.

Thus, France associated herself with the popes in the cult of the Roman saints.[1] Then a remarkable thing happened, the full significance of which can be grasped only in the context of the period. In 736, at the time of Leo the Isaurian's persecution, Pope Gregory III had established, in the chapel of St. Peter already referred to, a festival of all the saints. In 835, during the persecution of Theophilus, Pope Gregory IV decided that this Feast should be celebrated by the whole Christian world on November 1. So we see that the feast of All Saints was originally an atonement offered to the saints for the insults lavished upon them by the iconoclastic emperors.

VIII

It was not only through frescoes, mosaics and icons studded with silver or gold that the popes kept up their devotion to images. They also had hangings woven, and these were embroidered with scenes taken from the Gospels or the lives of saints.

It is a fact well worthy of notice that, until the iconoclastic dispute, the *Liber Pontificalis* rarely makes mention of hangings being presented by the popes to the churches in Rome. Those that are mentioned are usually gifts sent by the eastern emperors or by great dignitaries of the Byzantine court. One gains the impression that Constantinople had maintained her monopoly of silk – that marvel whose secret she had stolen from China in the time of Justinian. But when the fugitive monks came to Rome they seem to have brought with them the art of weaving rich materials for the sanctuary. At the height of the persecution the *Liber Pontificalis* speaks for the first time of an altar-cloth on which the Nativity was represented: Zacharius had had it made for St. Peter's. There were, therefore, workshops in Rome capable of turning out cloths decorated with religious scenes. These skilful weavers must have been easterners, for such cloths are distinguished in the inventories by their makers' Greek names. The popes constantly had recourse to their talent and, from Zacharius onwards, we find innumerable references in the *Liber Pontificalis* to these historiated fabrics.

We cannot form the least conception, today, of the magnificence of the Roman basilicas in Carolingian times. Between the columns of each arcade rich eastern cloths were suspended, elegantly decorated on both sides. In the centre a silver crown known as the *regnum* was suspended; sometimes the crown was replaced by a chalice. At Santa Maria Maggiore, suspended between the columns, there were forty-two of these silver chalices, the gift of Pope Paschal. The greater churches of Rome had altar-frontals consisting of bas-reliefs in chased silver; the altars themselves were draped with cloths, richly embellished with gold

[[1] Not only France. It must be borne in mind, here and elsewhere, that the author was writing mainly for a French public.]

embroidery and precious stones. These hangings were changed according to liturgical needs and the scenes exposed – whether from the life of Jesus Christ or of the Virgin – corresponded to the great festivals of the year. Over the altar stood a canopy or baldaquin not (as it would be later) of marble, but of silver. Between the columns of the baldaquin, and arranged to be drawn along rods of precious metal, there were curtains, adorned with crosses, flowers, lions, eagles and oriental monsters. A crown combined with a cross, both of gold or silver, hung above the altar. An iconostasis sheathed in silver separated the priests from the congregation, and this was surmounted by icons half hidden under incrustations of precious metal, while Christ, the Virgin, apostles and angels formed a row above the architrave. Curtains of figured silk fabric could be used to close the iconostasis completely, so shutting off a sort of Holy of Holies. Other hangings surrounded the sanctuary, and a huge curtain, sometimes decorated with sacred subjects, hung before the door of the church. Innumerable silver lamps illumined the interior: they bore Greek names, a *hexaphoti* being a lamp with six wicks, an *enneaphoti* one with nine. Great silver chandeliers in the shape of crowns or crosses were suspended by chains: one of these at St. Peter's carried thirteen hundred wax candles. These countless lamps, hanging at different heights above the ground, threw a complex network of light and shade throughout the church. In front of the *Confessio* where the bones of the martyrs lay, golden lamps were kept burning. At St. Peter's the door of the *Confessio* was of gold and the steps leading down to it of silver; gold bas-reliefs surrounded the Apostle's tomb, which rested on sheets of gold.[1] In all the basilicas the pavements, made of ornamental marbles, were as rich as those of the Byzantine churches. The walls were faced with marble. The gold of the great mosaics which filled the apses matched the magnificence around them. Everything glittered in the lamp-light; it shone no less in the light of day, for the ancient basilicas were infinitely better lit than now. The 17th century, seized with a sudden passion for a 'dim religious light', blocked up more than half the windows in all these old churches.

Such was the splendour of the basilicas in which Charlemagne set foot. The palaces and temples of pagan Rome were falling into their final decay, the patrician villas were crumbling to dust, but the churches brought new beauties before the eyes of men, with all the added enchantment of colour. By their very magnificence they refuted the heresy of the iconoclasts.

The end of the persecution was now approaching. On the death of Theophilus his wife, the empress Theodora, who had never ceased to deplore the emperor's violence against those who believed in images, determined to re-establish their worship. Thus two women, Irene and Theodora, triumphed on two separate occasions over the iconoclasts. Their sensitive natures were depressed by the bare church walls, and they divined, with their feminine instinct, all that art can add to the appeal of the faith.

[[1] The full story of the *Confessio* of St. Peter's, as told by Toynbee and Ward Perkins in *The Shrine of St. Peter*, Chapter 7, is a useful complement and corrective to this highly coloured description evidently drawn from an early but not wholly reliable source.]

Theodora, as Regent, deposed the iconoclastic Patriarch of Constantinople and then convened a Council at which the supporters of the images carried the day. On March 11, 843, a solemn service was held in St. Sophia to celebrate the great victory which now, at last, was final. Still today the Greek Church observes the anniversary of this triumph as a festival.

The heresy was defeated and art was free to resume its splendid career. On that great day the steadfastness of the popes reaped its reward. The days of iconoclasm form one of the great chapters in the history of the papacy, and one too often forgotten today. For more than a century the eastern emperors did but intensify the violence of their persecution, but the popes, convinced that truth was on their side, remained unshaken. Rome, once again, became the champion of civilisation. As a result, while art remained sterile at Constantinople, it blossomed in Rome. Bigotry had its usual effect: it exalted the very thing it set out to destroy. So true is it that the Roman artistic revival was due to the conflict itself, that we find art becoming suddenly impoverished there as soon as the heresy is defeated. Mosaics disappear, those of San Marco being the last; and we have to wait two hundred and fifty years until another mosaic appears in a Roman church.

The papacy, seeking to glorify the images, appealed to all artists – Greeks and Latins alike. There is therefore no cause for surprise if the frescoes and mosaics carry a deep imprint of eastern art. The popes, with a touching sense of tact, wished to give the Greek artists the consolation of practising an art which had earned them persecution and exile. This collaboration of Greeks and Latins had, for them, a great symbolic significance.

Seen in this light the art of the 8th and 9th centuries will, I think, seem much more interesting. If we really want to understand these old Roman churches, which have so much to teach us, we must enter them with History as our companion and guide.

CHAPTER SEVEN

The Emperor Otto III: His Roman Adventure and His Saintly Contemporaries

[TENTH CENTURY]

San Bartolomeo dell'Isola; San Sebastiano in Pallara; Castel Sant'Elia; Grottaferrata

I

IN THE 10th century, as in late classical times, the Aventine was the hill of the great Roman families. It enjoyed a wider horizon, purer air and a summer sun less scorching than most of Rome. The monks – that second aristocracy – had several communities near the houses of the nobility. Two of these were famous: that of Santa Maria Aventino (lately placed under the Cluniac rule by St. Odo) and that of SS. Boniface and Alexis. The latter was a cosmopolitan monastery where, alongside the Latins, Greeks and Slavs were to be found, and from which missionaries set forth to evangelise the Baltic coasts. Today St. Mary's on the Aventine has become the Priory of the Knights of Malta, built to Piranesi's designs; as for Sant'Alessio, it is an 18th-century church in which nothing recalls the distant past, except perhaps the epitaph of Crescentius let into a wall of the cloister.

In the monastery of St. Boniface, at the end of the 10th century, there was an extraordinary man who was to attain to sainthood through martyrdom; this was Adalbert, Bishop of Prague. Exhausted by his unrelenting struggle against the paganism of Bohemia – a country still untamed – he had come to Rome seeking a little rest. His ardent, self-sacrificing soul had a profound influence on other passionate natures. His conversation had deeply stirred the young emperor Otto III, who was then in Rome and whose palace stood right beside the monastery of St. Boniface. After his consecration he had sent, as a gift to his neighbours the monks, the magnificent mantle which he had worn on the day of the ceremony. It was embroidered with apocalyptic scenes – a tremendous theme which gripped the imagination of the time and was soon to gain general currency in the world of art. Thus had the young emperor, moving forward in St. Peter's at the service, been surrounded by the terrors of the Last Day.

Everything about this young man was strange; everything about him astonished the Romans, and astonished his compatriots, the Germans, even more. Son of a princess of Constantinople, accustomed since childhood to look up to Hellenic civilisation, contemptuous of

Germanic barbarism, he had adopted Byzantine ceremonial in his Roman palace. The dignitaries of his court had Greek names, and he took his meals alone, wearing a golden cloak, sitting at a sigma-shaped table on a raised platform. All this pomp was an indication of his vast ambitions, for he aspired to nothing less than the mastery of the world. He had near him a man of immense learning who passed for a magician in that ignorant age, namely the Frenchman Gerbert – humanist, mathematician and astronomer. With his deep classical culture and passionate admiration for the ancient world, he had brought home to the young Otto the splendour of the Roman Empire and implanted in him the desire to revive it. But what he wished to revive was not merely the empire of Charlemagne, too restricted for his dreams, but the vaster empire of Justinian. Gerbert took pleasure in humouring his pupil's dreams and when he became pope in 999 he took the name of Sylvester after the great pope of the triumph of the Church. In this way he sought to show that he would labour for the well-being of the world like a new Sylvester, side by side with a new Constantine.

A miniature in the library at Chantilly represents Otto III seated on the imperial throne (59).[1] A young, handsome and dignified figure, he holds in one hand a long sceptre, in the other the orb inscribed with a cross. A number of women wearing crowns approach the emperor and offer him lesser golden globes. They represent the nations, come to do homage to their sovereign. We can feel the grandeur of this conception – this dream of a great Christian empire united by love. It illumines – if with a melancholy light – these two distant figures, Otto III and Sylvester II, in the darkness of the 10th century. They dreamed of that unity which men had sought – but sought in vain – since the fall of the Roman Empire.

Biding his time until the right moment should come for world conquest, the young emperor had to gain control of Rome. In his absence the patrician Crescentius had led a revolt, had driven out the German pope, chosen a new pope and prepared the city to resist attack. The Romans hated these foreigners who periodically came down from the Alps, treated Italy as a subject country, levied taxes and appointed popes. They revolted; but the Germans, with their well-disciplined troops, always kept the upper hand. Crescentius, besieged in the Castel Sant'Angelo, put up a courageous defence; but, after a long siege, the old fortress was taken and Crescentius beheaded. His body and those of the twelve heads of the city wards were hung from gibbets on top of the Monte Mario so that all Rome could see them from afar.

Nevertheless, the emperor allowed Crescentius to be buried in San Pancrazio on the Janiculum, where his epitaph, transcribed by Baronius, was long visible. It told that Crescentius came of an illustrious family, that he was handsome, that he governed Rome with wisdom

[[1] The Chantilly miniature, a detached page from a MS. of the *Registrum Gregorii* still preserved in Trier, dates from *c.* 983 and has usually been considered to represent Otto II. A very similar scene (extending, however, to a pair of miniatures occupying opposite pages) occurs in the somewhat later Gospels of Otto III at Munich and is assumed to represent that emperor himself, while the provinces are identified as Roma, Gallia, Germania and Sclavonia. The emperors' features in the two miniatures are hardly to be distinguished.]

and made the city powerful, until that day when, betrayed by fortune, he met his end. Strange to say, not a word in these twelve Latin verses tells of his heroic struggle against the foreigner. No doubt his family were afraid of rousing once more the emperor's wrath. Rome, however, was no less faithful to her hero's memory. It was in vain that Otto styled himself 'Roman' in his proclamations to the people, in vain that he declared his love for the Eternal City and his 'dear sons'. Nothing could make men forget this tragic episode at the opening of his reign.

Otto III had allowed his passionate nature to prompt an act of merciless violence, which, however, he soon came to regret. He was assailed by feelings of remorse. There were two elements in his character: sometimes he was Caesar Augustus, the mighty emperor and future master of the world; sometimes the humble devotee, trembling for his soul's salvation, forgetful of the earth in his concentration on heavenly things. His mother, the Byzantine princess, had given him his sense of personal grandeur, but it was to his grandmother, St. Adelaide, that he owed his humility. Hence the strange contrasts of his personality. After having Crescentius put to death he undertook a pilgrimage to secure heaven's forgiveness for his brutal act. He journeyed on foot to the sanctuary of St. Michael in the Monte Gargano. This wild mountain overlooking the Adriatic, with its deep forest and its mysterious cave where the Archangel had left his foot-prints, was then one of the holy places of Christian Europe. In fear and trembling men entered this gloomy sanctuary, whose threshold bore the inscription from the Bible: *terribilis est iste locus.*

The young emperor had a craving for religious emotion. We find him at Monte Cassino and at Subiaco, following the trail of St. Benedict. In Rome he was known to disappear for days together, hidden hermit-like in a cell near the church of San Clemente. Gerbert, his master, instructed Otto in the things of this world, but three great ascetics, three future saints –Romuald, Nilus and Adalbert – imparted to him their heavenly learning. These three men shared a restlessness of spirit which prevented them from staying for long in any one monastery or hermitage. They kept searching for the place where the perfect life could be led, but could never find it. It is difficult even to follow the movements of St. Romuald. We find him near Venice, then at St. Michel de Cuxa in the south of France, where he persuaded the Doge Orseolo, who had also become an anchorite, to follow him; then in Istria, then in Hungary. Later he reappears in Italy: in the forest of the Camaldolesi, where he founded a monastery; near Ravenna, where he lived in a hut among the marshes; and finally, in the Val de Castro near Camerino, where he died in the wilds. It was at Ravenna that Otto III saw him; he was overwhelmed by the supernatural stature of the ascetic who had attained to the highest level of non-attachment and already seemed a stranger on earth. Determined to follow his example, Otto promised him soon to lay down the imperial crown and then to concern himself, as a simple Christian, only with the salvation of his soul.

St. Nilus too was a nomad monk. A Greek of Calabria, he entered the Basilian monastery of Rossano before starting on his wanderings. We meet him at Capua, at Monte Cassino, at Valleluce near by, at Serperi near Gaeta and finally almost at the gates of Rome, at Grottaferrata, where he died at the age of ninety-six. Convinced that there was no stable dwelling in this world, he was perpetually travelling hither and thither in Italy. Otto III visited him at Serperi. He admired the simple huts of his disciples grouped around an oratory. 'The tents of Israel in the desert!' he exclaimed. 'Those who dwell in them are not citizens who stay, but pilgrims who pass on.' He had long conversations with the patriarch, and asked him to say if there was anything he would like. St. Nilus, laying his hand on the young man's breast, answered, 'You will die one day, like all men, and God will judge you. I only ask one thing: that you should think of your soul's salvation.' Otto, his eyes full of tears, put his crown between the old man's hands to show him that he would willingly cast it aside to win eternal life. In a period of deep moral degradation when monks no longer observed the rule and bishops had lost all sense of responsibility, Romuald and Nilus emerge as shining lights. In the darkness of the 10th century we may say there were neither poets nor writers nor philosophers, for those few who could be mentioned were incapable of touching men's hearts. There were none but these ascetics and a few great monks of Cluny to maintain human values, for men were fast slipping back into that aboriginal mire from which humanity, by slow degrees, had risen.

Otto was influenced by both these burning spirits, but it was perhaps Adalbert who touched him most deeply of all. This restless Slav, wandering through Italy, France, Bohemia, Hungary and Poland, had a real passion for self-sacrifice. His whole soul longed for martyrdom. At that time, martyrdom was not difficult to achieve among the peoples of eastern Europe. Adalbert sought it in Prussia, on the Baltic. He was killed as he preached the Gospel to the pagan people of those coasts, and his head was exhibited on a stake, like a trophy. The Duke of Poland bought back his remains from the barbarians and laid them in the cathedral of Gnesen.

Otto III was stirred to the depths by the death of his friend, who, transfigured in his eyes, had not only become a saint but, at the same time, Otto's own heavenly patron. Without delay (probably in 998) he had work started on a church in Adalbert's honour on the island in the Tiber: he could see its walls rising from his palace on the Aventine. But soon he wished to go and pray at the new saint's tomb at Gnesen, and he left Rome for Germany and Poland. He brought back to Italy, as the most precious of all treasures, a relic of St. Adalbert. But before returning to Rome he stopped at Aix-la-Chapelle to do homage at another tomb – that of Charlemagne. There we find him, true as ever to his divided nature, now carried away by mystic ecstasies, now by his dreams of universal dominion. He went to ask Charlemagne himself for his secret. We are told that he had the tomb opened and gazed upon the great emperor, still seated on his throne, sceptre in hand. A cross of gold shone on his breast: Otto did not hesitate to take possession of it, as an heirloom reverting to him by right. History, at this moment, attains the splendour of an epic.

He had already founded a church in honour of St. Adalbert at Aix-la-Chapelle; he founded another at Ravenna, a third at Subiaco. The building in Rome was completed; in it he deposited the relics of his friend, in whose name the church was consecrated. But, if certain chroniclers are to be believed, he further enriched it with a most notable relic – that of St. Bartholomew.[1] Returning from Monte Gargano, he had prayed at Benevento at the Apostle's tomb, and he wished to carry away his remains to render still more venerable the sanctuary on the island.

It is a romantic tale – fit for the *Golden Legend* – that St. Bartholomew's relics tell. It was said that the body of the apostle, who had been martyred in Armenia, was first brought by Christian hands to Dara in Mesopotamia. When the Persians invaded the Byzantine empire the sacred remains were carried as far as the Bosphorus, placed in a coffin and left to the mercy of the waters, which deposited them eventually on the shores of the island of Lipari. There a church was built which became a much-frequented place of pilgrimage until the Moslems from Sicily, after conquering the island, destroyed the sanctuary and scattered the Apostle's bones. A monk collected them again and took them to Benevento, and these were the relics which Otto III coveted. It was told in Rome that the people of Benevento, who could not resign themselves to the loss of their patron saint, had deceived the emperor and handed over to him the remains, not of St. Bartholomew but of St. Paulinus of Nola. The story adds that Otto, informed of the fraud, returned to Benevento at the head of an army and carried off the Apostle's relics by main force. As a result, the Tiberine island could glory in the possession at once of St. Bartholomew and St. Paulinus of Nola. However, the Beneventani never accepted a story which they always regarded as fabulous. They wrote books to refute it; Roman scholars wrote other books to prove the authenticity of their relic, and the dispute went on for centuries. About 1740 the Bollandists gave an account of the whole debate in the *Acta Sanctorum* without coming to a definite conclusion, but expressing the conciliatory view that the two churches, in all probability, shared the relics of the Apostle.[2] Thus it came about that St. Bartholomew continued to be venerated both at Rome and Benevento.

Meanwhile, Otto III did not take the monastic habit. His dream of worldly power definitely prevailed: he intended to be Caesar. He sent the Archbishop of Milan to Constantinople to ask, on his behalf, the hand of a Byzantine princess, a request which was favourably received.

But all of a sudden Tivoli rose against him and, after Tivoli, Rome. He was besieged in his palace on the Aventine and had to quit the city as a fugitive – that city which he loved so much, the only place where he could live. He travelled to Ravenna, then returned to the Roman Campagna to await the relief army which was coming down from the Alps. Sick and discouraged, his dreams shattered, he was struck down with fever at the castle of Paterno near the Monte Soratte. He fought the fever for a few days and then, after receiving communion from the hands of Pope Gerbert, he died on January 23, 1002. He was twenty-

[1] The chroniclers are not agreed as to the name of the monarch who brought the relics of St. Bartholomew to Rome. Some say Otto III, others Otto II. The papacy early came to a decision in favour of Otto III, as is proved by an inscription placed by Paschal II in 1113 above the door of San Bartolomeo dell'Isola.

[2] *Acta Sanctorum*, August, Vol. V, pp. 49–100.

six. He had expressed the supreme desire, since Rome repudiated him, to be buried at Aix-la-Chapelle, next to Charlemagne. As his coffin was being carried northwards, protected by his soldiers' arms, his betrothed, escorted by the Archbishop of Milan, had left Constantinople and was approaching the Italian shores.

II

There is much in this pathetic story, with its strange mixture of naïveté and splendour, to interest and to move us. The young Saxon's mystic strivings towards the eternal life, his passion for the beauty of the South and the Mediterranean sun, his love of Rome and of Greece, where he thought to find his ancestors; finally, these first gleams of humanism in the night of the Dark Ages – all these things grip the imagination and make a memorable tale. We cannot help wondering if Rome, where so many centuries have left their mark, bears any traces of this young dreamer's fleeting stay.

For centuries, under the portico of St. Peter's, a tomb could be seen before which Otto III no doubt often prayed: it was that of his father Otto II, who lay there in an antique sarcophagus. At the time of the destruction of old St. Peter's the bones of Otto II, gathered in a crude stone basin, were moved to the Grotte Vaticane, the crypt of the basilica. As for the marble sarcophagus in which the emperor had lain, it went to decorate a court at the Quirinal Palace and became the trough of a fountain in the neighbourhood of the kitchens. Such indifference to history at a time when Baronius was bringing the past to life again is astonishing. The grim amorphous tomb we see today in the Grotte Vaticane, thrust away into a dark corner, this sort of megalith, plastered over and painted black, is frightening – like the 10th century itself, when humanity sank so low. One thinks sorrowfully of the beautiful carved sarcophagus which had been deemed worthy of the ruler of the Holy Roman Empire. It must have inspired in Otto III some brief reflections on the uncertainty of great enterprises – for he could hardly forget his father's humiliating failure in attempting the conquest of Southern Italy – but any such thoughts must soon have been dismissed from his mind.

Otto III's palace on the Aventine (perhaps an old Roman house which had been restored) has disappeared without leaving a trace. But the church which the young emperor erected to his friend, St. Adalbert, still stands. Today it is called San Bartolomeo dell'Isola, for the Apostle's memory has long since eclipsed that of the Slav missionary.

It is difficult to visualise the island in mid-Tiber at the time when St. Adalbert's church was under construction. It still had the shape of a trireme, for the Romans had fashioned the two ends to resemble a prow and a stern, to recall the memory of a ship sent to Greece to bring back the Serpent of Aesculapius. The obelisk raised in the middle to resemble the mainmast of the ship was no doubt still standing. But the sanctuaries of the island were nothing more than heaps of ruins. The temple of Jupiter could still be identified, also those of Veiovis, terror of perjurers, of Faunus, protector of flocks and herds, of Aesculapius, god of healing, also that of the river-god himself, honoured on the island so often submerged by his waters.

Rome in the 10th century presented a scene of splendour and of desolation which we can hardly imagine. What was the Rome of Chateaubriand by comparison? Pilgrims might come there to do homage at the apostles' tombs, but they were held there by an enchantment. An unheard-of spectacle met their eyes: palaces half-stripped of their marble facing, patrician villas with their nymphaea (whose last remains disappeared only in the 16th century), streets paved with basalt slabs between crumbling porticoes, fallen statues lying by their pedestals, fragmentary walls to which exquisite frescoes still clung, great thermae whose towering vaults still sheltered dried-out pools, porphyry cisterns and figured mosaics. Still standing, too, were the circuses, theatres, amphitheatres, imperial tombs with their overwhelming masses of masonry, on which five centuries had made little impression; and here and there, on the hills, the remains of ancient sacred groves, with their sombre greenery. That Rome of dreams conjured up by Hubert Robert, where a sphinx lies beside a portico with columns blue-black from fire; where, under lofty vaults, one glimpses a distant panelled apse, crumbling under a growth of trees – such was the Rome of Otto III (60).

It was on the site of the temple of Aesculapius, at the southern extremity of the island, that St. Adalbert's church arose. Temples of Aesculapius were usually of modest dimensions, but they were surrounded by spacious porticoes where sick people came to spend the night. In their dreams the god appeared to them and they heard him prescribe the remedies that would cure their ills. In their mind's eye they no doubt saw an Aesculapius resembling his statue from the temple, which was found in the bed of the Tiber in the 16th century and is now in the Naples museum. The god, with an expression of kindly gravity, leans on a staff round which the serpent of Epidaurus is coiled. From this temple and its porticoes Otto III carried away the columns for his church.

The visitor who comes to this church hoping to see an ancient basilica is sadly disappointed. He sees nothing but a classical façade built in 1624 by Martino Longhi (55). Entering, he finds an interior which appears at first sight to belong to the 17th century. The chapels contain pictures and frescoes devoted to St. Francis of Assisi, St. Margaret of Cortona and St. Anthony of Padua, and the visitor guesses that the church has long been served by the Franciscans. Some very recent paintings decorating the surroundings of the altar recount the life of St. Bartholomew. Where, in these surroundings, can we hope to find Otto III and the uncouthness of the 10th century?

But first of all we must think of the vicissitudes suffered by this church in the course of centuries. Standing in the midst of the Tiber, it was flooded time and again. Little more than a hundred years after its foundation, under Paschal II, a restoration became necessary, and the same happened several times in the following centuries. But in 1557 the church was all but carried away in a flood. Such was the force of the current that it destroyed the old façade and caused the aisles to collapse. The relics were saved and placed for safety at St. Peter's, while the church, for several years, was left abandoned. It had to be reinforced and in part rebuilt. The 17th century busied itself removing all traces of the catastrophe, building chapels, painting walls and ceilings; Antonio Carracci and two Capuchin brothers were engaged on the task. The decoration was completed in the 18th and 19th centuries.

So one might imagine that nothing remains today of Otto III's work, but this would be a mistake. With a little trouble it can be found. The fourteen granite or marble columns from the temple and porticoes of Aesculapius still stand on either side of the nave. It is true that the capitals have been remade, but some of the bases are original. Two of them have the rich decoration of certain Corinthian bases in which the lower torus becomes a wreath tied round with ribands. The two rows of columns supporting the nave arcades certainly remain in position and give us the main lines of the original church. They show that the feeling for classical proportions, still so strong in the 9th century (as the churches of Paschal I show) begins to weaken in the 10th. The nave and aisles no longer have that splendid breadth which lent magnificence even to churches of modest size.

Nowadays the altar is approached by a flight of steps and overlooks the nave – as, in all probability, it always did. Since the end of the 8th century the use of crypts had become general in Rome, for people wished to approach the sacred tombs more closely, and touch them with their hands. These crypts with their underground chapel, their ambulatory and stairways leading down on either side, necessitated the raising of the choir.[1] The crypt of San Bartolomeo is now inaccessible, but fairly recent sources testify to the presence therein of small antique columns. It is obvious that the relics of St. Adalbert, St. Bartholomew and St. Paulinus of Nola were formerly kept in this crypt. Maybe they were already contained in the fine antique porphyry vessel which is now placed under the altar.

There is every reason to believe that the two chapels opening to the sides of the apse (but probably shallower originally) go back to the 10th century. Ever since Charlemagne's time this Syrian plan had become acclimatised in Rome. So the church differed only in its less fortunate proportions from those built by Paschal I in the previous century: it was very like Santa Cecilia, Santa Prassede and Santa Maria in Domnica. It carried on a tradition without, however, pointing the way to any advance.

But is there nothing here to recall the young emperor whose traces we are seeking? Can Rome have forgotten entirely one who loved her so much?

An inscription cut in 1113, in Paschal II's time, over the principal door tells the pilgrim that the relics belonging to the church were brought there by Otto III. These relics are mentioned by name: they are those of St. Bartholomew and St. Paulinus. Thus, at the beginning of the 12th century Otto III was still remembered, but the name of Adalbert had fallen into such complete oblivion that the very church dedicated to him now bore the name of St. Bartholomew.

A singular monument, the most curious in the church, also proves that Otto III was still a name in the minds of the Romans. It is a little marble well-head most oddly set in the steps

[[1] See discussion of the crypt and the *Confessio* *St. Peter*, 1956, Chapter 7.]
in Toynbee and Ward Perkins, *The Shrine of*

leading up to the choir (57, 58). Four figures are carved around it. They are not named in the inscription, but can nevertheless be identified. The first represents Christ, distinguished by a cross inscribed within the halo, the second St. Bartholomew holding the knife, symbol of his martyrdom, the third a bishop who might be Adalbert but is really, we shall see, St. Paulinus of Nola (57). The fourth figure, bearing crown and sceptre, is the emperor Otto III, represented alongside the two saints whose relics he had brought from Benevento (58).

What was the meaning of this strange monument? An artless inscription says, without giving us any information, that 'one here sees the saints arranged in a circle around the mouth of the well'.[1] Where did this well lead to? It has been suggested more than once that it enabled the faithful to let down, following the old Roman custom, pieces of cloth or 'brandea' to touch the relics in the crypt. But another inscription on the well, once deciphered by a German archaeologist but no longer legible, is phrased in these terms: 'Let him who is thirsty come to the fountain to draw from the spring a health-giving draught.' The well-head belonged, therefore, to a real well, and, examining it more attentively, one notices that it has been rubbed down by the well ropes. From this we must conclude that there was once a sacred spring in the church – as there was in many other Christian sanctuaries. Such a spring, welling up close to the relics of the saints, would pass on some of their healing virtue to the sick. Should we go farther and imagine that this was none other than the spring of the temple of Aesculapius? It could be so, since all his temples, according to Vitruvius, had to have their spring of fresh water. The Church of Rome has shown such skill in manipulating popular sentiment, has so often sanctified rites which it could not destroy, that one is almost tempted to accept the theory. It should be borne in mind that no attempt was made to orientate San Bartolomeo, which occupies the exact site of the temple; therefore the peculiar position of the well – in the middle of a flight of steps – seems to suggest that it already existed at that spot before the church was built. Possibly this well never ceased to attract the sick; it may have been enclosed, at an early date, in a Christian chapel later replaced by Otto III's basilica.

But what is the date of the well-head and its bas-reliefs? Not very long ago certain scholars tried to make it contemporary with Otto III, in which case the effigy of the emperor would have been carved in his lifetime.[2] If we accepted their conclusions, if we agreed that this well really went back to 998 or 999, it would be the earliest piece of medieval sculpture in Europe. It would become a key monument for historians of art, anticipating by nearly a century the figured capitals of Moissac and the reliefs of Saint Sernin at Toulouse. And since the carvings of our well-head show a certain feeling for relief, a certain understanding of drapery, they cannot be regarded as the first experiment of a new art. On the contrary, they show a proficiency already of long standing, which would push back farther still the real

[1] Os putei s(an) c (t) i circu(m) dant orbe rotanti.

[2] Geza de Francovich in *Bollettino d'Arte*, November 1936, pp. 207–224; and O. Homburger in *Jahrbuch der Preussischen Kunstsammlungen*, 1936, pp. 130–140.

beginnings of medieval sculpture. This monument, however, is unique in Rome. Nothing of the kind existed before it, and not until a century and a half later was another work even remotely comparable to it produced – i.e., the great candelabrum at San Paolo fuori le Mura. Rome remained hostile to sculpture longer than any other Italian city; she possessed no storied tympana, nor did a single statue adorn the portals of her basilicas. In the 12th century, when the churches of Lombardy as well as those of southern Italy were embellished with sculpture, Rome remained faithful to those antique decorative forms, the fresco and the mosaic. Is it likely that she pioneered a new departure in art in the 10th century and produced one of the earliest works of European sculpture?

An examination of the monument does not support any such hypothesis. How could Otto III have been represented as we see him here in 998, while he was still alive? Contemporary miniatures show him as a beardless young man with short hair and refined features, while the well-head of San Bartolomeo shows a man of mature age, long-haired, with beard and moustache. The heavy cap he wears has nothing in common with the graceful foliated crowns of the 10th-century emperors. The monarch holds a disc on which is represented a church with its tower – the church of St. Bartholomew which he is offering to God. Now we know that this tower – rising to the left of the church as in the carving – dates only from the 12th century. We may add that the letters of the inscription no longer have that antique firmness and dignity which was still preserved in the 10th and even early in the 11th century. In the cloister of Sant'Alessio on the Aventine the epitaph of the Patriarch Sergius, dated 981, and that of a Massimi ancestor, dated 1012, still resemble the beautiful inscriptions of Roman times, for their characters are pure in form, abbreviations are few and the whole layout is a joy to the eye. At the well of San Bartolomeo we sense another – and a medieval – epoch.

There seems to be no need, then, to modify the traditional date of this little monument. Everything goes to show that it was produced well on in the 12th century and is not, therefore, in any way exceptional. The artist imitated, as far as he was able, the single figures under arcades which occur on certain Christian sarcophagi.

So the effigy of Otto III was carved more than a century and a half after his death. Though his features had been forgotten in Rome, his name was still remembered. The papacy was the faithful custodian of traditions and memories of the past, and by these reliefs it sought to honour the young emperor to whom it owed both the church he had founded, and some precious relics. Next to him were placed the figures of Christ and of those saints whose remains he had brought to Rome – St. Bartholomew and St. Paulinus of Nola. These are the saints named in the 12th-century inscription over the door. The bishop among the figures cannot therefore be St. Adalbert, whose memory was so early effaced, but must be St. Paulinus, who is still honoured at San Bartolomeo.

III

We must admit that it is difficult to evoke Otto III and Gerbert at San Bartolomeo. But is there not some other church in Rome decorated in their own time, a church which they themselves entered, and whose frescoes they would have admired? All things are possible in Rome and, sometimes, to search is to find.

Climbing the Palatine by the little-used lane of San Bonaventura we find, half hidden in the box and wistaria, the church of San Sebastiano in Pallara.[1] It stands on the site of the gardens of Adonis, laid out for Domitian in the oriental manner. It may well be that some of the plants sacred to the young god – mallow, fennel and barley – still grow there. Near this spot tradition placed the scene of St. Sebastian's martyrdom under Diocletian. Baronius thought he had found the steps, in front of the church, on which the saint, who was believed dead, appeared to the astonished emperor, and was sent a second time to execution. The church is only a large chapel in which, at first sight, there seems to be nothing ancient. Over the door an elegant escutcheon, concave like a tilting-shield, displays the bees of the Barberini family. This is because the church, which had long been abandoned and ruinous, was put in repair by the Barberini pope, Urban VIII. An undistinguished nave without aisles, a cupola carelessly frescoed (displaying Virtues borrowed from Ripa's *Iconologia*), an enormous 17th-century altar – that is all we discover at a first glance. But, going round behind the altar and its reredos, we suddenly see an ancient fresco in the apse, and remains of paintings on the neighbouring walls.

The fresco in the apse is a very striking work. It shows Christ standing erect under a dark, blue-black sky, raising one hand in a gesture of welcome and holding in the other the scroll of the Law. He dominates all the smaller figures around him. On his right is St. Sebastian dressed in rich eastern stuffs, and St. Lawrence with his gridiron on the ground before him; on his left St. Stephen and another martyr, St. Zoticus, who (like SS. Sebastian and Stephen) is clothed and tonsured as a deacon. The scene is framed by two palm-trees, on one of which sits the phoenix, symbol of the Resurrection. Twelve sheep make their way from the two holy cities of Jerusalem and Bethlehem towards the Divine Lamb, placed under the feet of Christ. The model for this fine composition is not far to seek. It is the famous mosaic in Santi Cosma e Damiano which represents so majestically a group of four saints with Christ in the centre. There, too, a pair of palm-trees (one with the phoenix) frame the scene, and the twelve sheep advancing towards the Lamb of God form a frieze under Christ's feet. This masterpiece of the 6th century continued to influence art-works in Rome for hundreds of years. Mosaic-workers of Paschal I imitated it in the 9th century at Santa Prassede and Santa Cecilia, those of Gregory IV at San Marco (see Chapter 6). As we have seen, the painter of San Sebastiano was still being inspired by it, and the same was true of others in later times.

But what is the date of this fresco at San Sebastiano? It can be established within a few

[[1] Also called San Sebastianello, San Sebastiano in Palatino, or San Sebastiano alla Polveriera.]

years. An inscription, half obliterated nowadays but copied in its entirety in the 17th century, gives us the name of the donor. He was a certain Peter, a well-to-do medical man of the 10th century, whose name is recorded in several documents.[1] He built the church whose apse is still standing and decorated it. As he died shortly before 998, the fresco must be anterior to that date by a few years.

The painter of San Sebastiano was not content to imitate the mosaic of Santi Cosma e Damiano, but extended it. Below the frieze of lambs he added a large additional field, which he peopled with hieratic figures. The Virgin stands in the middle, her hands open and raised before her in the manner of an *orans*. She is flanked by two angels bearing the sacred banner and the seal. They are accompanied by four crowned female saints. One can hardly imagine anything more solemn than these seven symmetrical figures, facing directly forward, whose rigid pose seems fixed for eternity. All these figures – Virgin, saints and angels – wear splendid Byzantine costumes, stiff with pearls. Through the immobility of the figures, and through the richness of their attire, the painter has given his fresco the impressiveness of a mosaic.

The end-wall and the adjoining surfaces in the nave were similarly covered with paintings, of which little now remains, though in the 17th century they were largely intact. At that time people were beginning to have scruples about destroying the works of the past, and it was a common practice, before the destruction took place, to describe or to copy them. While considered barbarous, they were yet vaguely felt to be worthy of respect. Thus, at the time of the partial reconstruction of San Sebastiano a draughtsman (unfortunately an incompetent one) was given orders to copy all the frescoes which were still visible. From his mediocre water-colours, preserved in the Vatican Library, reproductions were made some years ago which are exhibited in the choir of the church. They show scenes of the Passion together with various incidents from the martyrdom of St. Sebastian and St. Zoticus. The donors, too, had themselves painted: Peter the doctor could be seen offering his church to St. Sebastian, while his wife presented some object not now identifiable to St. Zoticus. Some of these subjects have an oriental stamp, and the Passion scenes especially betray the influence of models which are not to be sought at Constantinople but in Asia Minor, especially in Cappadocia.

The terminal wall (above the opening of the apse) had a double frieze. On top, one saw the four-and-twenty Elders of the Apocalypse, kneeling on one knee, each offering to God his crown, carried on veiled hands. Below, an extraordinary scene was unfolded, of which vestiges still remain: a number of muscular old men carrying on their shoulders haloed figures stretching their arms towards heaven (69). What does this mysterious scene signify? The solution is provided by a stained-glass window at Chartres. There we see the four major prophets carrying the four Evangelists on their shoulders, which means that these prophets' teaching served as a basis for that of the Evangelists. At San Sebastiano in Pallara

[1] They have been published by M. Fedele in *Archivio della Reale Società Romana di Storia Patria,* Vol. XXVI (1903), pp. 343 ff.

the idea is the same, but conceived more broadly: all the prophets carry all the apostles to show that the prophetic books were the foundation of the apostolic teaching as a whole. The New Testament rests upon the Old, but the apostles, raised up on the prophets' shoulders, see farther than they. Certainly a fine conception, but one which, interpreted and represented literally, becomes too weird for words.

So the window at Chartres, which seems to have inspired the sculptor of the portal at Bamberg (where French influence is so obvious), was itself inspired by an earlier model. The idea was not born in the famous theological school of Chartres – as one might reasonably have supposed – but came from farther afield. Should we conclude that a canon of the cathedral brought the idea back from Rome at the beginning of the 13th century? There is nothing impossible in the theory. I must say, however, that I have found no record at Chartres of such pilgrimages to Rome.[1] It is true that two of the windows are devoted to Roman saints, St. Eustace and St. Sylvester; but their legend is narrated according to the text of the cathedral lectionary. In St. Sylvester's window there is not even any sign of the pope's victory over the dragon – an episode which a traveller returning from Rome could not have failed to include, since pilgrims were shown the spot (in the Forum) where the monster was chained in his subterranean cavern. A statue in the south portal of the cathedral represents the pope St. Clement with his miraculous chapel under his feet; but it was only necessary to read the canons' service-book to know the legend of the chapel under the sea, from which the waves retreated every year. We may therefore suppose that ancient models, now lost, inspired both the Roman fresco and, two centuries later, the stained-glass window at Chartres. Moreover, we can understand very well why, at San Sebastiano, the apostles and prophets have been brought near to the Elders of the Apocalypse: it is because, for the early Doctors, the twenty-four Elders of St. John's vision symbolised the twelve prophets and the twelve apostles taken together. These prophets of San Sebastiano, athletic, half-naked figures, each carrying an apostle on his shoulders, were one of the strangest works of their period in Rome.

The whole of this great fresco-cycle, of which only the last remains exist today, was seen by Pope Sylvester and by Otto III. In fact, in the year 1001 a Synod met at San Sebastiano in Pallara. Its purpose was to put an end to a difference which had arisen between two German churches. Both the pope and the emperor were present. After having listened to the reading from the Gospel, and some passages from the Fathers, they called upon St. Bernward to speak – Bernward the bishop-artist of Hildesheim, Otto III's old tutor. So these three distinguished men sat together in the church of San Sebastiano; and before their eyes, in all their freshness, were the frescoes which we can still contemplate today. We know with certainty, therefore, what art was like in Rome at the end of the 10th century: a mixture of ancient Roman traditions and influences from the East. If – as is probable – Otto III had San Bartolomeo decorated with frescoes, they must have been very similar to these.

[1] On the other hand, a bas-relief in the south portal of the cathedral, showing pilgrims collecting miraculous water at the tomb of St. Nicholas, recalls the pilgrimage to Bari.

IV

I had read about a church at Castel Sant'Elia, not far from Monte Soratte, dating from the reign of Otto III. Its apse and transepts were said to be covered with 10th-century frescoes, the work of two Roman artists – the brothers John and Stephen – aided by their nephew Nicholas. Not only were these frescoes contemporary with Otto III, but, if certain scholars were to be believed, the painter John was that 'Johannes pictor' whom the young emperor took with him to Germany to decorate the church at Aix-la-Chapelle. Otto III had certainly followed the Via Flaminia several times when travelling between Rome and Ravenna; he liked monks and monasteries; and he could easily have stopped at Castel Sant'Elia, a Cluniac priory not far from the old road, and seen the Roman painters at work.

So there was a 10th-century church near Rome, almost contemporary with San Bartolomeo, but intact, and much better calculated to call up the century of Gerbert, Crescentius and Otto. The trip would be worth making.

Between Rome and Nepi there stretches a grand but melancholy piece of country. Leaving the city, one still sees some ruined tombs by the roadside; then the great solitude opens up, intersected by ravines, unpopulated and almost treeless. Now and again ancient basalt paving-slabs show through the Via Flaminia.[1] No living thing meets the eye, except an occasional peasant on his mule. To the right appears the beautiful outline of the Sabine hills, to the left, in the far distance, the Monti Cimini. Monte Soratte rises in isolation like an Egyptian pyramid, sculptured like one of the mountains in Greece. This is the land of the Etruscans, gloomy and mysterious, where thunder-claps call man to prayer. Here the gorge of Civita Castellana, the ancient Falerii, guards its old tombs and Nepi, another Etruscan city, raises its ruined walls not far away.

The church of Castel Sant'Elia is not easy to find, and seems to hide itself from view. A high cliff overlooks it, and the church itself seems in turn suspended above the depths of the ravine (63). The Benedictine monastery, built on the same narrow shelf, has long since disappeared, but the church is intact. Seen from outside, its nave, aisles and transept stand out plainly; it is simple to the point of austerity, a group of dark cypresses providing its most effective embellishment.

What was known of this monastery of St. Elias? Very little. After being burnt down by the Saracens, it had been given, around 940, to St. Odo, who was then disseminating the Cluniac rule in Italy. According to several archaeologists, the church had been rebuilt in the second half of the 10th century, and decorated with frescoes towards the end of that same century; it appeared, therefore, to be a monument of exceptional importance, one of those very rare churches of the 10th century preserved in their entirety.

Such was the ready-made doctrine with which I left Rome for Castel Sant'Elia. It began to be shaken, however, as soon as I examined the façade. This façade, with its sober blind

[[1] This is no longer so, but impressive tracts of the Roman Via Flaminia, with its honeycomb paving of dark stone slabs, can still be seen immediately alongside the modern road in its higher reaches.]

arcades framed by vertical strips of Lombardic character, with its three doors surmounted by relieving arches, was unmistakably north-Italian: the work, not of a Roman, but a Lombard architect. In the 10th century doorways like the one I was looking at in the middle of the façade were not to be found in Lombardy. The arch, instead of being simple, was recessed in three orders, like three arches one inside the other. The elaborations of Romanesque art were beginning to appear here: such a doorway could not be earlier than the first quarter of the 11th century.

This first observation was bound to make me uneasy, and I reassured myself by the thought that the façade – as so often – might have been completed long after the church proper. Now the interior had to be examined, and at a first glance it seemed not inconsistent with the early date assigned to it (64, 65). The antique columns borrowed from a pagan temple, the exposed roof-timbers, the rough masonry of the walls, the narrow windows – everything, in fact, in this severe interior recalled the century of the Ottos. I found it quite natural to evoke the memory of the young emperor; but the spell was broken when I noticed a detail which had so far escaped my attention. The nave arcades, instead of being simple like those of the earlier Middle Ages in Italy, were double, the outer arch being reinforced by a second somewhat narrower one below. This was a feature of Romanesque architecture. Northern Italy, explored so carefully by Kingsley Porter, does not offer a single example of nave-arcades in two orders before the second quarter of the 11th century.[1] Since these double arches corresponded perfectly with the triple orders of the entrance-doorway, it became evident that façade and nave were planned at the same time. Both were built at the beginning of the Romanesque period, that is to say in the early years of the 11th century.

Would the frescoes confirm this conclusion? That was the next question to examine. They occupy the apse and the transepts, those of the apse being well preserved, those of the transepts (devoted to the Apocalypse) partly destroyed.

The apse-fresco has great dignity. It shows a standing Christ under a sombre blue sky, raising his right hand and carrying in his left the scroll of the law. On his right are Paul and Elias – the soldier-saint martyred in the mines of Cilicia; on his left Peter and an unidentified saint. Two palm-trees frame the scene and, under Christ's feet, twelve sheep, forming a long frieze, are approaching the Mystic Lamb. The whole strikingly resembles the composition at San Sebastiano already described. They derive from the same prototype: the 6th-century mosaic of Santi Cosma e Damiano. We have shown that the San Sebastiano frescoes dated from the end of the 10th century. Could those of Sant'Elia be of the same period?

At San Sebastiano we saw, immediately below the frieze of sheep, a broad frescoed field

[1] The earliest example is at Lomello, about 1025. Several archaeologists consider that the arches in two orders at San Pietro, Tuscania (formerly Toscanella) go back to the 8th century. In their view this would be a unique exception to the rule. I personally disbelieve in such exceptions. Since the church was altered in the 11th and 12th centuries, we may reasonably suppose that the double arches date from that time.

occupied by hieratic figures: the Virgin and accompanying saints face directly forward, solemn and motionless. At Sant'Elia we have a similar field containing similar figures, but they have lost something of their majesty. The women saints still wear their splendid eastern robes, but no longer stand full-face: they form a procession and move forward with heads slightly inclined. To either side a further frieze unfolds, in which we recognise the Elders of the Apocalypse. They too are advancing, and each, with a mighty gesture, raises his chalice heavenwards: this is a new motif in art. At San Sebastiano also there was a frieze of the twenty-four Elders, but, like those of the old mosaics in Rome, they carried crowns in their hands instead of chalices. In the first Christian centuries, and in Carolingian art, the Elders carry crowns; in Romanesque art they have chalices – symbolic, according to St. John, of the prayers of the saints. Thus the art of Sant'Elia was open to new ideas and, at the same time, was beginning to awake from its century-long immobility. This first glance, superficial though it was, inclined me to put it later than the art of San Sebastiano.

A more attentive examination supported this impression and changed it into a certainty. At Sant'Elia the frescoes of the apse are divided into upper and lower tiers by a most elegant decorative band. Octagons with curved sides alternate with quatrefoils, all being joined together by graceful arabesques, and the whole strip has crenellated borders. Now, when studying the paintings in the lower church of San Clemente I noticed that one of the frescoes (the well-known subject of the child recovered by its mother in the chapel under the sea) was surrounded by an identical band. Not only was the design the same, but the two decorative strips were interrupted in the middle to make room for a circular medallion containing, at Sant'Elia, the mystic lamb, and at San Clemente, the bust of a saint. There were still other resemblances. I had noted with some surprise at Sant'Elia, in the border of the apocalyptic frescoes, motifs of a purely antique character: birds, apples and pomegranates, baskets of fruit with cloths symmetrically festooned. These were the first signs of the fascination which antique art, and the frescoes still visible on the old walls, were beginning to exercise. Here again, similar subjects could be found at San Clemente.

The date of the San Clemente frescoes is known: they were painted soon after 1084. Are those of Sant'Elia contemporary? It may be so, but I personally consider them a little earlier. Though closely related in their subject matter, the two sets of frescoes differ in spirit. In these frescoes at San Clemente, dealing with the lives of Pope Clement the Roman and of St. Alexis, we notice touches of humanity and sensitive realism: the mother presses the lost child's cheek against her own; the servant leads the blind man with anxious care; the wife of St. Alexis throws herself on the body of the poor beggar, whom she has just recognised. These curious frescoes, in which everyday realism begins to mingle with the hieratic gravity of tradition, point the way to a liberation in art. We have the feeling that a younger artist has appeared, one familiar with the traditions of the Roman school and its decorative repertory, but more gifted than his masters. John and Stephen, the painters of Sant'Elia, belong to the previous generation, and their work may be earlier by twenty-five or thirty years. Our conclusion is that these frescoes, attributed by certain antiquarians to the 10th century, really belong to round about the middle of the 11th. They were probably painted a few years after the completion of the church, about 1050 or 1060.

We see, therefore, that the name of Otto III cannot, after all, be called to mind by the visitor at Sant'Elia. The frescoes date from half a century after his death, and the painter John, whom he took with him to Aix-la-Chapelle, was not the John of Sant'Elia. Moreover, re-reading the texts which relate to these facts, I noticed that Rupert's *Chronicle* calls Otto's *Joannes pictor* a Lombard, 'gente longobardus'.[1] On the other hand, John, Stephen and Nicholas, when they signed the frescoes at Sant'Elia, informed us that they were Romans.[2]

The church of Sant'Elia, which has survived the centuries without any later embellishment and remains today much as it was nine hundred years ago, is none the less one of the most interesting monuments of central Italy. It offers nothing to take us back to Otto III, but it does help us to visualise the century of Gregory VII.

V

The centuries go by and the memory of Otto III seems to be completely lost. But nowhere in the world is so little forgotten as in Rome. Not far from the city, on the slopes of the Alban Hills near the ancient Tusculum, there was a monastery where the memory of the young emperor was always fresh: the abbey of Grottaferrata, founded by St. Nilus. It was built on Roman ruins, which were thought to be those of Cicero's villa.

Greek monks still receive the visitor today, as they did nearly a thousand years ago. There are Greek inscriptions over the doors, and one might think oneself in a monastery of Thessaly or Phocis. A Byzantine mosaic adorns the entrance to the church; it shows Christ between the Virgin and St. John the Baptist and a Greek inscription on the architrave thus admonishes the faithful: 'You who enter God's house, leave here the intoxication of your thoughts.' Was there ever a better description of the perpetual seething in men's minds, of that vapour which ceaselessly rises from the depths to screen the infinite from one's view? This solemn doorway seems to promise an ancient church beyond, but, alas, it leads us into

[1] *Monumenta Germaniae Historica*, S.S. VIII, p. 267 and IV p. 729.

[2] While a very ancient picture of the Last Judgment, at the Vatican, was being cleaned, the painters' names were revealed: they were called John and Nicholas. There can be little doubt that these were two of the artists of the Sant'Elia frescoes. The picture was commissioned by an Abbess named Constantia. The fact that SS. Paul and Stephen occupy the places of honour in the Last Judgment scene points to Constantia having been the Superior of the Convent of St. Stephen, built beside the atrium of San Paolo fuori le Mura. The picture, therefore, was painted in Rome. The study of the inscriptions (which have very characteristic abbreviations) places the date of the picture about the middle of the 11th century. The date 1050–1060, to which I attributed the Sant'Elia frescoes before the discovery of the picture, will now appear, I think, even more probable. The picture in the Vatican was studied by M. Redig de Campos in *Rendiconti della Pontificia Accademia Romana di Archeologia*, Vol. XI, 1936, pp. 139 ff.

a stucco interior restored in the 18th century. However, a Greek mosaic, left untouched by some miracle, still glows at the far end of the church, allowing it to retain a little of its former dignity. The Apostles are seated as the pentecostal rays of fire descend on their heads; in their midst stands the empty throne of the Master, whose thought at that moment comes down to them, but who henceforth will be present only in their hearts.

The church communicates with a large chapel. It is here that St. Nilus is buried, along with one of his first successors, St. Bartholomew of Rossano; and it is here that we shall meet the shade of Otto III.

In the first years of the 17th century Cardinal Odoardo Farnese, patron of the abbey, adorned this chapel magnificently. The Farnese always remained faithful to their great family traditions. On the recommendation of Annibale Carracci the cardinal chose, to decorate the chapel walls with frescoes, a young artist who had already proved his ability in Rome. This was Domenichino, who was now asked to glorify the two saints whose remains lay in the chapel. The old story of St. Nilus and of Otto III had not long since been honourably resurrected in Baronius's *Annals*, where the cardinal could have read it. The story is told with charm and vivacity, due largely to those long quotations from the old annalists which often enliven the pages of Baronius. Moreover, the monastery had preserved the Greek lives of the two saints, which the monks read every year, on their respective anniversaries. These lives, which had been translated by Cardinal Sirlet, were brought to Domenichino's notice by the novice-master.

The scenes chosen were nearly all visions and miracles: an epileptic child healed through the prayers of St. Nilus; Christ crucified taking one arm from the Cross to bless the saint who kneels at his feet; the Virgin appearing to SS. Nilus and Bartholomew to give them a golden apple; St. Bartholomew at harvest-time driving away a storm; the same saint building the monastery, when his presence arrests the fall of a column. Only two incidents are other than miraculous – the meeting of St. Nilus with Otto III and the old hermit's death, surrounded by his disciples. All these subjects seem to have been chosen by the monks, who were accustomed to hearing them read in the choir. It is strange that they should have forgotten one of the most moving stories from the saint's life. At the age of ninety he did not hesitate to come to Rome from the neighbourhood of Gaeta to save the anti-pope Philagathus. The nominee of Crescentius, Philagathus had fled from Rome on the return of Otto III and the Austrian pope Gregory V, Gerbert's predecessor. But he was taken prisoner and mutilated with that ferocity which the West learnt, in those days, from the East. His nose and ears were cut off, his eyes put out and they threw him into a dungeon. 'Give him to me,' said Nilus, addressing the pope and the emperor, who had respectfully seated him between them; 'I shall take him away and together we shall lament our sins.' The emperor wished to refuse nothing to the saint, but the pitiless pope was not only unmoved by his prayers but had Philagathus mounted back-to-front on a donkey and given over to the insults of the populace. The old saint returned in indignation to his solitude.

Such as they are, these seven frescoes by Domenichino were long numbered among the masterpieces of Italian painting. In Stendhal's time travellers felt obliged to go to Grottaferrata to admire them. Stendhal himself had made the journey five times to let them sink into his consciousness. He called them 'sublime'. The fact is that the glory of Domenichino waxed without a pause from the 17th century to the early 19th, from Bellori to Lanzi. His renown became established slowly and surely, like a scientific truth. Domenichino was a second Raphael, at times greater than the first. In a century of improvisation and new departures he seemed calm, collected, self-assured. Bellori had said of him that he 'could paint souls'. A century later, Lanzi wrote as follows: 'His figures have something about them so sweet, so sincere, so loving, that they inspire us to love the good . . . Each one of them occupies precisely its appropriate place in the composition. A light which enchants the soul is spread everywhere, but it brightens on those faces which are the most beautiful of all and which draw to themselves the eyes of the heart. It is a joy to run over every element of his compositions and to see how each one plays its part. We need no interpreter: every person lets us know, by his attitude and his expression, what he is thinking and what he is saying. Had they the power of speech they could not speak more clearly to our ears than they speak to our eyes.' Thus the art of Domenichino, a direct emanation of the soul, expressed all that is most noble in man.

Our contemporaries, who do not wish to find thought in a picture, but rather the sensuous pleasure given by a harmonious play of colour, have little time for Domenichino. They are put off by paintings which are meant to express so many things. They cannot share the sentiments of Bellori and Lanzi. There are few in these days who make the trip – so simple now – to Grottaferrata. Yet, having gone, they come back less disappointed than they may have feared. It is true that the colours, retouched by Cammuccini in 1819, are unattractive, but the spectator cannot fail to be struck by the fervour in the two saints' faces and the inner force which impels them towards Christ and the Virgin; by the astonishing realism of the epileptic boy's rolling eyes. The dignity of the composition as a whole and its accuracy in detail, the combination of careful thought with flights of fancy, of knowledge with ingenuousness – all this ends by arousing even the most prejudiced visitor's interest.

For my part, I found real pleasure in studying the meeting of Otto III and St. Nilus (61). My thoughts were already full of these great figures of the 10th century, so I was curious to know how Domenichino had dealt with them and their times. One thing he felt deeply was the beauty of the episode itself. The young man wearing his crown, who bows before St. Nilus with a tender respect and gently takes the old hermit's arm, quite forgets that he is the emperor. The old man with his faltering step and bent back bows too. He would be embarrassed by such honour were it not that his human charity reassures him. This emperor, he feels, is a man, and one whose soul he must help to save.

The composition of the fresco is most successful, even though at variance with the classic rules of art. The two main figures – emperor and saint – are not placed in the middle but right to one side. The emperor's suite – all the pomp of the Holy Roman Empire – follows behind him. His dignitaries and his men-at-arms serve to emphasise the honour he is doing to the old saint, whose modest escort amounts to two or three accompanying monks.

A painter of our times would be much perplexed if called upon to represent the court of Otto III; in spite of a few miniatures, it is most difficult to imagine what these people of the year 1000 looked like. This is where Domenichino gives rein to his fancy. He wants to give his contemporaries some idea of the lapse of time, without confronting them with anything hopelessly unfamiliar. His armour-clad horsemen are something like Romans, something like 16th-century knights. The standard-bearer holds aloft in the breeze a flag of the Holy Roman Empire, adorned with the double-headed eagle, which comes from the time of Charles V. The long trumpet and the curved trumpet of the musicians seem to be taken from Trajan's column, whereas the short trumpet, with coloured cloth hanging from it, belongs to the period of the Italian republics. History was told like this by Shakespeare, the great contemporary of Domenichino's youth. In 1608, when the painter was just beginning his frescoes, *Coriolanus* was finished, *Cymbeline* in preparation, and *The Tempest* already taking shape in Shakespeare's mind. No doubt Domenichino's ignorance of Shakespeare was complete, but, like him, he mixed history and romance. Here, in Otto's suite, is a comely young woman disguised as a knight: we can imagine her as Rosalind, sword at her girdle, in the forests of the Ardennes. Here is the little page holding up his master's cloak, and here the court dwarf, shorter than the emperor's sword and shield. The three trumpeters are three rustics worthy of *A Midsummer Night's Dream*. Nowadays we should probably not think of judging the sounds produced by each musician from the degree of tension in their faces. Bellori, devotedly analysing every beauty of the fresco, did so, and found that one produced a shrill, another a powerful, and the third a solemn note. Nor perhaps would we notice that one of the young people of the emperor's entourage is listening to what his neighbour says without, however, taking his eyes off the old hermit, 'so that he exercises simultaneously his hearing and his sight'. We are not interested in the same things. What gives us more pleasure today is being introduced by the painter to a world much like the world of Tasso or of Shakespeare. But the real beauty of the fresco lies elsewhere: in the attitude of the emperor, humbly abasing his omnipotence in the presence of sainthood.

And so Otto III's sojourn in Rome was not in vain: he built a church which still stands and he inspired a fine work of art. Many a potentate has come to Rome and left no trace there at all!

CHAPTER EIGHT

Pope Gregory VII and the Churches Destroyed by Robert Guiscard

[ELEVENTH CENTURY]

The old bronze door of San Paolo fuori le Mura; Santi Quattro Coronati; San Clemente; San Saba; San Lorenzo in Lucina; San Silvestro in Capite

I

AT THE beginning of the 11th century the Church, weary of its century-long struggle against human instinct, seemed to be returning quietly to nature. Priests and bishops lived with concubines and cared for nothing but the things of this world. All ecclesiastical offices were bought and sold. Since the Church had become involved in the feudal organisation of the period, the bishop had to receive his investiture at the hands of his suzerain, and obtained it only at a price. Such clergy were in no way fitted to teach those Christian virtues which they did not practise.

The popes tried to eradicate these abuses; they forcibly separated a few priests from their women and deposed some simoniac prelates; but their efforts were in vain, because the most powerful section of the clergy was against them. The German bishops said: 'Let the pope get angels to rule his Church.'

Some people then realised that there was only one remedy: to liberate the Church from the practice of feudal investiture – to make it free so as to make it holy. The bishops, chosen by the Church itself and not by local potentates, should be the worthiest, not merely the richest, candidates. As soon as the shepherd had the apostolic spirit, the reform of other malpractices could begin.

The papacy freed itself first. The German emperors had been nominating the popes, but their choice was rarely fortunate. In 1059 Nicholas II convoked a Council and laid down rules for the election of future popes: it was decided that they should henceforth be nominated by the cardinals, not by the emperor. This was an innovation of tremendous import. Among the signatories at the foot of the decree one name shines like a beacon – that of Hildebrand, the future Gregory VII. As the pope's adviser he no doubt had much to do with this reform, in which we detect his spirit.

It was next necessary to liberate the Church as a whole from the trammels of feudalism.

This mighty struggle between the pope and the emperor, which involved the future of Christendom, began in 1073, when Hildebrand became Gregory VII.

As an aid to his conduct of affairs, the new pope had written down twenty-seven guiding principles among which the following may be quoted:

> The Church of Rome was founded by the Lord alone.
> Only the pope of Rome has the right to be styled 'universal'.
> His name is unique in the world.
> He only can use imperial insignia.
> His feet alone are kissed by all princes.
> He can be judged by no man.
> No man can reverse his decisions, but he can reverse the decisions of all others.
> He is empowered to depose emperors.

The man who, without hesitation, committed these amazing words to the parchment was the son of a poor countryman. He was puny in outward aspect and his soul was burdened with sorrows. He wrote to St. Hugo, the great Abbot of Cluny, of whom he was very fond: 'I am filled with infinite sorrow and grief unfathomable. . . . Long have I asked God to take me away from this world. . . . My life is but a ceaseless dying.' As man, he was weighed down with wretchedness; yet as pope he felt himself invincible. All the divine power of the papacy was in him. No human being ever brought more heroic courage to the defence of what he called 'justice', that is to say, freedom to establish God's kingdom on earth.

The struggle of this defenceless pope against the most powerful monarch in Europe is one of the great spectacles of history. In 1075, at the Synod of Rome, Gregory VII solemnly forbids all priests to accept a church at the hands of a layman. The German emperor, Henry IV, ignoring the papal decision, goes on investing priests. Reproached by the pope, the emperor retorts by assembling twenty-four bishops at Worms and having him deposed. Unhesitatingly, Gregory VII in turn deposes and excommunicates the emperor, absolving his subjects from their oath of allegiance. Henry IV's initial indifference to the sentence of excommunication turns to astonishment and then to alarm as he finds himself abandoned by degrees. He realises that the lightning has struck him. Almost alone, he flees from Germany, crosses the Alps and comes down to do penance before the pope at Canossa. A solemn moment indeed. Not for nothing have men remembered the incident: this once, in the annals of history, the spirit had triumphed over brute force.

But Gregory's triumph was of brief duration. The emperor, pardoned and apparently repentant, immediately began preparing his revenge. Only a few years later the pope was besieged by Henry IV in Rome, and it was only Robert Guiscard's arrival that saved him. Gregory followed Robert Guiscard to Salerno and died shortly afterwards, believing that the cause was lost. He was wrong, however. Gregory's successors, fired by his example, did what he himself had failed to do and, hardly forty years later, the Church had gained its freedom.

II

What reminders did this heroic pope leave behind him in Rome? Had the great fighter any leisure for the enjoyment of art? On this point the documents are sadly uninformative.

However, one magnificent work of art, which was still standing rather more than a century ago, bore his name engraved upon it, namely the bronze door of San Paolo fuori le Mura (71–73). It can still be seen in the sacristy of the church, darkened, mutilated and half destroyed by the fire of 1823. The main lines are there, some engraved scenes can just be distinguished, but much is completely lost; of Hildebrand's name only a few letters remain. Happily a set of drawings made a few years before the fire has survived to show us the door as it was.[1]

The work belongs to the first part of Hildebrand's career when, before his pontificate, he was in charge of the abbey of San Paolo fuori le Mura. The fact that his name is followed, in the inscription, by the word *monachus* shows clearly enough that he was a monk, and it is strange that the contrary should have been maintained. For several years he acted for the abbot, who was away, then became abbot himself. It was his cherished desire to build up again this famous foundation, sanctified in past generations by the presence of St. Odo, St. Majolus and St. Odilo (all abbots of Cluny), but which had since become utterly decadent. In those days the wilderness started at the very gates of Rome, and grazing animals wandered freely into the great basilica, which was almost abandoned. Only a few monks remained in the monastery; these were served by women and observed no rule whatever. Hildebrand re-established monastic discipline and restored the abbey. Possibly the fresco, the last remains of which can be seen on one of the cloister walls, dates from his time; it represents the Last Supper and was formerly in the refectory.

The original door of the basilica was already at that time six hundred years old and doubtless in bad condition; it was replaced in 1070 by the admirable bronze door, of which now only the shadow remains. Inscriptions engraved in the metal tell its story, which was a most curious one. At that time there was a well-known family, living at Amalfi, whose members, as generation succeeded generation, were named alternately Mauro or Pantaleon. These were Amalfi's days of greatness. This picturesque little town, squeezed between mountain and sea, with its sparse population and abandoned harbour, was then a city of seamen and shipbuilders and enterprising merchants. Amalfi had trading stations in the East. The Pantaleons possessed a palace in the quarter of the Amalfitani at Constantinople and had amassed a huge fortune; being a very pious family, they showed generosity towards the churches. Pantaleon senior caused to be made, in Constantinople, the bronze door embossed with silver and enamels of Amalfi cathedral; Mauro, son of Pantaleon, ordered from the same workshop the simpler door of the church at Monte Cassino. Pantaleon, son of Mauro, had two doors cast and decorated at his expense in Constantinople: those of San Paolo fuori le

[1] They are to be found in Nicolai, *Basilica di San Paolo*, 1815. Other drawings of the door have been published by Seroux d'Agincourt in his *Histoire de l'Art par les Monuments*, Plates, Vol. IV.

Mura and of San Michele in the Monte Gargano, and both were sumptuously decorated with historic and biblical scenes. Was Hildebrand indifferent to the beauties of these doors at San Paolo, and content merely to thank Pantaleon for his princely gift? The inscription states the contrary. Long ill-deciphered, it was very convincingly interpreted by Father Grisar.[1] It reads thus: 'In the year 1070 of the Incarnation, in the time of the most saintly Pope Alexander, under the general direction of the venerable monk and archdeacon Hildebrand, these doors were executed in the imperial city of Constantinople, with the collaboration of the noble consul Pantaleon, who ordered them to be made'.[2] Instructions drawn up by Hildebrand must therefore have been sent from Rome to Constantinople.

The artist was asked to represent, first of all, the great Gospel scenes, then the martyrdom of the apostles, beginning with the twin patrons of Rome, Peter and Paul. Alongside the apostles, prophets carrying inscribed scrolls were to foreshadow the story of the Word made flesh. The door therefore demonstrated that Christ's religion had been spread about the world only by dint of sacrifice – a thought which was often, we may be sure, the subject of Hildebrand's meditations.

In matters of detail, the artist was allowed great liberty, the proof being that he remained faithful in every particular to Byzantine tradition. He began by summing up the Gospel in twelve scenes, according to an Eastern convention which was then relatively new. These were called the 'twelve great festivals' at Constantinople, for, in the East, religious art had gradually become an aspect of the liturgy. In 1070 the choice of the twelve festivals was not yet finally established. The doors of St. Paul's show the following: the Annunciation, the Nativity, the Presentation in the Temple, the Baptism, the Transfiguration, the Entry into Jerusalem, the Crucifixion, the Descent from the Cross, the Resurrection, the Appearance of Christ to the Apostles, the Ascension, the Descent of the Holy Ghost. A little later the Descent from the Cross and the Appearance to the Apostles were left out, and the Resurrection of Lazarus and the Death (or, as the Greeks said, the Dormition) of the Virgin inserted in their place. The door of San Paolo therefore has a special interest, for it takes us back almost to the origins of a practice which was to last – with minor modifications – for centuries. The composition of the scenes is no less interesting, since they are precisely dated, which is very unusual. This provides a fixed point of reference for Byzantine iconography. Certain scenes show features which link them to the past. The Baptism, for instance, still has the Jordan personified as in the earliest versions of this scene, and the pilgrims' cross in the middle of the river. But other scenes, such as the Transfiguration, have already taken on the changeless pattern of their final perfection. All the inscriptions are in Greek.

[1] *Civiltà Cattolica*, 1895, Vol. III, pp. 205–210.

[2] Instead of '*Alexandri Sanctissimi papae quarti et Hildebrandi . . .*', Father Grisar read '*Alexandri sanctissimi papae cum arte Hildebrandi . . .*' It is impossible that Alexander II should have been called Alexander IV in 1070, in his lifetime, because Alexander IV was a pope of the 13th century. The expression '*arte*', '*cum arte*', implying an intellectual collaboration, is found again in the inscription in the cloister of St. Paul's: it applies to the abbot who directed the work.

In the same way the death of the Apostles is wholly of Greek inspiration. I found conclusive evidence of this in studying the miniatures in the Menologium of Basil II at the Vatican – a famous manuscript dating from at least a century before the bronze doors. If we examine the death scenes of St. Thomas, St. Matthew or Luke the Evangelist on the door, and compare them with those of the Menologium, we find the corresponding subjects to be almost identical. Unfortunately the illustrations of the Menologium do not cover the whole year's calendar and the deaths of the other Apostles are not included. But we cannot doubt that the craftsman responsible for these designs had Greek models before him, for he follows the eastern, not the Latin, tradition throughout. Thus St. Bartholomew is not flayed alive but crucified; St. Andrew is not fixed to a cross but to a tree with widely spreading branches. The Prophets, Apostles and Evangelists, whose solemn figures complete the decoration of the doors, similarly conform in every detail to the tenets of Byzantine iconography. The Prophets' gestures and attitudes are those of the mosaics at Daphni, which are almost contemporary: they give the benediction with their right hand and carry in their left a parchment bearing the words of their prophecy (which may be unfurled and carried in both their hands). The Apostles can be recognised by the scroll of the law which they carry and the Evangelists by their book. Centuries later the *Painters' Manual* of Mount Athos still lays down that they should be represented in this manner. It is to be noticed that the verses inscribed on the scrolls of these purely Byzantine prophets are not in Greek but in Latin; no doubt they were included in the general plan for the decoration sent from Rome.[1]

Such was this admirable door, where the figures were outlined in silver and their faces brightened with coloured enamel – a work of technical perfection reflecting, too, a profound faith. Pantaleon, prostrate at the feet of Christ and St. Paul, asks the Apostle, in Latin, to remember this door and in memory of it to open for him, one day, the gates of heaven. And the bronze-caster writes in Greek: 'I, Staurachios of Chios, made this work with my hands. You who read this, pray for me.' It is moving to reflect that the great Hildebrand looked upon these doors which he had helped to plan, and admired them.

III

The restoration of the monastery of San Paolo fuori le Mura is the only artistic undertaking which we can attribute, with certainty, to Gregory VII. However, according to one inscription he dedicated an altar in Santa Cecilia; according to another he re-dedicated the ancient church of Santa Maria de Porticu, but we do not know if he had reconstructed or merely restored it. The *Liber Pontificalis* does not once mention his foundations or his gifts to churches. It must be said that this papal history, now reduced to a quite disheartening baldness, refers to not a single work of art during the long years between the death of

[1] Curiously enough three prophecies, taken from the Book of Kings, are in Greek: those of Elijah, Elisha and Ezekiel. Probably the artist, having a few more spaces to fill in, copied a Greek model in which these prophets were shown together, along with their prophecies.

Sylvester II (1003) and that of Gregory VII (1083). Nevertheless, some 11th-century documents name a certain number of Roman churches for the first time: S. Salvator de Bardonia (1053), S. Salvator de Terrione (1053), S. Laurentius juxta Gradata (1056), S. Laurentius in Sassi (1066). There are still others, mentioned, however, only in passing, in connexion with the gift of a garden or a vineyard, or on a list of sanctuaries dependent on St. Peter's;[1] nowhere is the date of their foundation given, and we cannot tell what century they belong to. However, the 11th century, as far as Rome is concerned, does not seem to have been productive. In 1045, when he ascended the pontifical throne, Gregory VI had to appeal to Christendom for funds to restore St. Peter's, which was threatening to collapse. William, duke of Aquitaine, was almost the only person to respond. About 1050, as we have seen, San Paolo fuori le Mura was in no better state than St. Peter's. It was scarcely possible to think of building new churches when not even the old ones could be kept in repair. The architectural poverty of the 11th century in Rome contrasts with its wonderful fruitfulness in France and in other parts of Italy. Raoul Glaber's remark is true: 'After the year 1000, the Christian world covered itself with a white mantle of churches.' It is enough to mention, among a host of others, a few in France – Caen, Mont Saint-Michel, Saint-Germain-des-Prés in Paris, Saint-Etienne at Nevers, Conques, Saint-Sernin at Toulouse; a few in Italy – St. Mark's at Venice, San Miniato in Florence, Pisa cathedral and the famous church at Monte Cassino, then the artistic centre of southern Italy.[2] During these years, when the Christian world was in travail, Rome created nothing. Seemingly the popes, absorbed in their great struggle, had no leisure for the arts.

IV

The truth is that the reign of Gregory VII was distinguished rather by the destruction than the building of churches. It is the ruins that recall the memory of this great man today.

The tragic events of the last years of his pontificate are well known. Henry IV wanted to take his revenge for the humiliation of Canossa. After having an anti-pope elected, he came down to besiege Gregory VII in Rome; he took possession of the various quarters of the town one after another and was preparing to attack the Castel Sant'Angelo to which the pope had retired. Gregory VII seemed doomed, but, intrepid as ever, he had renewed his sentence of excommunication against the emperor. The crisis seemed imminent, for Henry IV now had the Roman populace on his side.

One morning in May, 1084, it was suddenly learned that Robert Guiscard was arriving from southern Italy with an army of thirty thousand Normans. True to his oath, he had come to succour the pope. He established his troops outside the Porta San Giovanni, but

[1] See Huelsen, *Le Chiese di Roma nel Medio Evo*, Florence, 1927.

[[2] Let us add some English examples, all begun in the 11th century: St. Albans, Durham, Canterbury, Winchester, Gloucester, old Westminster Abbey.]

circled the city in the night and entered by the Porta Flaminia. As both Germans and Romans attempted to oppose him, he set fire to the quarters of San Lorenzo in Lucina and of San Silvestro, advanced as far as the Castel Sant'Angelo, freed the pope and took him to the Lateran. Henry IV immediately evacuated the town and the Normans' victory seemed assured when the Romans, now roused to resistance, attacked them once again. A second battle was fought between the Lateran and the Colosseum and that whole quarter burnt down. The victorious Normans gave themselves up to every sort of violence, and they made prisoners, whom they carried off in their retreat and sold into slavery. The only safe place for the pope was Salerno, where he could remain under Robert Guiscard's protection. There Gregory followed him, but he survived the drama only by a few months. It is said that he uttered these words on his death-bed: 'I have loved justice and hated iniquity; therefore I die in exile.' 'Holy Father,' replied one of those present, 'a pope cannot die in exile, for he has received all the nations of the world as an inheritance from God.' Legendary words, perhaps, which yet express the new stature of the papacy, raised by Gregory VII above all the powers of this world.

Gregorovius, in his *History of the City of Rome in the Middle Ages*,[1] has represented the conflagration started by Robert Guiscard as one of the great catastrophes of history. According to him, most of the town was destroyed, even the Aventine being reduced to a wilderness. Many historians have repeated his statements without realising how grossly exaggerated they are. It is true that a contemporary, Guido of Ferrara, writes of Robert Guiscard burning most of the town ('maximam urbis partem'), but Guido, bishop of Ferrara, lived a long way from Rome and was in any case a sworn enemy of Gregory VII. Malaterra, in his *History of Sicily*, expresses himself on the same lines, but he does not seem to have known Rome, for he places the Porta San Giovanni by the Tiber. The *Liber Pontificalis*, which was based on Roman documents, alone gives precise information. From it we learn that Robert Guiscard first destroyed the quarter containing the churches of San Lorenzo in Lucina and San Silvestro, after which, when the conflict was renewed, he set fire to the region around the Lateran and the Colosseum. The fire did not, therefore, involve the major part of the town.

To prove that almost the whole town had been annihilated Gregorovius cited two elegies by Hildebert, bishop of Le Mans, on the ruin of the Eternal City. Hildebert was at Rome in 1107, twenty-eight years after the fire. Re-reading his poems carefully, I have discovered absolutely no allusion in them to the destruction wrought by the Normans. The poet is brooding in a melancholy vein on the collapse of empires, and could have written exactly the same verses thirty years earlier, before the fire. In the first of these elegies he writes: 'Rome, thou art but a ruin, yet nothing can be compared with thee. In thy fallen state thou dost let us guess thy greatness when standing erect. It has taken centuries to bring thy glory to nought. The Caesars' palaces and the temples of the gods have crumbled away in stag-

[[1] English edition translated from the 4th German edition by Mrs. G. W. Hamilton, 8 vols., London, 1894–1902.]

nant waters. Fallen in ruin is this city, man's masterpiece, which made Araxes tremble, and which now Araxes laments. . . .' Clearly, this is a meditation, going far beyond mere contemporary history.

The second elegy has the same generalised character. The poet makes Rome speak; she admits that her decadence began on that day when she embraced the true faith; her palaces and temples have collapsed, yet she was never greater than in her ruin: 'When I was intact,' she says, 'I ruled bodies; ruined, I rule souls. The standard of the Cross has brought me more power than the eagles, Peter more power than Caesar; my kingdom was on earth, now it is in heaven. My glories have been reduced to nothing that my citizens should not rest their hopes in them, that they should never forget the might of the Cross. What so precious do I owe to the military genius of Caesar, to the devotion of consuls, the eloquence of orators? Their labours let me gain the world; the Cross has given me heaven.' [1] Hildebert of Le Mans is a sort of Chateaubriand meditating on the ruins of Rome; what he sees is not the work of man, but the work of centuries. No evidence can be drawn from these elegies to extend Robert Guiscard's ravages to the entire city. On the contrary, in the first poem I find some extraordinary verses in which one glimpses a city still adorned with statues: 'Man gave this town such greatness that the gods have failed to destroy it. These gods admire their own beauty there and would wish to resemble their own statues. Nature could never create gods as beautiful as the admirable images which man has been able to make of them. From these the gods have taken their features, and it is not their own divinity that men venerate, but the genius of artists.' Surprising verses, when we reflect that they were written, not in the 16th, but early in the 12th century. We see that the Middle Ages also were sensitive to antique art and we need no longer be surprised that the artists of Reims were sometimes inspired by Greece. Revealing verses, too, for they prove that statues of marble and of bronze still embellished medieval Rome and that Robert Guiscard had not destroyed everything.

One thing, however, is certain: he set fire to two churches near the Colosseum, for traces of the disaster have remained visible in both cases. These churches are the Santi Quattro Coronati (the Four Crowned Martyrs) and San Clemente (St. Clement).

The Quattro Coronati probably already existed in the 4th century, but the church burnt down by the Normans had been entirely rebuilt under Leo IV about the year 850. The fire destroyed the roof and part of the walls, but spared the crypt and the interior colonnades. With a little trouble one can trace the remains of the 9th-century church in the present building, and reconstruct it in imagination. It had a broad nave separated from the aisles by beautiful Ionic columns. Its proportions were those of the Carolingian churches in which classical traditions were still preserved: the width of the nave was twice the height of the columns; that of the aisles slightly less than the height of a column.

When, about 1110, Paschal II reconstructed the church he reduced it by more than half: it became only half as wide and one-third as long. The two rows of Ionic columns were

[1] *Patrologia Latina*, Vol. CLXXI, col. 1409.

incorporated in the outer walls of the church, where some of them can still be seen, and a new avenue of columns, taken as before from an antique building but this time with Corinthian capitals, formed the new nave – a rather narrow one (76). The aisles, correspondingly narrow, were surmounted with galleries. The nave, narrowed down in the restoration, was also greatly shortened, being left with only four columns on either side instead of the original twelve. The original aisles, now walled-in, became mere annexes; as to the abandoned portion of the nave, it became a picturesque open court forming the new approach to the church.

The disastrous damage sustained by the church was therefore only repaired in part, and the narrow nave and aisles leading up to the great apse of the old church give a strange impression. The visitor becomes aware of some puzzle to which only history provides the solution. The church of the Quattro Coronati was, in fact, the witness of great events. It perpetuates the memory of the sack of Rome by Robert Guiscard and thus of that most tragic chapter of the Investiture controversy.

Was San Clemente, the near neighbour of the Quattro Coronati, destroyed at the same time? The early antiquarians did not think so. San Clemente, with its charming atrium, its colonnades, its *schola cantorum*, its pulpits, its marble bench round the apse and bishop's throne, seemed the perfect model of the Early Christian basilica. This is what Clement XI himself implied in the inscription placed over the entrance-doorway at the beginning of the 18th century, which says: 'This ancient church has escaped the ravages of time.' It was indeed easy to make this mistake, so well has the church (in spite of its heavy ceiling) preserved its purity of form and classic dignity (75).

The error persisted until the middle of the 19th century. In 1857 excavations [1] brought to light, underneath the church, another and far more ancient basilica, and this proved to be the church which Robert Guiscard had destroyed. A careful study showed that the fire (traces of which were found on the Via Labicana side) had left the church standing, and that for several years it was hoped to save it. Some of the inter-columnar spaces were provided with piers for reinforcement, and these – to reduce their disturbing effect – were decorated with frescoes. The death of St. Alexis and scenes from the legend of St. Clement were executed in these spaces soon after 1084. But the stability of the church continued to give cause for anxiety; moreover, it was now much lower than the neighbouring streets, whose level had risen. For these reasons a reconstruction was decided upon at the beginning of the 12th century under Pope Paschal II, and the lower basilica, well buttressed and filled in with rubble, served as a platform for the new church. This, however, as in the case of the Quattro Coronati, was planned on a reduced scale: the apse was smaller, the nave and aisles narrower. Whatever could serve to adorn the new church had been removed from the old. The 6th-century marble choir-screen formed, with minor adjustments, the new *schola cantorum*. Did they also transfer the mosaic from the old to the new apse, or were they content to copy it? It is difficult to be sure. It may be that the splendid green scroll-work on a gold ground, so

[[1] Conducted by Father Mullooly, Prior of the Irish Dominican community.]

true to 5th-century models, is original, but the small figures in the volutes and the crucified Christ in the centre of the composition are medieval (89).

We have seen that at San Clemente, since the discovery of the lower church, the marks of Robert Guiscard's destructiveness can be seen as clearly as at the Quattro Coronati. Were any other churches burnt down in the same area, as, for instance, the old basilica dedicated to SS. Peter and Marcellinus? There is no evidence of it. In the reconstruction of 1750 the only memento of earlier times is a 13th-century inscription stating that Pope Alexander III restored the church and consecrated it in 1256. If it had been affected by the fire of 1084 it would hardly have been left a century and a half before restoration, for the two martyrs, Peter and Marcellinus, were greatly venerated in Rome. The pope St. Damasus had sung their praises and told the story of their heroic sacrifice just as he had heard it, as a child, from the mouth of the executioner himself.

But a new problem arose some years ago. Several scholars advanced the theory that San Saba also was burnt down by the Normans.[1] The reason was that in 1901 a more ancient church had been discovered, as at San Clemente, under the existing one. If the conclusion drawn was correct, the fire must have spread well beyond the region of San Clemente and the Quattro Coronati, and reached the distant slopes of the Aventine. If so, Gregorovius was proved correct, as regards this particular area at least.

But of what period are the two superposed churches of San Saba? The underground church, decorated with frescoes purely eastern in style,[2] is most certainly that of the Greek monks who had been established on the pseudo-Aventine since the 7th century. After the destruction by Robert Guiscard it was supposed to have been abandoned for more than sixty years and rebuilt at a higher level when the Cluniac monks were installed there by Pope Lucius II in 1145. This is what the texts seem to suggest, but the building itself tells a different story.

No archaeologist had studied the upper church with due care until the task was undertaken by Father Lestocquoy, chaplain of San Luigi dei Francesi. In 1929 he examined every part of the building with the greatest care.[3] Certain features of the plan, the system of construction and the decoration prompted him to give up the traditional theory and to conclude that the upper church was built, not by the Cluniac community in the 12th century but by the Greek monks themselves in the late 9th or early 10th. He drew attention, in this connexion, to the two subsidiary apses required by the eastern liturgy (66), to the Byzantine pulvins borne by the capitals, to the Carolingian plan of the crypt, to the contemporary masonry (tufa blocks bonded with bricks) of the foundations, to the window-frames and the *schola cantorum* (the latter with interlaced designs) both of 9th-century type. Finally, he pointed to a dated sepulchral inscription which proved that burials were still taking place in the upper church in 994. The combined evidence of all these arguments seems to show that the upper church of San Saba dates, not from 1145, but from around 900. If so, it is clear

[1] Huelsen still put forward this hypothesis, in 1927, in his *Chiese di Roma nel Medio Evo.*

[2] They have been moved to the upper church.

[3] *Rivista di Archeologia Cristiana,* 1929, pp. 313 ff.

that the lower church, considered too small by the Greek monks, was demolished by them and reconstructed on a much grander scale, at a higher level. At the same time it becomes obvious that Robert Guiscard had nothing whatever to do with its destruction, and that the fire started by his soldiers did not reach the Aventine. So we find nothing in this part of Rome to substantiate the belief that the Normans extended their ravages beyond the vicinity of the Quattro Coronati and San Clemente.

There remains the area of San Lorenzo in Lucina and San Silvestro. According to the *Liber Pontificalis* 'it was destroyed, and reduced to nothing'.

[1]We need not doubt that the ancient church of San Lorenzo in Lucina was burnt down at the same time; however, the old 5th-century brick walls have not completely disappeared. Remains of them can be seen outside, and they look like those of Santa Maria Maggiore, which are contemporary. They can be recognised by their mortar-beds, which are as thick as the bricks themselves, and by the windows of ample size.[1] The church must have been left derelict for some years until reconstructed, at the beginning of the 12th century, by Paschal II, who undertook to remove all traces of Robert Guiscard's fire. According to an inscription a priest was trying, at this time, to obtain relics for the church, no doubt to replace those which had perished in the flames. The interior was transformed in the 17th century, but the portico with its Ionic columns and the campanile with its marble colonnettes still call to mind the times of Paschal II.

As to San Silvestro, the records are silent and the building itself reveals nothing, having been rebuilt at the end of the 17th century. But in explicitly mentioning San Silvestro in this burnt-out quarter, the *Liber Pontificalis* evidently intends to imply that it was one of the principal buildings destroyed. No doubt it was then that the old basilica, built by Stephen III to record his journey to France, disappeared. He had dedicated it to St. Denis and to his companions Rusticus and Eleutherius in order to show his gratitude to the country which had come to his rescue, and to Pepin the Short, who had stood by him. If the account of Benedict, a monk of Monte Soratte, is to be believed, Stephen imitated even the architecture and decoration of the French church. Later on the memory of St. Denis faded, his name dropped out and was replaced by that of St. Sylvester.

The area of San Lorenzo and San Silvestro was not as completely destroyed as the *Liber Pontificalis* would lead one to suppose. San Lorenzo was surrounded by antique monuments: it abutted on the Ara Pacis, whose beautiful reliefs were not yet buried in the ground, and stood close to a triumphal arch dedicated to Marcus Aurelius or (more probably) to Hadrian. Behind the church was still standing the great obelisk which Augustus brought from Heliopolis to serve as the gnomon of a gigantic sundial. The important point is that none of these things perished. The bas-reliefs of the Ara Pacis, in excellent preservation, are dispersed, but could be brought together again.[2] The obelisk was subsequently erected by Pius VI in front

[1] See Krautheimer in *L'Illustrazione Vaticana*, May, 1935, p. 217.

[2] This has been done, and the altar reconstituted [close to the Mausoleum of Augustus in Rome, between the Corso and the Tiber].

of the Palazzo Montecitorio with this poetic inscription: 'The divine Augustus, having subjected Egypt to the Roman people, made this gift to the sun.' As to the triumphal arch, it was destroyed in the 17th century by Alexander VII so as to widen the Corso – an exploit which he proudly recorded in an inscription; its reliefs now adorn the Palazzo dei Conservatori. Neither the marble nor the Egyptian granite were cracked by the flames, which do not even seem to have touched them. Robert Guiscard's fire was therefore of limited extent; it destroyed four churches and the neighbouring houses, which is a good deal, but not 'the greater part of the town'.

It must have been deeply distressing to Gregory VII to be rescued at such a price, and to see processions of Roman citizens, in chains, marching along the roads to the south. The father could do no more for his children, and he too was obliged to follow the conqueror. His grief must have hastened his death. It is a sad thought that only some burnt-out churches and their still visible remains enable us, in Rome today, to recall the memory of this great pope.

V

There did once exist a triumphal monument to remind men of his glory, and that of other popes who, with him, had fought for the liberation of the Church. For, after nearly a century, the Church emerged triumphant from the struggle. In 1122 the emperor Henry V, after resorting in vain to cunning and to violence, after setting up an anti-pope and imprisoning Paschal II, after being (like his father Henry IV before him) excommunicated, at last decided to sign, with Calixtus II, the Concordat of Worms. Thenceforth the bishop, pastor of souls, would be invested by the Church. From the Church, too, he would receive his crozier and his ring, but, as holder of fiefs and vassal of the Empire, he would afterwards receive his sceptre, symbol of feudal investiture, at the hands of the emperor. The distinction was a happy one which gave liberty of action to the Church while respecting the principles of feudalism. The pope only rendered to Caesar that which was Caesar's.

To celebrate this great event Pope Calixtus II constructed, in the Lateran Palace, a chapel combined with two adjoining rooms. In one of these rooms all the articles of the Concordat of Worms could be read, inscribed on the walls. In the chapel, above the Virgin and Child between angels, one could see the portraits of those popes who, in the course of eighty years, had fought for the liberties of the Church – Alexander II, Gregory VII, Victor III, Urban II, Paschal II, Gelasius II and finally Calixtus II himself – kneeling at the Virgin's feet.[1] They

[1] Opposite Calixtus II another pope knelt at the feet of the Virgin; his position showed that he too had worked at the decoration of the chapel. M. Duchesne, amending one of the inscriptions most ingeniously, has here recognised Anacletus II. It may seem rather odd that paintings begun by Calixtus II should have been completed by an anti-pope. But we must not forget that after the death in 1130 of Honorius II, the successor of Calixtus II Christendom hesitated in uncertainty between Anacletus II and Innocent II. The authority of St. Bernard had to be invoked, who decided that the real pope was

were accompanied by two popes of earlier centuries, glory of the Roman church and model for all popes: St. Leo the Great and St. Gregory the Great. Lastly, in the second room, some extraordinary frescoes expressed with a certain savage grandeur the victory of the seven legitimate popes over the anti-popes raised up by perfidy and hatred: the real popes, sitting in majesty on their thrones, had the false popes under their feet (70). The psalmist's words '*donec ponam inimicos tuos scabellum pedum tuorum*' had been taken literally and depicted literally: the vanquished enemy was a footstool under the victor's feet.

Ever since the 12th century this astonishing fresco had made a deep impression on pilgrims in Rome. Suger, Arnolphe de Lisieux and John of Salisbury all speak of it, and none of the three omits to mention the anti-popes trampled underfoot by the popes.[1] In the 16th century Onofrio Panvinio was still able to describe these paintings and to quote the verses inscribed under each figure.[2] Until recent years the fresco itself was only known from a bad 17th-century drawing, which gave a very imperfect idea of it.[3] But an earlier and much more faithful drawing, made for Onofrio Panvinio, was discovered and published in the 1930s; in it the defeated are quite clearly seen under the conquerors' feet.[4] An arrogant symbol it certainly is, but quite true to the medieval spirit.

For more than three hundred years, from the 13th to the 16th century, French artists depicted the early Christian martyrs with their persecutors under their feet. But Rome offers, as we have seen, the most ancient example of this triumphal group. Should we conclude that there was here a direct influence on French art? It would be difficult to prove it. Suger could have brought the idea to Saint-Denis, but there is no trace of it in what we can see, or what we know, of the great abbey he created. John of Salisbury was bishop of Chartres from 1176 to 1180, but if he inspired any works of art in his cathedral they disappeared in the fire of 1194. All we can say is that some years later, at the beginning of the 13th century, the first French representation of the apostles with their persecutors under their feet appears in the south portal of the reconstructed cathedral. Is it a reminiscence or a new, independent creation? We have to resign ourselves to uncertainty.[5]

We cannot too greatly regret the destruction of Calixtus II's monument with its frescoes –

Innocent II. Anacletus, considering himself the legitimate pope, may well have completed his predecessor's work and had himself represented in it (see Duchesne, *Liber Pontificalis*, Vol. II, p. 325). The chapel was dedicated to St. Nicholas. Reproductions of the old paintings are to be found in Lauer, *Le Palais du Latran*, 1911, pp. 163 ff., and in Wilpert, *Die Römischen Mosaiken und Malereien*, 1917, Vol. I.

[1] Suger, *Vie de Louis le Gros* (Ed. Molinier), p. 95. Arnolphe de Lisieux (Ed. Gilles), Oxford, 1844, Ep. 21, p. 109. John of Salisbury, Ep. 59, *Patrologia Latina*, Vol. CXCIX, col. 39.

[2] Onofrio Panvinio, *Le Sette Chiese*, p. 221.

[3] This drawing, made for Cardinal Rasponi and altogether unfaithful to the original, did not show the anti-popes under the feet of the popes.

[4] This picture, precious for the confirmation of the text which it affords, was published in *Rivista di Archeologia Cristiana*, 1935.

[5] Let us bear in mind that there had been an image of St. Michael with the defeated dragon under his feet at the Monte Gargano since Carolingian times. This image, born in Italy, soon became widely known in France.

one of the great memorials of history. In 1747 Benedict XIV sacrificed it to the beauty of the great open space in front of the Lateran Palace and the new façade of the basilica. Of the whole precious ensemble we have nothing left but drawings. Examining the one showing the frescoes in the chapel we notice a surprising detail: all the popes standing under the Virgin's throne have a nimbus and are thus considered to be saints. It was thought, therefore, that in defending the rights of the Church they had earned the same merit in the eyes of God as the Fathers had earned in defending the faith. Rome understood full well the magnitude of their struggle with the emperors and had deemed them worthy of the highest award of all – the prize of sainthood. These champions of 'justice', as Gregory VII put it, were not distinguished one from another: standing erect, with short beard and conical tiara, the book in their left hand and their right raised in benediction, theirs was the solemnity of an abstraction. They were the papacy itself, immutable. Even had the frescoes been preserved they could have told us nothing of Gregory's physical appearance. But what matter the features of a man who was but an ardent soul and an invincible will?

CHAPTER NINE

Saint Bernard in Rome

[TWELFTH CENTURY]

Associations with: Santissimo Nome di Maria; San Bernardo alle Terme; Santa Maria Scala Coeli (Abbazia delle Tre Fontane); Santa Croce in Gerusalemme

SAINT BERNARD came to Rome twice, in 1133 and 1138. On the first occasion he accompanied Innocent II, whom he had recognised at the Council of Etampes as the real pope. He hoped to see him triumph at Rome as in France. But his rival, the anti-pope Anacletus II, was master of St. Peter's, and he defended it to such good effect that the emperor Lothair, even though he had an army, had to get himself crowned by Innocent II at the Lateran. This city of Rome of which St. Bernard must often have dreamed, and which he now found divided against itself, distressed him deeply. He pronounced this severe judgment on the Romans: 'They are a people who do not know what peace is and who live in the midst of disorder; a violent and intractable people who will only give in when resistance is no longer possible.' [1]

This first visit of St. Bernard's to Rome, when he may not even have been allowed to pray at St. Peter's tomb, probably remained with him as a bitter memory rather than a sweet one.

When St. Bernard returned to Rome in 1138, summoned by the pope, part of the town was still in the power of Anacletus. Innocent II held another section of the city and so could issue his bulls from Rome, but not from St. Peter's, which remained in his rival's possession. Nothing seemed to have changed in five years, and Bernard no doubt wondered sadly whether all he had done for Innocent II was not to prove in vain. He had been a few weeks in Rome when, on January 25, 1138, he learnt that Anacletus had just died, rather suddenly. He thought this meant deliverance from the schism and exclaimed: 'the wretch has been swallowed up by death and by the Pit. Let all those like him perish likewise.' But he counted too hastily on his triumph; the schismatic cardinals met and elected a new anti-pope, who took the name of Victor IV. However, times had changed; the Romans were beginning to tire of the schism, and Victor saw his supporters dropping away one after another. Soon he had no courage left to carry on the struggle. One night he had himself brought to St. Bernard, to whom he announced that he was prepared to abdicate. The saint took Victor forthwith to Innocent II, and introduced him stripped of his papal insignia.[2]

[1] *De Consideratione*, Lib. IV, cap. II; *Patrologia Latina*, Vol. CLXXXII, col 773.

[2] *S. Bernardi vita prima*. Lib. II, cap. VII. *Patrologia Latina*, Vol. CLXXXIII, col. 296.

This time the schism was at an end and peace returned to the Church. Rome was in transports of joy and St. Bernard's departure was like a triumph. The entire populace escorted him and revived, in his honour, the splendid but long forgotten title of 'Pater patriae'.[1]

A magnificent work of art recalls, in Rome, the memory of Innocent II, St. Bernard's pope. It is the apse-mosaic of Santa Maria in Trastevere which the pope had made in 1140, a year and a half after his victory. It represents the Virgin, crowned, seated at the right hand of her Son, while saints in solemn attitudes stand by. Among them is a donor: it is Innocent II himself, bareheaded, the *pallium* on his breast, the church in his hand. There is therefore in Rome, not, assuredly, a portrait but an idealised image of the pope for whom St. Bernard fought for eight years.

But where shall we find St. Bernard himself? If the old Lateran Palace still existed we should no doubt see the great abbot of Clairvaux in the frescoes which Innocent II commissioned to commemorate the coronation of the emperor Lothair. It is unlikely that the pope would have forgotten to have that extraordinary man portrayed to whom he owed so much and whom he had himself called to Italy. He could not have allowed posterity to forget that St. Bernard had fought for his cause.

But the frescoes in the Lateran have long since disappeared, and we have searched in vain, in Rome, for any medieval work of art devoted to St. Bernard. His name was not, however, forgotten. The Knights Templar preserved, in their House in Rome, a tunic which St. Bernard had forgotten there and which, so it was said, worked miracles even in the saint's life-time.[2] Near Trajan's Forum there was a church bearing St. Bernard's name: it was medieval and may have been dedicated to him immediately after his canonisation in 1174. It was rebuilt in 1738 and is now called the 'Santissimo Nome di Maria', but St. Bernard has not been forgotten, for an 18th-century picture shows him in contemplation before the Virgin, who seems to be dictating his books to him.

Another church in Rome is dedicated to him, namely San Bernardo alle Terme. It is an antique rotunda with coffered dome, a sort of miniature Pantheon, which formed part of the Baths of Diocletian. At the end of the 16th century it was given to a Frenchman, Jean de la Barrière, the founder of the order of Feuillant, in which the spirit of St. Bernard was revived. These remote sons of Cîteaux had brought from France some notable relics of the saint. These were held in veneration by the people and the magistrates, on St. Bernard's festival, used to make a gift of four torches and a chalice to his church. According to a 17th-century scholar this was done 'in memory of the great services rendered by the saint to the city in its times of trial'.[3] Thus St. Bernard's sojourn in Rome was not yet forgotten in the 16th and 17th centuries. To these same centuries belong the three works of art now to be mentioned, which all relate to his residence in this city.

The earliest is to be seen in the little church of Santa Maria Scala Coeli standing in the

[1] *Patrologia Latina*, Vol. CLXXXIII, col. 296.

[2] *S. Bernardi vita prima*, Lib. II, 1, 2; *Patrologia Latina*, Vol. CLXXXV, col. 323.

[3] Piazza, *Emerologio di Roma*, Vol. II, p. 541.

poetic solitude of San Paolo alle Tre Fontane. This is the valley where St. Paul was beheaded and where his head, rebounding, was said to have caused three springs to gush forth. A monastery dedicated to SS. Vincent and Anastasius existed close to San Paolo and Santa Maria Scala Coeli. Innocent II gave this monastery to the Cistercians and, according to the legend, St. Bernard lived here for the few months he spent in Rome. One day, as he was saying mass in the church of Santa Maria, he had a vision of purgatory. Angels were taking up souls from thence and setting them on a ladder of light which led up to heaven. It was after this vision that the church took the name Santa Maria Scala Coeli. Unfortunately it was reconstructed, at the end of the 16th century, by Cardinal Alessandro Farnese. The picture over the altar dates from this period (1584). It is the work of an unknown artist, who shows St. Bernard on his knees contemplating the angels and the souls on the heavenly ladder (78).

Curiously enough, none of the old lives of St. Bernard mentions this vision, the derivation of which remains quite unknown. History raises a grave objection to the story. In 1138, when St. Bernard came to Rome for the last time, the monastery of SS. Vincent and Anastasius, long occupied by the Cluniacs, was completely deserted. The monks of Cluny had abandoned it, driven out by the fever. Only after St. Bernard's departure, in 1140, did the pope make over the monastery to the Cistercians.[1] They courageously came and established themselves there, but were sorely tried by the sickness. Their interesting church, of typically Cistercian plan, only dates from the beginning of the 13th century. Evidently, therefore, St. Bernard could not have lived at the monastery of SS. Vincent and Anastasius. There was nothing to attract him to it or to keep him there if he ever went.

Apart from this, it is strange that the legend should be unknown to the medieval authors, and we may suspect that it is in fact of later origin. I find it for the first time in the Pilgrims' Guide to the Seven Basilicas by Onofrio Panvinio which appeared in 1570, two years after the author's death.[2] A document quoted by Manrique in his *Annales Cistercienses* takes us back approximately to the same period. He tells us that he saw, in a Spanish Cistercian abbey which he calls Mons Salutis, some relics sent from San Paolo alle Tre Fontane, and an accompanying letter attested that they came from the church where St. Bernard had seen souls climbing the ladder to heaven. The letter, he adds, was about a hundred years old.[3] Since Manrique wrote in 1642 he was referring roughly to the period when Onofrio Panvinio himself knew the legend. It does not seem to have been accepted by everyone in the 16th century, for Cardinal Baronius makes no allusion to it in his *Annales*, where the life and miracles of St. Bernard are told at length. On the other hand, from the 17th century on-

[1] *S. Bernardi vita prima.* Lib. II, cap. VII; *Patrologia Latina*, Vol. CLXXX, col. 296, and E. Vacandard, *Vie de Saint Bernard*, Vol. II, pp. 65 ff.

[2] *De praecipuis Urbis basilicis, quas septem ecclesias vulgo vocant*, 1570. The Italian translation dates from the same year.

[3] Manrique, *Ann. Cisterc.*, Vol. I, p. 392, cap. VIII, 5.

wards the legend is accepted and endlessly repeated. Some learned writers of the 19th century, outdoing their predecessors, affirm not only that St. Bernard lived at the monastery of Vincent and Anastasius but that he himself settled his monks there.[1]

Evidently we cannot trace the sources of St. Bernard's vision. It was no doubt an oral tradition among the monks. But we can understand why it was first committed to paper and celebrated in art in the 16th century. For there was never a time when the doctrine of purgatory was so much in men's minds. It was rejected by the Protestants, affirmed by the Catholics, and was indeed one of the great subjects of religious debate in those times. To the arguments drawn from scripture were added those offered by history. The visions of the saints were freely quoted, especially those of St. Gregory, who had been able to see the souls delivered by his prayers. Hence the particular importance attached at that time to the tradition of the monks at SS. Vincent and Anastasius; hence the need to write down the story of the vision and to require of it a new argument for the controversy.

The Cistercians had another famous monastery in Rome – that of Santa Croce in Gerusalemme. Pope Pius IV established them there in 1561, and they are still there today. Their church was one of the Seven Roman Basilicas, and here all had to commemorate the Cross, of which they possessed the *titulus*, and St. Helena, traditional foundress of the church. However, the Cistercians, mindful of their history, did not hesitate to embellish the church, in the 17th century, with two pictures illustrating episodes of St. Bernard's stay in Rome. These pictures, placed above two altars in the right aisle, are little known, being in deep shadow and difficult to see at certain times of day. For us, who are seeking memorials of the great abbot of Clairvaux, they have a lively interest.

The first is a work of Carlo Maratta and must have been painted about 1660 (77). It shows St. Bernard leading Victor IV to the feet of Innocent II. The anti-pope, on his knees, offers the Holy Father his tiara, which a child carries on a cushion. Innocent II, his hand raised, makes a gesture of astonishment which will turn to a gesture of pardon. St. Bernard, standing in his white monkish habit, introduces the defeated Victor with grave dignity. The saint is the hero of the scene and the artist has happily expressed his character. He has made him almost youthful and given him an air of restrained ardour. His piercing gaze is on the pope, and a mysterious brightness floats about his head.

The second picture, by Giovanni Bonatti (a contemporary of Maratta) represents a curious subject.[2] Before leaving Rome, St. Bernard asked the pope, as his only reward, for some noteworthy relic. The pope had the head of the martyr St. Caesarius brought to St. Bernard, who was authorised to take away a portion of it, and he was content with a tooth. But the monks accompanying him vainly attempted to remove the tooth and broke several knives in the process. 'Let us pray,' said St. Bernard, 'for we shall only have that which the martyr is willing to give us.' After saying the prayer, the saint had only to put his two

[1] Nibby, *Roma nell' Anno 1838, Parte I, Moderna*, p. 756; Armellini, *Le Chiese di Roma*, p. 755.

[2] The picture we see today is a copy of the original, which has disappeared.

fingers on the tooth to remove it without effort.[1] This was the singular incident which the Cistercians of Santa Croce told Bonatti to depict.

Why, among so many well-known episodes of St. Bernard's life, should they have chosen that one? The reason was that a few years earlier a book had appeared which was read in every Cistercian monastery – the *Annales Cistercienses* of Manrique, formerly professor at Salamanca.[2] The two first volumes of this great history of the order (four volumes in all) had been published at Lyon in 1642. They were received with enthusiasm. The beginnings of the order and its subsequent progress are here described in such rich and learned detail that the work is invaluable, even if Manrique lacks the critical spirit of the Bollandists and the great Benedictines. His life of St. Bernard, which fills nearly a volume, was the one always read thereafter. All the traditions given credence by Manrique were accepted in the Cistercian monasteries. It was admitted, for instance, since Manrique's dissertation refuted the opponents of the miracle, that the Virgin had let her milk flow on to St. Bernard's lips.[3] Thus it came about that the Spanish Cistercians asked Murillo to represent this scene, of which he made a masterpiece. Several old medieval traditions, adopted by Manrique, were revived in the art of the 17th and 18th centuries. There was the Virgin announcing to the mother of St. Robert, founder of Cîteaux, that she was betrothed to her unborn child.[4] There was the scene of Christ coming down from the Cross to embrace St. Bernard. At Rome itself these two subjects are met with in the church of San Bernardo alle Terme.[5]

All the Cistercian abbots who were having their churches decorated had read Manrique. There is therefore no need to be surprised when we find, at Santa Croce, the episode of St. Caesarius' tooth side by side with the submission of the anti-pope Victor. These two stories illustrate, in Manrique's pages, St. Bernard's residence in Rome, and they are given almost equal prominence.[6]

Such are the few echoes, in the art of Rome, of St. Bernard's two periods of residence there. They have their interest. The two pictures in Santa Croce have reminded observant visitors for nearly three hundred years that the great Burgundian monk did come to Rome, that he brought peace to the Church, and that the Romans called him (as they might have called a victorious emperor) the father of their country.

[1] *S. Bernardi vita prima*, Lib. II, cap. 1, 1; *Patrologia Latina*, CLXXXV, col. 322.

[2] *Cisterciensium, seu verius ecclesiasticarum Annalium a condito Cistercio* . . . tomus 1. Lugduni, 1642.

[3] *Ann. Cisterc.*, Vol. II, anno 1153, cap. XII, 6 *et seq.*

[4] *Ann. Cisterc.*, Introd., cap. 2.

[5] The mystic marriage of St. Robert and the Virgin was also represented in a picture at Santa Croce in Gerusalemme.

[6] *Ann. Cisterc.*, anno 1138, cap. I, 7, and cap. III, 2.

CHAPTER TEN

Rome in the Later Middle Ages: the Persistence of an Ancient Architectural Tradition

[ELEVENTH TO THIRTEENTH CENTURIES]

Santa Maria in Trastevere (12th century); porticoes, pavements and towers

I

THE VISITOR to Rome who has just been admiring Santa Maria Maggiore thinks, when he enters Santa Maria in Trastevere, that this is another basilica of the first centuries (82). Everything he sees speaks of early-Christian times: the nave almost as broad as high, with its rich wooden ceiling; the aisle-width matching the height of the columns; the Ionic colonnade torn from a temple of Isis; the architrave and cornice of classical tradition.[1] The interior has not the grandeur of Santa Maria Maggiore, but the two are closely related, and at first sight it is easy to believe that they date from the same century. We imagine that we are looking at the original church of Trastevere, built on the very spot where, according to tradition, a spring of oil appeared on the day the Saviour was born.

However, if we take the trouble to read Pope Innocent II's epitaph under the portico we learn that he himself undertook the reconstruction of the church in 1140, the work being completed after his death in 1148. This evidence is confirmed by other texts. What we see, therefore, is not a basilica of the first centuries, but a medieval church which faithfully reproduces early-Christian models.

This is really astonishing, and the date 1140 gives food for much thought. In 1140, in France, Romanesque churches of extraordinary beauty and variety were rising in every province. The church of Saint-Denis, where the Gothic appears in all its novelty, was well advanced. The vault was everywhere the rule. In Italy itself this fever had caught on: far and wide, north and south, churches were arising very different from the old basilicas. The world was in transformation; around Rome there was change too; but Rome herself,

[[1] The modillions (small brackets under the cornice) though derived, like many other elements here, from classical buildings, are set unconventionally in pairs, which do not always match each other.]

indifferent to all that did not belong to her particular tradition, remained unshakably attached to her past. Never, perhaps, had she proved this faithfulness more clearly.

In fact, a strange renaissance of classical tradition is to be observed, beginning about the end of the 11th century. Instead of arches, the flat architrave (abandoned several centuries before[1]) reappears on the nave colonnades. This return to the architrave, that is, to pure Greco-Roman forms, can be noted in 1090 in the little church of Santa Maria in Cappella[2] dating from the time of Urban II, the great pope of the First Crusade. The architrave appears again, a few years later, at San Crisogono. This church was built in 1122 by the valiant Cardinal John of Crema, soldier and diplomat, the staunch champion of Calixtus II against the anti-pope Bourdain. It was after attacking Sutri and taking Bourdain prisoner that he built San Crisogono to commemorate his victory. He borrowed its columns from an antique building, since the original church, revealed by excavation, had none; therefore the architrave of San Crisogono cannot have been a reminiscence of the original building, and we see that it was deliberately employed in preference to the arcade. Less than twenty years later the architect of Santa Maria in Trastevere again preferred trabeation to arches. Finally, in the first years of the 13th century, when Honorius III had the western portion of San Lorenzo fuori le Mura built, the architrave was chosen again.

Rome was reverting to the architecture of the Caesars, not only in the features of the nave, but in the use of porticoes built against the façade. In the 12th century the open court or atrium, which since the earliest times had given access to churches, was finally disappearing.[3] Of its four colonnades, only the one running along the façade survived, and so became a simple portico. Thus the lower part of the façades of Roman churches remained hidden, as they had been in the past. These porticoed façades with their frescoes or mosaics and protective moulding of somewhat Egyptian aspect are certainly attractive, but they lack the unity of the western fronts of contemporary French and Lombard churches. Porticoes of this type are a 12th-century innovation, and they accentuate the classical character of Roman churches of the period, for their Ionic columns always support an architrave. The pleasing horizontal lines of these colonnades are enough to awaken memories of a world long since departed. Who has not felt the charm of these old porticoes, those, for instance, of Santi Giovanni e Paolo on its little-frequented square (26), or of San Giorgio in Velabro, tucked away in a forgotten corner of old Rome? (79).[4] The portico of San Lorenzo in Lucina, tastefully restored in recent years, is probably the oldest of all, for it goes back to the reconstruction by Paschal II, that is to round about 1100. The porticoes of Santa Cecilia (102) and

[1] Santa Prassede constituted an exception. Here the trabeated porticoes bordering an old Roman street were re-used.

[2] Also called Santa Maria ad Pineam. This interesting church stands near Santa Cecilia, in Trastevere.

[3] That of San Clemente was the only new one belonging to the 12th century.

[[4] Owing to the opening up of the Via del Teatro di Marcello, which draws a great amount of traffic to the area, this description is no longer quite applicable. The small square in front of the church remains, however, a relatively quiet spot.]

of Santi Giovanni e Paolo date from the early years of the 12th century; those of San Giorgio in Velabro and San Lorenzo fuori le Mura from the beginning of the 13th. Several of these porticoes have disappeared. It is only from old engravings that we know those of St. John Lateran and Santa Croce in Gerusalemme; at San Crisogono and Santa Maria in Trastevere they still exist, but are unrecognisably transformed. All these are 12th-century examples.

There was, then, a curious reversion to the forms of classical architecture, and we cannot but remember that, just at this time, the name of Rome was beginning once more to stir men's minds. In 1143, when Santa Maria in Trastevere was under construction, the Senate was revived while the municipal authorities were establishing themselves on the Capitol. The ancient formula '*Senatus populusque romanus*' had been brought into use again, and Arnold of Brescia, in his fiery speeches, called up in his hearers' minds the mirage of the Roman Republic.

II

If the architecture of Santa Maria in Trastevere is that of the old basilicas, its decoration, on the contrary, presents new features. The apse-mosaic shows a subject which was a novelty in the Christian art of Rome: it shows the Virgin, enthroned on Christ's right hand, sharing his heavenly triumph (86). If the subject is novel, the mosaic as such represents, as it were, a resurrection. For nearly three hundred years no mosaics had been made in Rome. The last, that of San Marco, was Carolingian, dating from the pontificate of Gregory IV (827–844). This sudden rebirth of the mosaic in the 12th century would be inexplicable unless we knew that the celebrated Abbot Desiderius had summoned mosaic-workers from Constantinople to decorate the church he had just reconstructed at Monte Cassino. This happened towards the end of the 11th century when, according to his biographer Leone di Ostia, Desiderius determined to re-establish the lost art of mosaic-making in Italy. A workshop was set up in Campania which gained a wide reputation. There seems every reason to believe that it was these Byzantine masters who re-instructed the Roman artists in the technique of the mosaic.

These local artists had been able to produce, since the beginning of the 12th century, works as fine as the beautiful apse-mosaic of San Clemente, which first testifies to the renaissance of this art. The work is wholly Roman and probably reproduced, with some picturesque additions, the ancient mosaic of the lower church, destroyed by Robert Guiscard. But one detail betrays a contact between the Roman and the Byzantine artists; the names of St. Peter and St. Paul are not accompanied by the Latin adjective *sanctus*, but by the Greek adjective '*agios* (89).

Two other mosaics soon gave evidence of the skill acquired by the new school: that of Santa Maria in Trastevere, begun soon after 1140, and that of Santa Maria Nova, completed about 1161 when the consecration by Alexander III took place.[1] There are differences

[1] This is the church next to the Forum nowadays commonly called Santa Francesca Romana.

between these three mosaics, but there are also, when we examine them in detail, striking resemblances. All three of them include, in their upper portions, a curious feature: a sort of large tent adorned with concentric bands is spread over the heads of the figures and resembles an open pavilion in the sky. This decorative motif, very classical in feeling, goes back to the earliest Christian times – a 4th-century example remains in the chapel of SS. Rufinus and Secundus at the Lateran Baptistery. It may be that the old mosaic of the lower church of San Clemente, imitated in the 12th century, also possessed this feature. In any case, we can say with certainty that the three mosaics of San Clemente, Santa Maria in Trastevere and Santa Maria Nova are the work, if not of the same artists, at least of the same school. Though trained in the craft by Byzantine masters, the Roman mosaic-workers immediately returned to the Roman tradition. In the apse, the twelve sheep issuing from Jerusalem and Bethlehem appear again, as do the apocalyptic beasts and the seven candlesticks on the sanctuary arch – subjects inspired, in both cases, by the Roman 6th-century mosaics.[1] We see how potent was the spell of the Eternal City's past.

In many ways the mosaic of Santa Maria in Trastevere is faithful to its early models. Its main lines are conceived – apart from the central group – after the pattern of the corresponding mosaic of San Marco. To the right of Christ and the Virgin we see St. Calixtus, St. Lawrence and Pope Innocent II carrying the basilica he has just reconstructed; to the left St. Peter, St. Cornelius, St. Julius and St. Calepodius. These particular saints find a place because of their relics preserved in the church; all stand full-face and motionless, as at San Marco. Above the sanctuary arch we see, as at San Marco, the four beasts and the candelabra of the Apocalypse and, on either side of the arch, two prophets. But at Santa Maria in Trastevere there is an unusual detail: by each prophet hangs a cage, with a bird inside (87). What is the meaning of this captive bird? The verses inscribed on the prophets' unfurled scrolls provide a clue. On Isaiah's scroll we read: '*Ecce virgo concipiet et pariet filium*' and on Jeremiah's '*Christus dominus captus est in peccatis nostris*'. Which means that Christ, in assuming the nature of man in the Virgin's womb, in imprisoning himself in the flesh so as to expiate our sins, was like a bird imprisoned in a cage through human malice.[2]

But the main interest of the mosaic is to be sought elsewhere. Its novel feature is the group of the Virgin and her Son seated in the middle on the same throne – a solemn scene for which there was no precedent. These two dignified figures seem to belong to a different race from the hieratic personages on either side, whom they dominate by their scale, and eclipse by their beauty. The Virgin with her long face, her soft eyes and finely cut mouth has an aristocratic grace which makes her almost human without detracting from her supernatural dignity. Crowned with a golden diadem, clothed in a golden robe, she shines like an apparition. The Christ-Child places his right hand tenderly on his Mother's shoulder and

[1] The latter subject has disappeared from Santa Maria Nova, but we know that it formerly existed. See Campiani, *Vetera Monumenta*, Part. II, p. 164.

[2] The two cages were formerly to be seen, near the two prophets, on the sanctuary-arch of Santa Maria Nova. See Campiani, *loc. cit.* Jeremiah's text is to be found in his Lamentations, IV, 20.

seems to be uttering the words written on the book in his hand: '*Veni, electa mea, et ponam te in thronum meum.*' [1] 'Come, thou whom I have chosen and I shall place thee on my throne.' And the Virgin answers with the words on her phylactery: '*Laeva ejus sub capite meo et dextera illius amplexabitur me.*' 'His left hand will be under my head and his right hand will encircle me.' Whence comes this dialogue, so full of tenderness? It is to be found in the *Liber Responsalis* attributed to St. Gregory the Great,[2] which contained all the antiphons recited in Rome in the course of the liturgical year. In this book the Feast of the Assumption is provided with a wealth of antiphons in the Virgin's honour, and few more gracious have been written. The first begins with these lines: 'I saw her in all her beauty rising like a dove over the streams, and the sweetest aroma was diffused from her clothes. She was surrounded by roses and lilies of the valley. . . . Who is she who rises up from the desert like the delicate spiral of perfumed smoke from myrrh and incense? Come, thou whom I have chosen, and I shall seat thee on my throne, for the King has desired thy beauty.'

Another antiphon, dispensing with veiled allusions, clearly refers to the Virgin's Assumption in the following words: 'Mary has been carried up into the sky; the angels rejoice and praise God. She has been carried right up to the celestial chamber where the King of Kings is seated on a starry throne.' [3]

It is in this latter antiphon that the passage inscribed on the Virgin's phylactery occurs. The text runs: 'Already the winter is past and the rains are left far behind. The great waters could not quench love. His left hand will be under my head and his right hand will encircle me.' In the quotations taken from these exquisite works some verses may be recognised from the Song of Songs, which surrounded the Virgin with all the poetry of Asia, transplanted by the Church into the archives of the Christian soul.

For centuries these charming lyrics had delighted the heart of man without inspiring any work of art. But at the beginning of the 12th century, all of a sudden, they appeared in material form. Did this first happen in Rome? I once advanced an hypothesis on the subject, which I may here be allowed to recall and expand.[4]

Until late in the 18th century there was, at Notre Dame in Paris, a stained-glass window representing the 'Triumph of the Virgin' presented to the church by Abbot Suger. It came from the old cathedral which preceded the present building (begun 1163), and had been preserved out of respect for the donor. We owe this information to Levieil, one of our last glass-painters. Unfortunately we do not know the exact date of the gift to Notre Dame.

[1] In the inscription we read *ponam in te thronum*, instead of *ponam te in thronum*.

[2] Some parts of it date from before, and some from after his time. The *Liber Responsalis* was being worked at up to the 8th century; on this subject see Batiffol, *Histoire du Bréviaire Romain*, p. 55. The text of the *Liber Responsalis* is to be found in the *Patrologia Latina*, Vol. LXXVIII, cols. 726 ff.

[3] The text is: '*Maria Virgo assumpta est ad aethereum thalamum in quo Rex Regnum stellato sedet solio.*' This inscription is not to be seen at Santa Maria in Trastevere, but may be read in Santa Maria Maggiore at the foot of the mosaic of the Coronation of the Virgin.

[4] In *L'Art Religieux du XII*[e] *Siècle en France*, pp. 183–184.

But perhaps it is not too rash to suppose that it took place before Suger decided to reconstruct the church of Saint-Denis and started concentrating all the abbey's resources for this great undertaking. Having been appointed abbot in 1122, he might have offered the window to Notre Dame forthwith, in token of homage. Now in 1130, at the time of the schism, Pope Innocent II took refuge in France and remained there for a considerable time. He came to Saint-Denis where Suger received him and where he held a magnificent Easter celebration; then he made his entry into Paris, where he stayed a few days. He could have seen Suger's window there and been struck with its novelty. For, how should we picture this triumph of the Virgin at Notre Dame if not as a solemn group showing the Virgin enthroned to the right hand of her Son – a subject as yet unknown? It is possible, therefore, that the pope remembered this splendid manner of honouring the Virgin when, soon after 1140, he commissioned the mosaic of Santa Maria in Trastevere. While it is not unlikely that Innocent II saw Suger's window, it is impossible that Suger should have seen Innocent II's mosaic, for he never went again to Rome after 1133.

An objection comes to mind. We have just seen that the magnificent group of the Son and his Mother seated on the same throne was born of the Roman liturgy. Could it then have been born anywhere outside Rome? And is not its origin written in the very verses which Christ and the Virgin present to the spectator? The argument may seem unanswerable, but it loses all force when we recollect that France, abandoning the old Gallican liturgy, adopted the Roman as the result of a decree by Pepin the Short – a decree confirmed in 789 by Charlemagne.[1] As early as 760 Pope Paul I sent to Pepin the *Liber Responsalis*, which contains the antiphons of the Assumption which we have quoted. In the 12th century, therefore, the Virgin was celebrated in France in the same manner, and in the same words, as in Rome, and this had already gone on for more than three hundred years. The antiphons of August 15 could therefore have inspired the French just as well as the Roman artists.

I can easily believe that these antiphons would have fired the imagination in France before doing so in Rome. It was, indeed, in northern rather than in southern lands that the worship of the Virgin found most favour from the 11th century onwards. I am not forgetting that an Italian, the saint and cardinal Peter Damian, had, about 1040 or 1050, spoken of the Virgin in a most unusual vein. This rough ascetic, who wore a hair-shirt and an iron chain, wrote hymns full of tenderness in honour of the Mother of God, but he remained isolated, and nothing goes to show that his compatriots followed his example. In northern France, on the contrary, the cult of the Virgin developed steadily and continuously. In the 11th century, both in England and in Normandy – countries then so closely united – a mysterious doctrine arose. It started from the belief that the Virgin, alone among all created beings, had by God's decree escaped the taint of original sin and that this new Eve came into the world spotless, like the first Eve when she left her Creator's hands. The festival of her Conception began to be celebrated in the churches of England and Normandy – an innovation passed over by Rome in silence. At the end of the 11th century, in northern Christendom,

[1] M. Duchesne, *Origines du Culte Chrétien*, p. 97, and Batiffol, *Histoire du Bréviaire Romain*, p. 81.

men's devotion to the Virgin was continually increasing. The prayers addressed to her by St. Anselm have a passionate intensity. The thought that Mary is the Mother of God throws the saintly Doctor into a kind of ecstasy. 'All nature,' he writes, 'is the work of God, and God was born of Mary! God created all things, and Mary gave birth to God!' [1] He celebrates this unique being in metaphors drawn from the most beautiful of the Bible. He expects all things of her: strength, succour, forgiveness; he loves her as he loves her Son, and in speaking of her exclaims: 'Let my heart languish for love, let my bones dissolve, let my flesh faint away!' Burning words such as these were no more to be overlooked; the new religious orders recorded them and exalted them. St. Bernard, in speaking of the Virgin, shows the same lyric impulse as St. Anselm. All the Cistercian monasteries were dedicated to the Virgin, and it was in her honour that Cistercians and Premonstratesians alike wore the white tunic. At Cîteaux the Virgin was first called Our Lady. And it was in the 12th century that our cathedrals – so many of them dedicated to her – began to rise from the ground.

The Festival of the Assumption celebrated the Virgin's ascent to heaven and exalted her triumph; but the Church remained silent as to the circumstances which surrounded, and which followed, her death. On the day of the Assumption it was even the practice to read a letter attributed to St. Jerome which stated that nothing was certainly known about the last moments of the Virgin's life. But the enthusiasm which was turning all hearts to Our Lady soon overcame any such scruples. From the beginning of the 12th century the old story attributed to Melito began to be honourably re-established. It had originally been made known by Gregory of Tours to the Church of the Gauls, in the 6th century, but had apparently fallen into neglect since then. Its return to favour is proved by one of Abélard's sermons preached at the Feast of the Assumption before the nuns of the Paraclete. This subtle dialectician with his critical mind, who had once roused the monks of Saint-Denis to indignation by trying to convince them that the apostle of Paris could not be the same person as Denis the Areopagite, accepts the apocryphal account of the Virgin's death without hesitation. He affirms that her body was carried up to heaven at the same time as her soul. Invoking the testimony of Gregory of Tours, he tells that, the Apostles being assembled at the Virgin's bedside at the moment of her death, Christ appeared in their midst to receive her soul. He adds that on the morrow the Apostles carried the Virgin's body to the tomb and remained there together until the moment when Jesus, appearing a second time, revived his Mother's body, which was then carried up to heaven by angels to unite with her soul. This was why the Virgin's tomb is empty, like that of Christ.[2] This sermon of Abélard's shows conclusively that the old legend, long set aside, had gripped men's imagination afresh. It soon made its appearance in art.

It will not now seem extraordinary that in northern France, where the cult of the Virgin had become so popular, Suger should have dedicated a window to her triumph before 1130.

[1] St. Anselm, *Orationes Patr.*, Vol. CLVIII, col. 956.

[2] *Patrologia Latina*, Vol. CLXXVIII, cols. 539 ff.

But we must draw attention, at this point, to an important fact. At Rome, where the Triumph of the Virgin appears for the first time about 1140, in Santa Maria in Trastevere, a century and a half went by before this subject was repeated. The second example, the mosaic by Torriti in Santa Maria Maggiore, is dated 1296 (88). What has France to show in the interval? An uninterrupted succession of Triumphs of the Virgin. This fine subject is seen shortly after 1160 in a stained-glass window of Angers cathedral, some decorative details of which link it with the school of glass-painters that grew up at Saint-Denis around Suger. In this window at Angers the upper medallion shows the Virgin enthroned on her Son's right, while the lower medallions represent her funeral and her Resurrection, according to the apocryphal story now again accepted. This is the earliest surviving example in French art. Almost at the same time the sculptors of Saint-Pierre-le-Puellier at Bourges also represented the death, miraculous funeral and Assumption of the Virgin.[1] Some years later, about 1185, the sculptors at Senlis introduced, into the beautiful tympanum of the cathedral, groups showing the Virgin's death among the Apostles, her Resurrection by the angels, and her heavenly triumph; and these scenes were soon repeated in the tympana at Mantes, Laon, Saint-Yved at Braine and (about 1200) at Chartres. From now on, and throughout the 13th century, the Triumph of the Virgin, which takes the new form of her Coronation, appears on the façades of nearly all our great cathedrals. First it is an angel who places the crown on the Virgin's head; later, Christ himself does so.

If any subject is indigenous to France, this one most certainly is. It is so little at home in Rome that when, after 150 years, it reappears in Torriti's mosaic at Santa Maria Maggiore, it does so in a French form. Christ crowning his Mother reproduces, in the technique of the mosaic, those splendid sculptured groups of the French cathedrals which had been made known, by means of ivories and miniatures, all over Europe.

But there is a further decisive proof of this French influence. While there is no example of the Triumph in Rome for a century and a half, there is one elsewhere in Italy, belonging to the end of the 12th century. In 1189[2] this scene was represented in the frieze of the sculptured choir-screen in the abbey-church of Vezzolano in Piedmont. Christ and his Mother, both crowned, are seated on the same throne in heaven and form the centre of the composition. Two scenes accompany the principal group: on one side the Apostles are laying the Virgin's body in the tomb, while, on the other, angels are resuscitating it. Below this frieze we see another containing a succession of figures whose names are indicated; they include Jesse along with the Patriarchs and the Kings of Judah, ancestors of the Virgin.

It is enough to inspect this ensemble carefully to recognise it as an adaptation of the tympanum at Senlis. We find the same scenes and often the same gestures. Christ and his Mother are shown in the same attitudes, and the angels lift the Virgin from the tomb in the same manner. Both compositions are completed by the Virgin Mary's ancestors, by patriarchs and kings, but instead of forming concentric semicircles, as at Senlis, they are arranged in a horizontal line. Even though the beauties of the original are lost in the copy,

[1] Now in the City Museum.

[2] The date is given by an inscription.

its derivation is evident. This is one more example of the quite extraordinary influence of the portal at Senlis.[1]

In Italy, therefore, we find three examples of the Triumph of the Virgin during the 12th and 13th centuries. Two of them – those of Vezzolano and of Santa Maria Maggiore – betray the influence of French originals. Is there not good reason to suspect that the third, that of Santa Maria in Trastevere, was also so inspired – inspired, in fact, by Suger's window in Notre Dame?

The objection has been brought forward that in Rome, ever since the early Middle Ages, the Virgin had always been shown wearing a crown; therefore the idea that she should be crowned by her Son would naturally arise in Rome.[2] It may be answered that the Virgin's traditional crown foreshadows in no respect the scenes of her Heavenly Triumph or of her Coronation. But is this crowned Virgin herself really peculiar to Roman art? France, less fortunate than Italy, has preserved none of her old Carolingian frescoes in which the Virgin was represented. But it may be observed that as soon as works of art again make their appearance, at the end of the 11th century, the Virgin is shown crowned. In the roughly-carved capital of Saint-Pons de Thomières,[3] anterior to 1100, the Virgin has a circle about her brow. On the capitals in the cloister of Saint-Etienne, Toulouse [4] (from about 1120) the Virgin, before whom St. Mary of Egypt is kneeling, wears a crown, and it is a crowned Virgin Mary whom the Magi are approaching. In the 12th century, in France, the Virgin constantly has a crown, as in a window at Vendôme, in the 'portail royal' at Chartres, in St. Anne's portal at Notre Dame in Paris and in the cloister at Fontfroide.[5] We gain the impression that this crowned Virgin is not a novelty, but maintains an old French tradition.

What conclusion can we draw? We have seen that the Virgin was exalted by the Church in France from the 11th century onwards and in the arts – more here than in any other country – from the 12th. The scene of the Virgin's Triumph in Heaven, side by side with her Son, while rare and isolated in Italy, early became widespread in France. We can hardly do otherwise, therefore, than conclude that this scene originated there. If we knew the date of the window presented by Suger to Notre Dame the argument would be clinched. I think it will be agreed, however, that everything points to the conclusion here suggested.

III

At Santa Maria in Trastevere another mosaic adorns the façade. G. B. De Rossi dates it to the middle of the 12th century, making it roughly contemporary with the Triumph of the Virgin in the apse. According to him, it represents, not the parable of the Wise and

[1] I have drawn attention to this influence in *Art et Artistes du Moyen Age*. The fact that the choir-screen of Vezzolano bears the date 1189 lends strong support to my attribution of the Senlis tympanum to 1185.

[2] Toesca, *Storia dell'Arte Italiana*, p. 1024.

[3] Now in the museum at Toulouse.

[4] Also in the Toulouse museum.

[5] In the museum at Montpellier.

Foolish Virgins, but a procession of female saints all with their lamps lit and all moving towards the Virgin, who is seated and gives suck to her Child. On these two points the great scholar's penetrating vision was at fault.

One of the reasons which led him to date the mosaic a little before 1150 was the presence of two kneeling donors at the Virgin's feet – donors whom he identified as Pope Innocent II, who began building the church in 1140, and Pope Eugenius III, who completed it in 1148. But, if we examine more attentively the vestments of these two little ecclesiastical figures, we find no trace of the pontifical *pallium*. Therefore they are not popes, but simply dignitaries of the Church. Moreover, the following entry, dating from the early 14th century, has been found in the register of deaths at Santa Maria in Trastevere: 'Death of the Canon B. de Molpiliis, who caused three images of Virgins to be made in mosaic above the door.' [1] Evidently this canon is one of the two donors who had the façade-mosaic executed in the course of the 13th century. Its style is in no way incompatible with such a dating. Though many of the figures have been restored – and clumsily restored – they seem, in their general outline, less Roman and more Byzantine than those of the Triumph in the apse. Now the 13th century, in Rome, is characterised by a recrudescence of Byzantine feeling, for in 1218 Pope Honorius III brought eastern masters from Venice to make a mosaic for the apse of San Paolo fuori le Mura. This influence remained strong in Rome until the end of the century, and a great artist like Pietro Cavallini could not escape it. If his faces are softer and more human than those of his masters, his colouring more refined, his iconography remains nonetheless completely Byzantine; the mosaics of the Virgin's life, with which he embellished the choir of Santa Maria in Trastevere in 1291, amply demonstrate this fact. Is the mosaic of the façade his too? This is very doubtful, for the Virgins are more hieratic than his and appear to be by another hand. They may be earlier – but if so only a very few years earlier – than Cavallini's work, because it is towards the middle of the 13th century that the Madonna giving suck to the Child first appears in Italy, under Byzantine influence.[2]

As to the meaning of the scene, there can be no real doubt about it. It is surprising that G. B. De Rossi and several antiquarians after him should have seen a procession of saints in these young women carrying lamps. They cannot be other than the Wise and Foolish Virgins; the restorers did not realise this, but they have not rendered the subject unrecognisable. While putting a crown on nearly every head and a flame in nearly every lamp, they nevertheless left two Virgins, on the Madonna's left, unaltered. Those two hang their uncrowned heads and there is no flame in their lamps. Such were, originally, all the five foolish Virgins, placed to the left hand of the Madonna and Child.

It has been objected that all these Virgins have haloes, while the foolish ones should not

[1] Cecchelli, *Santa Maria in Trastevere*, p. 138.

[2] See the icon from the Jarvis collection, New-Haven, reproduced by P. d'Ancona in *Les Primitifs Italiens*, fig. 63 (mid-13th century). The theme was of very ancient origin in the East, appearing as early as the 6th century in the monastery of St. Jeremiah at Saqqara. It reached France in Carolingian times – under eastern influence, as the ivory from Metz in the Bibliothèque Nationale proves.

have them. This is a mistake. As soon as the subject appears in western monumental art both the Foolish and the Wise Virgins are given haloes. They all have them on a capital in the Toulouse museum dating from the early 12th century. The same tradition survived into the following century, for the Foolish Virgins are haloed at the cathedrals both of Laon and Rheims. Apparently it was their virginity that the artists sought to honour. We see, therefore, that there is nothing to surprise us in the haloes of the Virgins at Santa Maria in Trastevere.

After this analysis we may conclude that the façade-mosaic is not of the 12th, but of the middle or late 13th century, and that it depicts no saints, but the parable of the Wise and Foolish Virgins. The Doctors attributed a deep significance to them at this time, associating them with the Last Judgment. The Wise Virgins, who had kept the flame of charity burning in their lamps, represented the Elect; the Foolish Virgins, who let their lamps go out, the Damned. Even their numbers had a mysterious significance: the five Foolish Virgins symbolised the pleasures of the five senses; the five Wise ones symbolised the five modes of inner contemplation. At Santa Maria in Trastevere, as in the French cathedrals, they foreshadow the great scene of the Last Judgment.

IV

At Santa Maria in Trastevere, after the mosaics, it is the rich pavement of the nave that most attracts one's attention. The visitor will already have seen similar pavements in the oldest Roman basilicas, including an almost identical one at Santa Maria Maggiore, and he readily imagines that this beautiful form of decoration is contemporary with the first Christian churches. This is a common mistake which needs to be corrected.

The pavements of the 4th- and 5th-century basilicas did not in any way resemble that of Santa Maria in Trastevere. The proof has been furnished by the discovery of a 4th-century example in the basilica at Aquileia. Here we find the usual elements of Roman mosaic-decoration: animals and birds in shapely panels against a light ground. It would seem a pagan work were it not that Jonah and the Good Shepherd give it a Christian character. The remains of pavements discovered in Rome in the lower churches of San Crisogono and San Clemente show us decadent antique traditions and are quite lacking in original elements.

These old pavements have nothing to do with those of Santa Maria in Trastevere and other similar churches, whose character is quite novel. Their basic decorative element is the circle. Sometimes a great round slab of porphyry is surrounded by four lesser discs; sometimes circles of equal diameter are knotted together by multi-coloured strands in graceful curves. Vacant spaces are filled up with fine mosaic-work consisting of tiny stars, squares, lozenges and triangles all forming a harmonious colour-scheme.[1]

What is the source of this highly refined art, of these carpets in marble? Without doubt, I think, they came from the East. The first essay in this manner is the floor of the little

[[1] See Edward Hutton, *The Cosmati*, 1950.]

chapel of San Zeno at Santa Prassede, which was decorated in the 9th century by Byzantine artists. But it was in the 11th century that the models destined to be imitated in Rome appeared at Monte Cassino. The master-craftsmen of Constantinople, called to Rome by the Abbot Desiderius, not only brought back to Italy the lost secrets of the mosaic but introduced at the same time the art of the polychrome pavement. The original pavement of the church at Monte Cassino has disappeared, but a partial record of it is provided by an old drawing. This represents only a fragment of the mosaic, and even that is restored, since close inspection reveals two French *fleurs de lis* and the five-petalled rose of Pope Urban IV (1261–64). Nevertheless, parts of it closely resemble the pavement-patterns of Santa Maria in Trastevere. It lacks the elegant connecting bands that link the circles together, but no doubt they were really present, for this is a typically eastern motif, of which examples remain in the monasteries of Mount Athos. The Byzantine origin of the Monte Cassino pavement and of those Roman ones which derive from it cannot be doubted. In them we find a last faint reminiscence of the splendid pavements of the imperial palaces, which the chroniclers compared sometimes to brilliant carpets, sometimes to flower-beds. In one of these halls the marble facing of the walls matched the floor so perfectly, both in pattern and colour, that this beautiful room (which was the empress's) was known as 'the Harmony'.

Mosaic pavements similar to that of Santa Maria in Trastevere are to be found in about fifteen other Roman churches.[1] Nearly all of them belong to the 12th and 13th centuries, and they are all so similar that it is very difficult to place them in chronological order. The earliest seems to be that of Santa Maria in Cosmedin, for it dates from the restoration, completed in 1123, undertaken by Alfanus in the time of Pope Calixtus II. The pavement of San Clemente cannot be much later, for the reconstructed church was dedicated in 1128. Then comes San Crisogono; an inscription informs us that the church and its decoration were finished in 1130. The mosaic pavements of Santa Maria Maggiore and of Santa Maria in Trastevere are contemporaneous, the former having been constructed about 1145, and the latter completed in 1148. It is highly probable that the floor of Santa Croce is also of these years, since the reconstruction was begun by Pope Lucius II in 1144. That of San Lorenzo fuori le Mura, on the other hand, is much later, for it dates from the construction of the western (anterior) church by Honorius III, between 1216 and 1227 (93).

These pleasing pavements also occur in some of the churches around Rome, but, except in the direction of Orvieto and Spoleto, they hardly extend beyond the limits of Latium. Rome, where marbles of all colours still abounded, and where a porphyry column, skilfully cut up, could yield numerous red discs for the pavements, was the natural centre for this eastern craft now acclimatised among the Latins. It survived unadulterated until the end of

[1] Santa Maria in Cosmedin, San Clemente, San Crisogono, Santa Maria Maggiore, Santa Croce in Gerusalemme, Sant'Alessio, San Benedetto in Piscinula, Santa Francesca Romana, San Giovanni in Laterano, San Giovanni a Porta Latina, Santi Giovanni e Paolo, San Gregorio al Celio, Santa Maria d'Aracoeli, Santa Maria in Domnica, Santi Quattro Coronati, San Lorenzo fuori le Mura, San Saba, La Scala Santa.

the Middle Ages. In memory we associate these beautiful pavements with the most venerable churches of Rome; they give them that mysterious and indefinable charm which is uniquely Roman. During the stations in Lent there is the added touch of the laurel-leaves strewn on the ground, and their bitter scent in the air.

V

As he leaves Santa Maria in Trastevere, the visitor will not fail to notice the campanile attached to one side of the church. It much resembles a whole family of Roman towers, some of which accompany the most ancient basilicas. Are they contemporary with these old churches? Are they more recent, and if so what is their age? And how old is the campanile of Santa Maria in Trastevere?

The problem is worth examining, for these brick bell-towers with their white marble colonnettes constitute, in their form and their colour, one of the beauties of Rome. They remind us of the holy city of the Middle Ages, the city of pilgrims, who saw these towers very much as we see them today. When were the earliest of them built? Their appearance has been explained on the basis of Gregory VII's liturgical reforms. He instructed the Roman clergy to return to the ancient usage and to celebrate mass at the traditional hours by night and day throughout the year. To summon the Chapter at such frequent intervals a bell-tower was necessary, hence the construction of a good many such towers from the 11th century onwards.[1] Possibly this explanation embodies a small element of truth, but every church in Rome did not have a Chapter of canons,[2] and it often happens that the most modest churches possess bell-towers. In any case, it was not in Gregory's time that they became so numerous, but in the following century. We read that in the 12th century the tower was loved for its beauty, the bell for its poetry. Every church hoped to have its campanile and its bells. Men loved to hear these voices, now solemn and now gay, floating down from the skies. On Christmas night and on Easter morning the whole town seemed to sing a hymn of joy. In Rome, as also in France, the 12th century was the age of bell-towers.

It is probable that the old Lombard campaniles, some of which (like that of San Satiro at Milan) go back to the 9th century, served as models for those of Rome; but the imitations are an improvement on the originals. In Rome the openings are more numerous and make the towers as a whole lighter; their proportions are finer and their storeys more clearly defined by means of cornices supported on white stone brackets. The use of brick gives these campanili a warm hue which is set off by the marble colonnettes of the windows and

[1] Serafini, *Torri Campanarie*, Rome, 1927. The text of Gregory VII's decree has been given by Dom Morin, *Revue Bénédictine*, 1901, p. 177.

[2] Gregory VII addressed his decree to what he calls the '*regularis auctoritas*', that is to say to the clergy subject to the rule. Dom Morin has very correctly translated this 'the regular canons'. The whole of the Roman clergy could not, therefore, have been affected.

sometimes also by coloured faience plates and enamelled Greek crosses let into the walls. Often the bricks of these campanili, borrowed from Roman buildings, have the patina of eighteen centuries. The colonnettes are nearly always antique too; one of those from the old bell-tower of St. Peter's, now in the Vatican museum, bears a Greek inscription in honour of Serapis of Canopus. The Rome of the Caesars lives again, in a different form, in the bell-towers, and their almost flat roofs harmonise with the horizontal lines of the city.

Few of these attractive towers remain exactly in their original form. Their numerous windows gave rise to fears for their stability, so that some were closed up by means of little walls imprisoning the columns. The lightness of the tower suffers, and we have to make an effort of the imagination to picture its original beauty. Some of them have been restored – a tricky undertaking, for it is only too easy to let the imprint of the centuries vanish away. And then, instead of a medieval monument battered by the passage of time, we see something from a World Fair.

The Roman campanili all look the same to a casual observer. In reality, however, we can distinguish three different types. In the first and simplest there are just two arched openings in each storey. In the archaic tower of Santa Maria in Cappella, built in 1090, the two openings are brought closer together, but not to the point of sharing a central colonnette (94). We see the same thing in the tower of San Lorenzo fuori le Mura (96), whose extreme simplicity suggests an 11th-century date, and in that of Sant'Agata dei Goti. Later, the two openings come to be separated only by a marble colonnette and so form a nicely proportioned double window. The campanile of Santa Rufina, in a forgotten corner of old Trastevere, is one of the most charming examples of this type (95).[1]

The towers with triple openings form a second category. The three windows are joined by two colonnettes whose trapezoid capitals are as long as the wall is thick. In the lower storeys the colonnettes are replaced by small piers, and at this level there may be only double windows. Most of the Roman campanili are of this type. It has been claimed, though not conclusively, that the tower of San Giovanni a Porta Latina (98) goes back to the 11th century, but all the rest are of the 12th, namely: Santa Maria in Monticelli, San Giorgio in Velabro (79),[2] Santa Pudenziana, Santa Maria in Cosmedin (80), Santa Cecilia (102), San Marco, Santi Quirico e Giulitta, Santa Maria in Campo Marzio. The tower of San Sisto Vecchio, however, belongs to the time of Innocent III – that is to say to the first years of the 13th century (104). It is not impossible that the round tower of Sant'Apollinare Nuovo at Ravenna, in which triple windows and decorative faience discs appear for the first time, may have inspired the Roman master-builders.[3] If so, these Roman towers were born under the combined influence of Lombardy and of Ravenna.

Thirdly, there are the towers with quadruple openings. These are fairly common in Rome, being found at Sant'Alessio, Santa Francesca Romana (103), Sant'Eustachio and San

[1] We may add San Benedetto in Piscinula and San Lorenzo in Piscibus.

[2] The top was reconstructed after a fire.

[3] Serafini, *op. cit.*

Lorenzo in Lucina.[1] It has been alleged that this type derives from the very ancient tower of old St. Peter's, built by Pope Stephen III after the coronation of Pepin the Short in 745.[2] Some 16th-century drawings do indeed show it as having quadruple windows with linking colonnettes in each storey. But was that really the 8th-century bell-tower? Had it not been restored if not rebuilt in the course of eight hundred years? When we learn that it was struck three times by lightning in a single century (in 1303, 1333 and 1352), which resulted even in the melting of the bells, some scepticism is surely justified. It must be added that the 16th-century drawings do not all agree and that one of them shows triple instead of quadruple openings in each storey. However attractive the theory, it will be seen to be untenable.

Similarly, we cannot accept without reserve the theory – ingenious though it is – that other such towers on the pilgrimage-routes of Italy were due to returned pilgrims imitating the old tower of St. Peter's. But it is true that the quadruple-windowed type occurs (if sparingly) on these pilgrimage-routes, as at Lucca, Arezzo and Assisi.[3]

In which of the three categories just discussed should we place the campanile of Santa Maria in Trastevere? One does not quite know how to answer the question, since it presents features which are exceptional in Rome (81). This is not obvious at first sight, for the openings have quite lost their original character. But careful observation soon shows that the top storey originally had the triple type of window, so one is at first inclined to assume that the lower storeys were similar and to class this tower in the second category. However, we discover with some surprise that the lower storeys really have quadruple windows and therefore belong to the third category. At Rome, where towers remain so true to type, this peculiarity offends the eye, as a verse with faulty metre offends the ear. The oddity is probably to be explained (but not justified) by assuming a resumption of work after an interval. This bell-tower was built in the course of the 12th century, for its cornices merge with those of the church walls themselves.[4]

The visitor exploring Rome notices, not without surprise, that there is no fixed position for the towers of the old basilicas. They may adjoin either the apse or the façade, they may be on one side of the church or the other and they may stand quite isolated. The campanile is a delightful *hors-d'œuvre* not integrated, however, with the church. Never do we find that feeling for order and unity so characteristic of the French churches, whose western towers coalesce with the façade in one grand composition, and whose central tower over the crossing forms a lofty crown to the whole.

Such are the features of Santa Maria in Trastevere which (limiting one's view to the 12th century) attract the art-historian's attention. From the 13th century onwards many generations left their traces in the church, but these later additions do not concern our subject.

[[1] Santi Giovanni e Paolo (100) should be added. In all these towers the quadruple windows take the form of two separate pairs.]

[2] Serafini, *op. cit.*

[3] Serafini, *op. cit.*

[4] The campanile of San Crisogono also presents a mixture of two different types, but it was deformed by 17th-century alterations.

CHAPTER ELEVEN

Memories of Saint Dominic

[THIRTEENTH CENTURY]

San Sisto Vecchio and Santa Sabina

ONE WINTER morning I was going to San Sisto Vecchio, which stands at the foot of the Coelian not far from the Appian Way. It had rained overnight and the sky was still threatening. The Roman sky nearly always has that lovely colour of oriental sapphire described by Dante; but when the strong sea-winds start blowing it soon assumes an air of deepest gloom. Yet to me it is never more beautiful than then. Perhaps because I first saw Rome, many years since, under such a sky; or perhaps because these sombre greys harmonise so perfectly with the ruins, with the cypresses, with the sombre and solemn history of the Eternal City. The new houses near the Lateran stood out against the inky sky, strangely white like Moslem tombs. Alas, these same houses concealed from view those glorious wide horizons which used to greet my youthful eyes – the great wilderness of the Roman Campagna traversed by long lines of aqueducts, hastening towards the mountains. One of the greatest beauties of Rome, one which should have been preserved with the same respect as a Michelangelo fresco, had gone for ever.

Leaving St. John Lateran, I took the path which runs down towards the Appian Way keeping just inside the Aurelian walls. I had not been this way for a long time. The path used to pass through gardens shut in by reed-fences, and it retained, like all this part of old Rome, a rustic charm. I found it lined with the houses of a workmen's quarter, and for a moment imagined myself transported to some northern industrial town. But all of a sudden the huge ruin of Caracalla's baths rose against the sky, and I knew that I was in Rome.[1]

I came to that pleasant park known as the 'Archaeological Promenade',[2] where, among evergreen oaks and laurels, two old churches stand. One of them is called San Sisto Vecchio, the other Santi Nereo ed Achilleo, and both are dedicated to martyrs. Ancient Christian traditions here add their poetry to the beauties of the scene. Santi Nereo ed Achilleo was called *titulus fasciolae* in ancient times, meaning 'the church of the bandlet'. It was told, in explanation of this name, that St. Peter, fleeing from the Mamertine Prison, dropped at this spot the bandage he had used to protect his sore leg from the irons. He continued along the

[1] The face of Rome changes so quickly that, since these lines were written, the workers' quarter has disappeared and the path has been broadened into a road.

[[2] Passeggiata Archeologica.]

Appian Way when, after the first milestone, he beheld Jesus carrying his Cross. Then the famous words were exchanged: 'Lord, whither goest thou?' To which Jesus replied: 'I go to Rome to be crucified a second time.' St. Peter, ashamed of his weakness, went back into the city to die there.

Another celebrated conversation took place, so it is said, on the exact spot where the church of San Sisto now stands. In the year 258, during the persecution under Valerian, Pope Sixtus II was led by the soldiers to the catacomb of San Callisto to be beheaded there. The deacon St. Lawrence awaited him on the Appian Way to bid him a last farewell: 'Father,' he said, 'whither goes thou without thy son? Priest, whither without thy deacon?' 'My son,' answered St. Sixtus, 'I am not deserting thee; greater struggles await thee; thou shalt follow me in three days.' After his execution St. Sixtus was buried in the cemetery of St. Calixtus, in the crypt of the martyred popes. The marble slab which bore his name and closed his *loculus* has not been found, but it is known that he rested near Anteros, Fabian, Pontian, Lucia and Eutychius, and we can still see, scratched on the plaster, the ardent invocations addressed to him by the faithful. Later on, when the catacombs were abandoned, the pope's body was carried to San Sisto; a relic of St. Lawrence was placed close by, and so these two martyrs of the same persecution found themselves side by side in death.

If I had come to San Sisto in search of an ancient basilica I should have been sadly disappointed, for this church (104), reconstructed in the 18th century, exhibits only stucco facings, shell-ornaments and heads of angels. It was not, however, the period of its foundation that drew me to the church but rather the 13th century; what I wanted to see was the remains of the old monastery, adjoining the church, where a great saint had lived. For the charm and the attraction of San Sisto – to those who love the Middle Ages – lie in its associations with St. Dominic.

One of the scenes from the predella of Fra Angelico's *Coronation of the Virgin*, in the Louvre, tells with delightful ingenuousness the story of a certain miracle of St. Dominic (106). Two angels, light as spirits and robed in sky-blue, are bringing bread to the Dominicans, who are seated at an empty table. On that day they had given all they possessed to the poor and nothing was left in the monastery for the evening meal. Nevertheless, St. Dominic told the brothers to take their places at table and to listen to the reading as usual; then he began to pray. 'Whereupon,' says the *Golden Legend*, 'two beautiful youths came in with two pure white napkins full of loaves. Beginning with the juniors, one to the right and one to the left, they gave each brother a most perfect loaf. When they came to the Blessed Dominic they gave him too a whole loaf and then, bowing their heads, they disappeared.' The scene of this story from the Miracles of St. Dominic was Rome – was in fact the very monastery of San Sisto Vecchio where I was standing.

St. Dominic, having left his battle-ground of Languedoc where he had been fighting the heretics, had come to Rome to ask the pope's authorisation for his Order. Innocent III at first hesitated, but one night, in a dream, he saw St. Dominic supporting on his shoulders the

Lateran basilica, which was falling down (105). He felt this dream to be a sign from heaven and no longer hesitated to grant the saint's request.[1]

The following year St. Dominic came again to Rome with some of his monks from Toulouse, and Innocent's successor, Pope Honorius III, gave the church of San Sisto to the new Order. It rose in one of the most deserted parts of medieval Rome, that Rome of the 13th century full of splendour and melancholy where the ancient sanctuaries stood in solitude. The surrounding scene was made up of ancient tombs and ruins and the vegetation on the slopes of the Coelian hill. Innocent III had just restored the church and made the surrounding monastic buildings habitable. It was he too who built the campanile which (but little modified) we see today, and which St. Dominic saw in his time. These old towers of dull-red brick, with their narrow windows and little white marble columns which catch the sun, are one of the beauties of Rome. They call up, by their mysterious and powerful incantation, the *aurea Roma* of the medieval pilgrims.

St. Dominic and the brothers of his community lived in this poor monastery, where they sometimes ran short of bread, but the saint's rousing speech, and some extraordinary miracles of which word went round, attracted new disciples. As their numbers increased continually, the pope gave the Order a new and bigger monastery on the Aventine – that of Santa Sabina, which has eclipsed San Sisto Vecchio. At Santa Sabina everything is preserved – the ancient 5th-century basilica where St. Dominic prayed, the cell in which he meditated, the refectory in which he sat (28, 107). Even his orange-tree still scents the old cloister where he planted it.[2]

The monastery of San Sisto was not abandoned, but became, instead, a convent of Dominican nuns. The pope desired that St. Dominic should place a certain number of nuns under his severe rule, that they might serve as an example to other communities. The sisters of Santa Maria in Tempulo accepted the Dominican discipline and agreed to be enclosed within the walls of San Sisto, but on condition that they might bring with them the image of the Virgin from their old church. It was one of those ancient eastern Madonnas said to have been painted by St. Luke. So venerated was she that the local populace had determined to prevent her removal by force. So it was at night that St. Dominic came to effect the transfer to San Sisto, and all the nuns followed, bare-footed and in deep silence, to take possession of the convent along with their Madonna. St. Luke's Virgin is no longer at San Sisto, but has twice migrated since. In the 16th century, when the Dominican nuns abandoned

[[1] The dream of Innocent III is illustrated in the altar-piece at Pisa (here reproduced) by Francesco Traini (1344–45). The identical tradition attaches to St. Francis, who approached the same pope at about the same time to obtain approval for his new Order. The pope's dream in relation to St. Francis has been represented more often: first, in an altar-piece by Guido da Siena dated 1275 and, later, in various fresco-cycles, including Giotto's at Assisi and Benozzo Gozzoli's at Montefalco.]

[2] This beautiful monastery of Santa Sabina, part of which belonged to the State, was made over as a whole to the Very Reverend Father Gillet, Master General of the Preaching Friars, who restored it with much good taste.

their old convent on the Appian Way – rendered uninhabitable by the malaria – they took their ancient picture to Santi Domenico e Sisto on the Quirinal. This beautiful Byzantine Virgin was to be seen there until comparatively recent years, with her big eyes, refined nose and hair confined by a Syrian head-cloth, bearing a decorative star. In 1928 the nuns moved a second time, exchanging Santi Domenico e Sisto for the Monte Mario, and they took their Madonna with them.

St. Dominic sent some of his French nuns to join the Roman community at San Sisto Vecchio and to instruct them in the new rule. He himself constantly visited his spiritual daughters, and not a day passed without the support and encouragement of his words. At that time there was a young nun in the convent called Sister Cecilia, who listened to the saint's daily teaching with passionate interest. She later became Mother Superior of the Dominican convent of St. Agnes at Bologna. There, in her extreme old age, sixty years after her stay at San Sisto, she recounted her youthful memories to one of her own nuns, Sister Angelica, who wrote them down. This was the golden legend of San Sisto, full of marvels and of poetry, one of those books the visitor should read if he would taste the full charm of the old convent.[1]

After so many years Sister Cecilia still saw the luminous features of St. Dominic, which she describes just as they were painted by Fra Angelico. 'He had a handsome face and beautiful eyes. His brow and his looks radiated a splendour which compelled respect and love. He was always filled with sweet serenity, except when moved by the sufferings of his fellows. His hands were delicate, his voice fine and well modulated. He had not lost a hair; his monastic crown was intact, with but a few scattered white hairs.' Sister Angelica, who gives us this attractive portrait based on Sister Cecilia's recollections, apologises for her bad writing. 'Excuse the style,' she says to her readers, 'for I know nothing at all about grammar.' She was certainly not ignorant, however, of the art of pleasing, for her agreeable Latin has the same simplicity, the same naïve charm that distinguishes that of Giacomo da Voragine, the contemporary author of the *Golden Legend*. Sister Cecilia, who inspired her, had forgotten nothing of what she had seen and heard. According to her, more miracles had occurred at San Sisto than in almost any other place in the world. There St. Dominic had commanded the forces of nature. One evening Sister Cecilia saw him return, wearied by a long and rough day's preaching, during which he had converted a sinner. It was so late that the nuns no longer expected him; they were already going up to the dormitory when the bell announced his arrival. They came down again at once and gathered around him. He asked for a little wine for himself and at the same time had a cup filled for the nuns. It was passed round from hand to hand, and each one drank from it, yet, marvellous to relate, it still remained full. This cup was inexhaustible, like the charity of St. Dominic himself.

Meanwhile the night was so far advanced that the nuns and their prioress exhorted the

[1] The text of St. Dominic's miracles as told by Sister Cecilia is to be found in Mamachi, *Annales Ordinis Praedicatorum*, 1756, Vol. 1, cols. 247 ff.

saint to remain at San Sisto and not to go on to Santa Sabina. To press on could be dangerous, for it meant threading the solitudes of the Aventine in the darkness, relieved only by the little lamps of Santa Balbina and Santa Prisca. One might meet anything at this late hour, and there was the frightening possibility of bad spirits appearing from their haunts among the ruins and ancient tombs. However, St. Dominic was not to be persuaded, for he had been miraculously warned that one of his monks at Santa Sabina, Brother Jacob, in-intended that very night to throw off the monastic habit and quit the community. St. Dominic therefore went on, but on the threshold a beautiful youth, stick in hand, appeared beside him and acted as his guide. When they arrived at Santa Sabina the youth, having noiselessly opened the door, suddenly disappeared, and St. Dominic realised that his companion had been an angel (an episode perpetuated by a fresco above the entrance). As he went in, the saint met Brother Jacob who was at that moment about to leave the monastery. In vain he implored him to be faithful to his vow; the rebellious spirit would listen to nothing. Then St. Dominic began to pray; and when he rose again the brother threw himself at his feet all in tears, asking his forgiveness.

In the 1920s nothing had yet changed in this corner of Rome since St. Dominic's time. One would have hesitated to walk at midnight from San Sisto Vecchio to Santa Sabina, following in the darkness the paths on the empty Aventine. Now a whole new town has arisen on the hill and St. Dominic would not recognise his retreat at Santa Sabina, where, after the labours of the day, he could return to the silence of the Thebaid. The Eternal City is born once again and Rome is becoming a great European capital; but artists lament that city of enchantment which has ceased to exist, where the old churches rose in isolation from the barren ground.

Though he lived at Santa Sabina, St. Dominic never ceased to pay visits to the nuns at San Sisto, and that old convent contains many reminders of him. A Dominican nun in white and black, just like a Sister Cecilia of seven hundred years ago, receives the visitor at the convent gate and seems to take him right back into the 13th century. Entering the old conventual building, we hope to find a cloister, gracefully rhythmic with fine colonnettes, instead of which there are brick piers and tall arcades, classic in style. I could no longer find, adjoining this cloister, the refectory where the monks were served by angels, and was beginning to wonder what had become of the Middle Ages, when at last I found them. I saw, opening on to the reconstructed cloister, a fine chapter-house divided into nave and aisles by pillars which were certainly those of St. Dominic's time. It was a remaining fragment of the monastery rebuilt by Innocent III at the beginning of the 13th century. Originally the chapter-house probably had a timber roof, since replaced by stone vaulting; yet it evoked the distant past most powerfully. The far end is slightly raised, and there it was that St. Dominic used to sit when his first Italian followers gathered together, to hear him expound the rule and be kindled at his fire.[1]

[1] Some time ago this chapter-house, which had retained its primitive character, was transformed by the nuns into a chapel.

I noticed that this ancient hall was covered with modern frescoes. In general, 19th-century religious painting is no better in Rome than in France. In some of the famous old basilicas we are distressed to find, next door to their splendid mosaics on a golden ground, frescoes which are wholly wanting in inspiration. Before examining those before me I reflected sadly on how Fra Angelico had lived in Rome, and how eternally regrettable it was that the Superior of his order never asked him to tell the story of St. Dominic's life on these venerable walls. It was about that time that Angelico painted the chapel of Nicholas V in the Vatican; he might have produced another marvel at San Sisto.

Lingering but briefly over these unnecessary regrets, I began to look at the frescoes, at first with indifference and then with sympathy. I saw four women saints of the Dominican order: St. Rose of Lima, St. Catherine of Ricci, St. Agnes of Montepulciano and St. Catherine of Siena, recognisable by her crown of thorns. There was something about them so pure that one could not help being reminded of the Umbrian and Sienese painters. This was no imitation, but a work as truly religious as those of earlier centuries, for it was the creation of a fervent and devoted spirit. Farther on I saw St. Dominic and St. Francis of Assisi, both on their knees, clasping each other in a brotherly embrace.

Who was the artist who worked here in the middle of the 19th century (when religious art in general was so uninspired) and produced these figures which, surprisingly, are moving? It was a young Frenchman, Father Besson, who had just entered the Dominican order as reorganised by Lacordaire. He had been competently trained in the studio of Paul Delaroche, but a journey in Italy revealed to him the beauty of the Primitives, whose work, he discovered, harmonised perfectly with his own religious nature. Lacordaire said of him: 'He was a soul incomparably pure; a second Angelico of Fiesole.' He entered Santa Sabina with a kindred spirit, the architect Piel, and he painted the frescoes at San Sisto between 1852 and 1856. He was unable to put the finishing touches to his work, for his superiors sent him to the East, to the Dominican mission at Mosul, where he was to end his days. With heroic abnegation he sacrificed his art to his duty of obedience. Had he stayed at Santa Sabina, he would have prayed brush in hand, as did Fra Angelico at San Marco in Florence.

The work of the great Dominican painter was continually in his thoughts, and he twice showed his indebtedness by imitating the master. Departing but little from Angelico's model, he painted the angels who served the brothers at their empty table, and Peter and Paul appearing to St. Dominic, who kneels in prayer; in the latter St. Peter offers him a staff, St. Paul a book, and both of them urge him to preach the Gospel across the world. When first entering this chapter-house I had regretted Angelico's absence from the walls, without doubting, however, that some trace of him would be found there. Assuredly, Father Besson is not Fra Angelico; as a pupil of Paul Delaroche he could not altogether withstand the ways of the school. His rather dull colours and heavy shadows have nothing in common with the celestial harmonies of Angelico, who, true to his name, seems to have caught glimpses of a world far different from our own. He does not possess the irresistible sincerity of that unique artist, who paints just as he breathes. Yet in spite of some defects, which are those of his time, there is a depth of feeling in Father Besson's work which does remind one of Fra Angelico.

In three big frescoes he has shown three miracles of St. Dominic of which San Sisto was the scene – all three resurrections from the dead. The saint restores to life a child brought to him by its mother; and again the architect of the cloister, killed by the collapse of a wall. Finally, he resuscitates a young man, nephew of Cardinal Orsini, who had just died as the result of a fall from his horse. It is the deep faith of St. Dominic that gives these frescoes their beauty. Before the dead child whom his mother brings forward Dominic simply raises his eyes to heaven, confidently awaiting the miracle. But he is on his knees by the lifeless body of the architect, his hands open, his eyes fixed on the invisible, imploring the divine mercy with his whole soul. His prayer has been heard, for life is returning to the dead man, who extends his hand like a shipwrecked seaman sinking among the waves. In the episode of the young Orsini Dominic stretches his arms towards heaven, transported by his faith, commanding Death; and the young man, drawn up from the depths by an irresistible force, begins to raise himself from the ground. Some nuns have fallen to their knees and tremble as they watch the miracle.

Among modern, 19th-century pictures in the churches of Rome I know of none to compare with these for intensity of feeling. It gave me pleasure to think that they were the work of a Frenchman.

For centuries, France has contributed nobly to the embellishment of the Roman sanctuaries. How many times, visiting one of these churches, have I been surprised to come across the work of a compatriot! Sometimes it was a picture by Simon Vouet, Mignard or Parrocel; sometimes a statue or bas-relief by Legros, Théodon, Adam or Houdon. At St. Peter's three of the finest pictures translated into mosaic are by Poussin, Valentin and Subleyras. Frenchmen have built churches in Rome; the Santissimo Nome di Maria, which, with its companion church Santa Maria di Loreto, makes so pleasing a setting for Trajan's column, was the work of Derizet, an 18th-century French architect (109).

There are also works executed by Italians but sponsored by the French. It was Cardinal d'Estouteville, Archbishop of Rouen, who had Sant'Agostino built in Rome in the style of the Renaissance, while at the same time he was building the choir of Mont-Saint-Michel in pure 15th-century Gothic. Benedict Adam, a judge of the ecclesiastical court, had the little polygonal chapel of San Giovanni in Oleo constructed, at the spot where St. John was plunged into boiling oil. We still read the prelate's motto '*Au plaisir de Dieu*' over the door.

Rome owes San Luigi dei Francesi to the kings of France, as also the Trinità dei Monti, with its majestic stairway and its tall façade, glowing pink in the sunset. It owes San Nicola to Lorraine, San Claudio to the Franche-Comté, Sant'Ivo to the Bretons. We cannot help remembering that Michelangelo's admirable *Pietà* was commissioned by a French cardinal. Rome was long a second fatherland to Christians; all catholic nations wished to make their contributions to its beauty, and none did so with greater zeal than France.

When I left San Sisto Vecchio the wind had blown the clouds away and the ruined palace of Septimius Severus on the Palatine was outlined against a clear blue sky. Walking along the Appian Way (which begins close by among the trees), I reflected that this convent of San Sisto, so rarely visited today, was really one of those privileged places where the 13th century lives on. Little remains, it is true, from those times, but the imagination calls up what is missing. The more one knows, the more Rome's beauties can be appreciated and enjoyed. A church which reveals nothing at a first visit can be brought to life again by a little study – a fact which San Sisto, among others, illustrates well.

CHAPTER TWELVE

The Italian Gothic and One Gothic Church in Rome

[THIRTEENTH CENTURY]

Fossanova and the other Cistercian churches; the Gothic of Siena, Florence and Milan; Santa Maria sopra Minerva in Rome

THE OLD road from Rome to Fossanova runs along the slopes of the Monti Lepini, once inhabited by the Volscians. It overlooks the plain but is itself overlooked by a succession of fortresses: Norba, with its cyclopean walls; Sezze, the ancient Setia, founded by Hercules and proud to show the Nemean lion in its coat-of-arms; Piperno or Privernum, home of the amazon Camilla. The spring is late this year, but the asphodel is coming into flower – that lover of stony places and of tombs which the ancients therefore associated with the dead and the gardens of the world beyond.

The abbey of Valvisciolo stands by the road. The church with its groined vaults and rough rectangular piers (to whose cornice, doing duty for a capital, simple pilaster-strips run down) shows us Cistercian architecture at its most austere. The cloister, encumbered with buttresses, has lost its harmonious lines.[1] Three or four monks inhabit this solitary place, where malaria once prevailed in summer. It sometimes happened that one of the wild herdsmen from the plains, having killed a man in some vendetta, would come knocking at the monastery door at night to ask for absolution. The road, bordered with cactus, assumes an African character. In the distance the Monte Circeo (Circe's mountain-promontory) seems to evaporate between the light of the sky and the light of the sea. Soon we leave the hillside road which overlooks the dried-up Pontine marshes and penetrate the mountains. Then the valley opens and we see before us a French church, erected by the Cistercians (116).

We have reached Fossanova but might well think we were in Burgundy. Everything here is French except the lintel over the main door, which has fine Roman mosaic-patterns in the style of the Cosmati. The elegant half-capitals of the aisle-walls are connected one with another (as in Burgundy) by mouldings which rise in the form of an arch to frame the windows of the aisle. The beautifully proportioned interior has a spiritual quality shared by few Italian churches (111–113). The groined vaults are generally plain, ribs being introduced only at the crossing. There is no painting, no ornament except some stylised foliage in the

[[1] But has recovered them as the result of the restoration undertaken in 1958–59.]

capitals, no other beauty than the mysterious harmony of numbers. It is one of those churches where the medieval spirit appears in its untrammelled purity. The monastic community with their architecture, their chant and their rule created, between heaven and earth, a world more perfect, to them, than our own. This highly spiritual architecture served as the auxiliary of prayer and of meditation. The cloister has the same sobriety (108). One side of it, however, was later reconstructed in a different spirit: the patterned columns, the elaborately sculptured capitals where crowned heads mingle with the foliage, the ornamental bases, all speak of the approaching 14th century. Here we already feel remote from the austerity of the early days of St. Bernard. An extension of the cloister, opening on to the flowers and lemon-trees of the garden within, contains the basin in which the monks performed their ablutions before and after food. This delightful little pavilion with its almost Moorish grace so charmed Cardinal Aldobrandini in the 16th century that he turned the basin into a table and had his meals served there. The refectory where Pope Innocent III dined with the monks in 1208, after the consecration of the church, is a spacious one suggesting a large community.

In the adjoining guest-house the room where St. Thomas Aquinas drew his last breath on March 7, 1274, has become a chapel, and a relief of the Bernini school shows him dictating his commentary to the *Song of Songs* on his death-bed. He had come up from southern Italy on his mule, along the Appian Road, on his way to the Council of Lyons, that famous Council which also led to St. Bonaventura's death. These twin lamps of learning and holiness of the 13th century were extinguished almost at the same moment. Such long journeys under the sun and the rain were exhausting to these men of prayer, accustomed to their cells.

The church of Fossanova presents the typical Cistercian plan, that is a nave with aisles cut across by a transept, from which extend eastwards the choir and side-chapels, all rectangular. This plan, which the Cistercians had already introduced into Burgundy and parts of France, but which remained as yet unknown in Italy, was to become extremely popular there. Inside, the salient features are the pointed nave-arcades and the square piers, to which semi-columns are applied on all four faces. The transverse arches of the main vault are carried on the long semi-columns rising from the inner faces of the piers, but these, instead of running right down to the bottom, stop short in a simple corbel about 3 metres from the ground, in the Burgundian manner. The interior is well lit, for there are not only the nave and aisle windows, as well as those of the transept, but two rose-windows – one in the façade, one surmounting the three lancets in the flat eastern wall of the choir.

Externally the outline of the church is very simple, being enlivened only by the projecting aisles and the row of buttresses (simple ones; the flying buttress does not appear). Over the crossing there rises an octagonal bell-tower – an unusual addition to an early Cistercian church. The former western porch has been destroyed (but see 117).

Fossanova shows us the birth of the Gothic; its church, begun in 1187, is still of the 12th century. In the first years of the 13th century the Cistercians built another monastery at Casamari, in the hilly region of Frosinone. The church there is similar to Fossanova, with the difference, however, that the vaulting, which is groined (except in one bay) at Fossanova, is here furnished with ribs (114, 115). The progress made in Burgundy is faithfully reflected, and Casamari is a pure Burgundian church of the beginning of the 13th century.

This simple and logical architecture seemed likely to attract Italian architects. Nevertheless, those of Rome remained indifferent to it – even though many fine churches in this style appeared to the north and some also to the south of Latium. In the north, during the 13th century, the Cistercians built one at San Martino near Viterbo. Here Burgundian architecture shows itself still more advanced: with its pillars alternately robust and slender, its sexpartite vault either completed or planned, San Martino resembles Saint-Seine-l'Abbaye, Pont-sur-Yonne and, in some respects, Notre-Dame at Dijon. It is all the more surprising that Rome did not accept the Gothic style which was being adopted in the neighbourhood. The Cistercian monasteries were centres from which French art radiated. Around Fossanova more and more Gothic churches were built, and those of Priverno Sezze, Sonnino, Terracina and Fondi all show Burgundian influence more or less clearly. Some may have been built by the Cistercians themselves, but most were the work of Italians whom they had trained. In these parts palazzi, porticoes, even houses, assumed a Gothic appearance.[1]

The influence of Casamari and of its closely similar offspring Santa Maria Arabona in the Abruzzi extended throughout the mountainous regions of central Italy from Subiaco to Tagliacozzo and Sulmona. In the other direction, San Martino helped to give Viterbo its Gothic character.

The popes were well acquainted with the Cistercian churches. Innocent III had consecrated Fossanova, and Honorius III, accompanied by two archbishops and eleven bishops, consecrated Casamari in 1217. The 13th-century popes so often went to stay at Viterbo that they could not have been ignorant of San Martino. In spite of this, they showed little interest in the new architecture and did not accept it in Rome. The fact was that the popes always looked back into the past, and for them the old basilicas of Constantine's era remained the perfect model for the Christian church. They continued to copy them, and as late as 1220 Honorius III built the anterior basilica of San Lorenzo fuori le Mura in the style of the 4th century. The spirit of antiquity was always alive in Rome and renewed itself from century to century. And so we are quite surprised, after all, when a veritable Gothic church does suddenly appear there towards the end of the 13th century. This is Santa Maria sopra Minerva – a unique phenomenon in Rome and so all the more worthy to engage our attention (119).

In truth, Santa Maria sopra Minerva is not a Roman but a Florentine work. And to understand it we must explain briefly how Gothic art reached Florence and what local character it took on there.

Tuscany had known the Cistercian Gothic since 1218, at which date the abbey of San Galgano, near Siena, began to be built. The beautiful abbey-church, now in ruins, repro-

[1] Camille Enlart, in his *Origines Françaises de l'Architecture Gothique en Italie*, 1894, had the merit of bringing all these facts to light.

duces Casamari; yet certain ornamental details, and the use of brick in the upper parts of the building, betray Italian workmanship. San Galgano made Gothic art known at Siena. Siena cathedral takes after the Pisan Romanesque in its round-arched arcades, its dome and its black-and-white striping. On the other hand, it shows the following Burgundian characters: ribbed vaults; compound pillars; a flat eastern wall to the choir, with triple lights surmounted by a rose-window; a cornice across the façade; a round-arched central portal with pointed ones on either side.[1] We discover, in fact, from the church accounts, that Cistercian monks of San Galgano worked there, which confirms what is told by the architecture itself. It is not surprising, therefore, to find several French details in the domestic architecture both of Siena and San Gimignano.

The monks of San Galgano, having already introduced Gothic art to the Siena region, carried it to the surroundings of Florence when, in 1237, they rebuilt the abbey of San Salvatore a Settimo. And Florence itself was not slow in adopting the new style.

Then something of great significance occurred, which ensured the wide diffusion of Cistercian architecture in Italy for more than a hundred years. The mendicant orders, created not long since by St. Francis and St. Dominic, adopted this architecture. There were natural affinities between the Order of Cîteaux, strictest of medieval times, and these new apostles of poverty, the Franciscans and Dominicans. The austerity of the Cistercian church, where nothing was sacrificed to ornament, seemed ideally suited to them.

The earliest churches of the mendicant orders have not come down to us. They may have been built by brothers converted from Cîteaux, among whom the Franciscans and Dominicans, who as yet possessed no such specialised craftsmen, could recruit architects and stonemasons. What seems certain is that the Cistercian plan was adopted for these first Dominican and Franciscan churches, for the oldest ones now surviving show it already well established. The eastern ends of these churches are identical to those of the Cistercians; the rectangular choir opens on to the transept and is flanked by two, three or even up to five chapels on either side, these too being rectangular.[2] As for the nave, it is often without aisles and covered by a wooden roof with exposed timbers. Of this type are San Domenico, the church of the Preaching Friars, and San Francesco, that of the Friars Minor, both at Siena. Simplicity could hardly be pushed to greater lengths; but it was not always so, for some Franciscan and Dominican churches were vaulted throughout.

The most beautiful of the Gothic churches of St. Dominic's order, and the purest in style, is Santa Maria Novella in Florence, begun in 1278, completed about 1350 (118). The Cistercian plan is here faithfully reproduced, not only in the transept and choir, but equally in the nave and aisles. The whole church has Gothic ribbed vaults, and the profile of their ribs is Burgundian. The church of San Galgano served as the architect's model, yet quite a different

[[1] The implication that all these features are of early 13th-century date is somewhat misleading, even if Burgundian influence is still apparent in them. The main vaults, the lower part of the façade and the eastern extremity of the choir belong to a reconstruction of the early 14th century.]

[2] In northern Italy both choir and chapels are sometimes polygonal instead of being rectangular.

effect is produced. Indeed, when visiting Santa Maria Novella it is difficult to think of a Cistercian church at all. What is it that makes so great a difference? It is worth considering this question, for the explanation will also show us how the French Gothic becomes transformed into the Italian Gothic.

The different impression is due to differences of proportion. If we first examine the pillar, we find it resembles those of the Cistercian churches, being of square section with applied semi-columns; yet instead of giving an impression of strength, it gives an impression of lightness. In fact, it measures only 1·5 instead of 2 metres in diameter; moreover, the four semi-columns almost touch, so that the rectangular core, whose corners have been chamfered, scarcely appears at all. In plan, the pillar of Santa Maria Novella almost makes a quatrefoil. The architect wanted to reduce the solids to the advantage of the empty spaces. No less significant is the distance between successive pillars of the nave arcades. In the Cistercian churches this distance averages 3·75 metres.[1] At Santa Maria Novella it amounts to nearly 9 metres in the first two bays counting westwards from the transept. But then a curious thing happens: the builders were not satisfied with these dimensions, ample though they already were, and the bays which follow each other towards the western wall become progressively wider, measuring over 11 and nearly 13 metres.[2] Thus the Italian proportions diverge more and more from the French.

Necessarily, these widely-spaced arcades had to be very tall. They are, in fact, more than 16 metres high, while those of the Cistercian churches do not exceed 7·5 metres. The remarkable thing at Santa Maria Novella is the striving towards greater space. It is true that the architect adopted the Cistercian plan, with its nave and aisles, but we feel that he wanted to unite these aisles with the nave, so that the eye could take in at a glance the entire width of the church, forming a single open space. It was to produce this effect that the architect made his pillars so tall and slender and spaced them so widely. He succeeded, for the spectator in Santa Maria Novella is not aware of a nave 13 metres wide accompanied by aisles 6·5 metres wide; he sees one great hall 26 metres across. Here, therefore, we meet again that correspondence between width and height which strikes one so forcibly in the Pantheon and in Santa Maria Maggiore at Rome. In Santa Maria Novella we recognise the Italian, which is also the classic, genius, with its feeling for ample space, for restfulness rather than heavenward striving, for a due equilibrium between height and breadth. Thus in the height of the Gothic age we find the spirit of antiquity persisting in Florence, as it persisted in Rome. Michelangelo called Santa Maria Novella his *fidanzata*; he found in it that calm, that pure grace not unmixed with pride, which he would have wished to find in the girl he loved – had he ever met her.

Our architectural historians have generally been rather hard on the Italian Gothic.[3] It is

[1] This is not measured from axis to axis, but represents the actual width of the open space between the pillars. The same applies to the figures given for Santa Maria Novella.

[2] The last bays go back to 12 metres.

[[3] On the subject of the Italian Gothic the reader is recommended to consult also J. W. Franklin, *The Cathedrals of Italy*, 1958.]

held against the Italians that they failed to understand the real character of French architecture, that cunning art of pure science and logic, the most perfect evolved by man since the Greeks. This reproach might be deserved if the Italians had set out to reproduce French art. But they never did accept the complete system, the close interdependence of whose parts does indeed seem to have escaped them; all they did was to borrow certain elements from it, which they used in their own way. The Italians adopted the ribbed vault (which incidentally they had long used, without seeing in it the germ of a new style), but nearly always rejected the flying buttress. They replaced it by a little sustaining wall built on the transverse ribs (or arches) of the aisle-vaults and hidden under the aisle-roofs – an insufficient support which necessarily led to the use of that unfortunate expedient, the iron tie-rod. The use of the ribbed vault combined with sustaining walls and iron ties would have made it possible to pierce the nave walls with large windows; however, they introduced nothing more than little *oculi* or simple undivided lancets. While, in France, the wall gradually disappeared to make way for an enormous expanse of glass, Italy, faithful to classical taste, regarded the solid wall as an object of beauty in itself, and felt that her bright skies rendered large windows needless. The Gothic clustered pillar – of rectangular section with four applied semi-columns – was accepted at Siena but soon underwent a transformation. We see it contracted at Santa Maria Novella, of polygonal section at Santa Croce in Florence and, finally, reduced to a simple column at Santi Giovanni e Paolo in Venice. From the 14th century onwards the genius of the Renaissance was in evidence.

But the Italian spirit made itself manifest more especially in its conception and its treatment of space. The desire for ever-larger spaces is indeed the secret of the Italian Gothic. It is enough to compare the cathedrals of Reims and Florence to realise the tremendous contrast between northern and southern art. At Florence, in a nave 76 metres long, we see on either side only three free-standing pillars from which rise the four immense arches 19 metres in width and 25 in height. The number of supports has thus been reduced to the absolute minimum in relation to the available space. And the huge openings in the arcade have the effect of closely uniting the nave with the aisles. The eye takes in, at a single glance, what seems to be one great aisleless hall 40 metres across.[1] Moreover, the nave vault rises to 40 metres from the ground. Thus we encounter once more, in the cathedral of Florence, that antique law of equality between width and height which we noticed at Santa Maria Novella. So it happened that the sense of classical rhythm and proportion, incorporated in the Italian genius, was mysteriously preserved through the centuries.

At Reims we find a shorter nave than at Florence, measuring only 67 metres. Here, instead of four broad bays as at Florence we count no less than nine compound pillars and nine arches in the lesser space. The distance from pillar to pillar is only 7 metres, the height of the arcade 16·4 metres. This is why we cannot, at Reims, take in the nave and aisles at a single glance; the nave is a separate entity. Above this nave (14·6 metres wide) the vault is poised at a height of 38 metres, as compared with 40 at Florence. Though actually a

[1] Within a few centimetres, the width of the nave is 20 metres; of the aisles 10 metres.

little lower than the Florentine vault, that of Reims appears to be far higher because it rises from a narrower base. Everything combines to create an effect of height at Reims, an effect of breadth in the Italian church. The architect of Florence cathedral cared so little for the soaring effect of his nave that he introduced, above the arcades, a heavy projecting balcony giving a pronounced horizontal emphasis. The sense of aspiration, the mystic impulse of the northern Gothic, are wanting. The Florentines regarded their cathedral as a splendid hall full of light and air where, after mass, it was pleasant to converse in the shade.

The only genuine Gothic cathedral in Italy – that of Milan – is completely Italian in its spaciousness. Its nave is as wide as at Florence, that is, it exceeds by more than 5 metres the nave-width of Reims. This broad nave is accompanied by two pairs of aisles each 9 metres across, so that the overall width of the cathedral is no less than 56 metres, against just over 30 at Reims. There was a certain incompatibility between this excessive width and the real genius of the Gothic. It was impossible for Milan cathedral to be at once a northern and a southern church. Hence the dramatic history of its construction, and the continual succession of architects summoned alternately from France and Germany. All were amazed at a scheme of proportions so diverse from anything they knew, and many offered new projects, only to see them rejected or thwarted by the Italian master-masons after endless debate. In spite of all opposition, the dimensions were maintained and the cathedral completed. But, as a result, we simply cannot realise that this great broad church is as tall as Beauvais cathedral. This dwarfing of the cathedral, so laboriously achieved, is really to be attributed to a secret struggle between the genius of the Middle Ages and that of the Renaissance. The history of the Italian Gothic proves to us that one and the same spirit – that is to say, the spirit of antiquity – never ceased to prevail in Italy, from the Early Christian basilicas to St. Peter's.

It is curious to find signs of this same spirit in southern France. The old nave of Toulouse cathedral, aisleless, as broad as high, provided only with small openings (until a rose window, copied from Notre Dame, was inserted in the façade) is as unGothic in feeling as Florence cathedral, in spite of its great ribbed vaults. The same may be said of hundreds of other aisleless churches in the south. The sublimity of the real Gothic cathedral, irresistibly soaring heavenwards, illuminated with unearthly light from its great windows, is the creation of northern France.

After this long digression we can now return to Rome – to Santa Maria sopra Minerva. Here we find an imitation of Santa Maria Novella in Florence, yet it is easy to understand why even well-informed visitors fail to notice the resemblance.[1] For the impression given by the two churches is wholly different: the Minerva is gloomy and full of dark shadows at certain times of day; its vault seems low, and the chapels opening off the aisles, added in comparatively recent times, have modified the original proportions. In this church we do not experience the restful atmosphere which is created at Santa Maria Novella by the ample

[1] The resemblance escaped Camille Enlart's penetrating eye; he thought he saw, in Santa Maria sopra Minerva, reminiscences of Casamari and of San Francesco at Assisi.

space and the soft light. For one thing, it is not quite the church it once was. In the 17th century its architecture was deemed barbarous and Carlo Maderna did his best to make it look like a classical church. In the region of the choir he replaced the original pointed arches by round ones; he also cut rectangular windows in the upper nave walls and reconstructed the apse. In the 19th century medieval art, once more respected all over Europe, was no longer an object of disdain in Rome. The Dominicans resolved to restore their church to its original aspect, and the work was started under Fra Giovanni Bianchedi, a member of the Order, in 1848. The restoration is for the most part convincing, though we may accuse the architect of excessive zeal. It was useless, for instance, to cover the upper reaches of the nave with decorative paintings; still more useless to give the pillars a facing of marble, which at a certain level becomes sham marble; such glossy surfaces are foreign to the severity of Gothic art. These unfortunate embellishments drive Santa Maria Novella still farther from our thoughts when we enter the 'Minerva'.

Nevertheless, the analogy between these two churches turns out, on analysis, to be very striking. The transverse measurements are, within a few centimetres, the same, the Minerva having a nave 12·75 metres wide against 13 metres, and aisles 7 metres wide against 6·5. The pillars of the nave arcade, like those in the first (eastern) bays at Santa Maria Novella, are spaced at intervals of about 9 metres, but this distance remains fixed, instead of increasing progressively towards the west. The square pillars with their four attached semi-columns are similar in the two churches, and the same rose windows admit light to the nave.[1] These resemblances are close enough to have led scholars to suppose that the same architect built both churches. Santa Maria Novella was begun in 1278, Santa Maria Sopra Minerva in 1280. The former was formerly attributed without hesitation to the Dominicans Fra Sisto and Fra Ristoro, though a more careful examination of the original documents has thrown some doubt on this conclusion. To attribute the Minerva to the same architects (as has been done) means raising one hypothesis upon another. An examination of the monument does not support the theory. Without a doubt the Minerva is an imitation of Santa Maria Novella, but rather a heavy imitation. To be aware of the difference it is enough to compare the pillars of the two churches. As already mentioned, those of Santa Maria Novella have the rectangular core reduced to the minimum, even its corners being smoothed down, so that the semi-columns come near to touching and in section almost form a quatrefoil. At the Minerva, nothing of the sort: the rectangular pillar retains its full dimensions, its flat faces extending well beyond the semi-columns. The diameter of the whole pillar is only 1·5 metres at Florence, more than 2 metres at Rome. How could so sensitive an architect, working on a second church in Rome, have renounced these refinements?

While the Minerva shows, in plan, all the generous proportions of the Florentine Gothic, and its spacious interior has real dignity, its height seems inadequate. In fact, the vault rises to hardly more than 20 metres, compared with 26 at Santa Maria Novella. We must not forget, however, that the Minerva was vaulted only in the mid-15th century when medieval

[1] The Minerva's rose windows are a restoration, but undoubtedly a well-founded one.

ideals were being gradually forgotten; its arches and its vaulting are accordingly rather flat, compared with the narrower and bolder forms of the church in Florence. Did the original design provide for as high a vault as that of Santa Maria Novella? One may well wonder. At the Minerva the shafts attached to the different faces of the pillars, which support respectively the arches of the nave arcade and the transverse ribs of the main vault, are all a metre shorter than in Florence. This suggests that the architect did not intend his vault to rise as high as in his model.

But here we meet a possible objection. Were not these shafts originally taller? Father Berthier, to whom we owe a monograph on the Minerva, tells of two conflicting opinions on the subject. Some authors declare that the level of the church was raised in order to avoid the floods of the Tiber, whose levels are marked on the façade. In this case the pillars would have lost part of their height. According to others, on the contrary, researches have shown that the height of the pillars never changed, and that they rise from the original ground level. Whom are we to believe? [1] It is a pity that Father Berthier did not try to resolve the problem by a few soundings. An uncertainty remains which only excavation could dispel. We should then know for certain whether the Minerva followed Santa Maria Novella not only in width but also in height, at least as far as the springing of the vault. As for this late vault, it has had the effect of altering the proportions for the worse. It also necessitated iron ties, which the architect of Santa Maria Novella, with his greater competence, had spurned.

The Minerva, then, like Santa Maria Novella of which it is the offspring, belongs to the family of Cistercian churches, as can be seen from its nave with aisles, its transept off which the rectangular chapels open and its typical vaults and pillars. The church owes its local character to the peculiarly Italian proportions discussed on an earlier page.

It was the only Gothic church in Rome, and it did not found a school. In any event, how could it have been imitated? The church was not completed when the popes' exile to Avignon began, which was followed by the sad period of the great schism – a sterile and almost barbarous century when not only were no new churches built but old ones were allowed to fall into ruin. The 15th-century popes were long occupied simply in repairing the ruins. When at last new churches arose the Renaissance had already penetrated to Rome, and medieval art, which had scarcely been known there, was already forgotten. In the new architecture of the Renaissance Rome recognised that spirit of antiquity which was truly hers.

However foreign to local tradition the Minerva may have been, Rome became attached to it from the moment when the relics of St. Catherine of Siena – the young saint so greatly beloved of the Romans – were brought there. Cardinals and patricians (among whom the

[1] I must say that the second view is to me the less convincing. The bases of pillars and shafts, which are too small for their height, are not medieval but of a period when classical forms had returned to favour. They have been re-made. These bases appear to date from the time when pillars and shafts were shortened through the raising of the church floor. Excavation would reveal their original height.

Orsini must be mentioned) were anxious to contribute the costs of new vaults and chapels, and of the new façade. Five popes were buried there. Leo X, the great pope of the Renaissance, lies close to an illustrious humanist, Cardinal Bembo. There is Clement VII, who witnessed the sack of Rome from the heights of the Castel Sant'Angelo. Then Paul IV, the severe reformer and implacable enemy of the heretics, buried not far from Filippino Lippi's fine fresco, which shows St. Thomas triumphing over the heretic at his feet. The last two are Urban VII, who reigned only a fortnight, and Benedict XIII, of the Orsini family, who wished to rest in a church dear to his ancestors and embellished by his own efforts.

For nearly four hundred years the monuments to Roman cardinals and nobles appeared one after another in this sumptuous place of burial around the tomb of St. Catherine; they tell the story of funerary sculpture from the end of the Middle Ages onwards. Great artists helped to embellish the church. Fra Angelico painted an altarpiece[1] and was himself buried here: there are always fresh flowers on his tombstone. Filippino Lippi's Triumph of St. Thomas has an almost Raphaelesque dignity; he also painted an Annunciation for the church in which the Virgin, proud and gracious as a young queen, blesses Cardinal Carafa, listening at the same time to the Archangel's words. Michelangelo contributed his sculptured Christ holding the Cross, nude like an athlete, calm as a hero.[2]

A stranger in its architecture, Santa Maria sopra Minerva, enriched by so many generations, has become one of the great sanctuaries of Rome.

[1] It has long since disappeared.

[[2] The bronze drapery was added later.]

THE ILLUSTRATIONS

1 The Colosseum (1st century AD and later)

2 Temple of Antoninus and Faustina enclosing 17th-century church

4 (*opposite*) Constantine's Arch (early 4th century)

5 (*opposite*) Constantine's 'Basilica' (4th century)

3 Via Biberatica – an ancient Roman street

6 Tomb of Cecilia Metella on the Appian Way

7 Sant'Urbano – built in a temple of Bacchus

8 Interior of the Pantheon

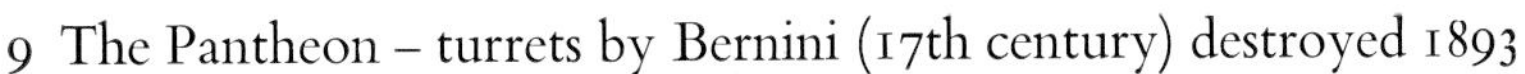

9 The Pantheon – turrets by Bernini (17th century) destroyed 1893

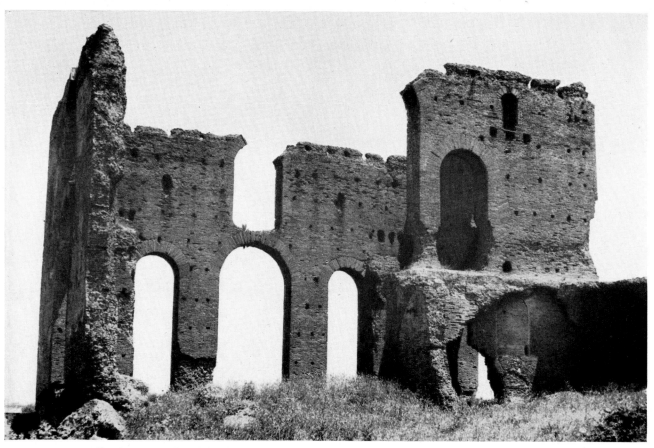

10 Villa dei Quintili (2nd century AD)

11 The Aqua Claudia – linking Rome with the Alban Hills

12 Torre Appia – medieval watch tower in the Campagna

13 Torre delle Milizie (13th century)

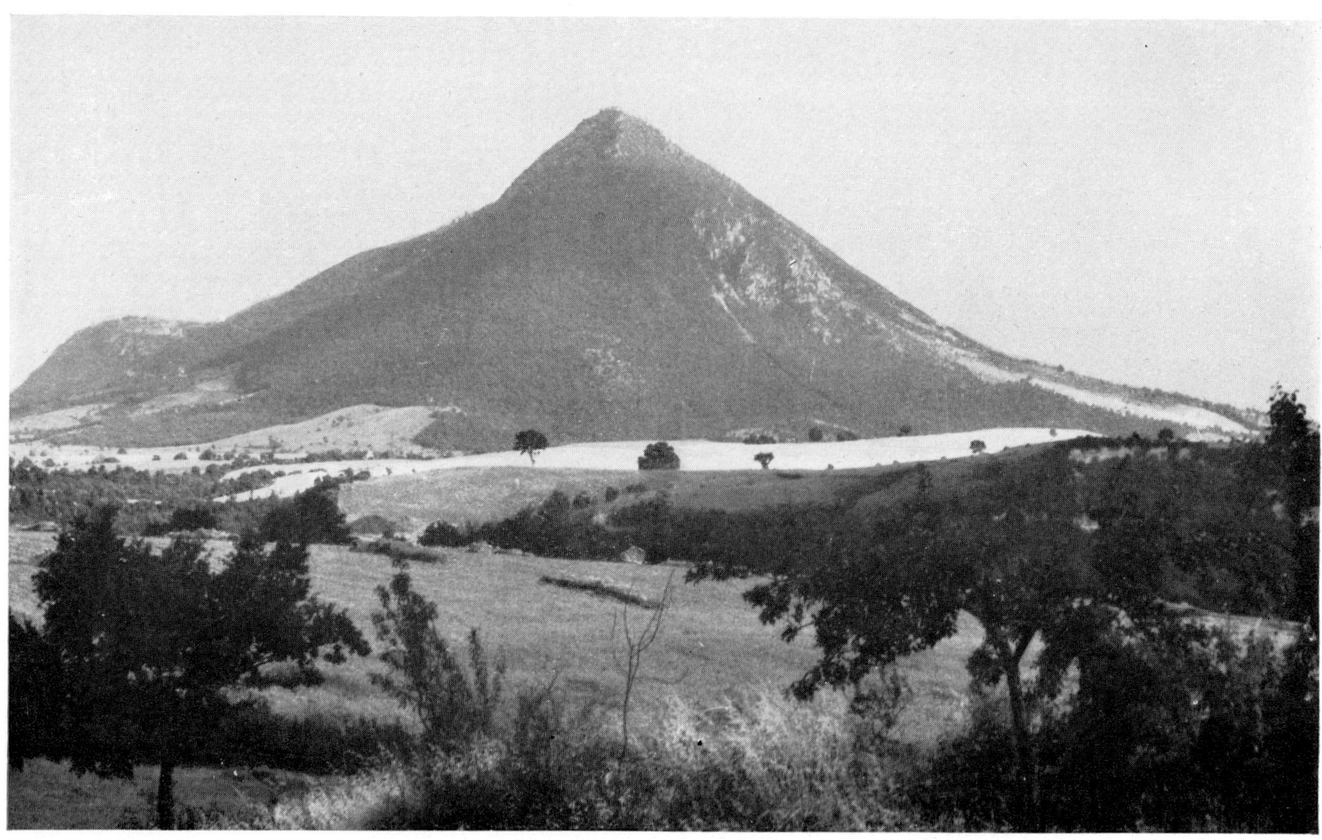

14 Monte Soratte – a landmark twenty-five miles north of Rome

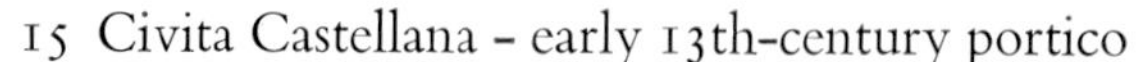

15 Civita Castellana – early 13th-century portico

16 Norma – medieval cliff-top village

17 Sermoneta – hill-top town thirty-five miles south-east of Rome

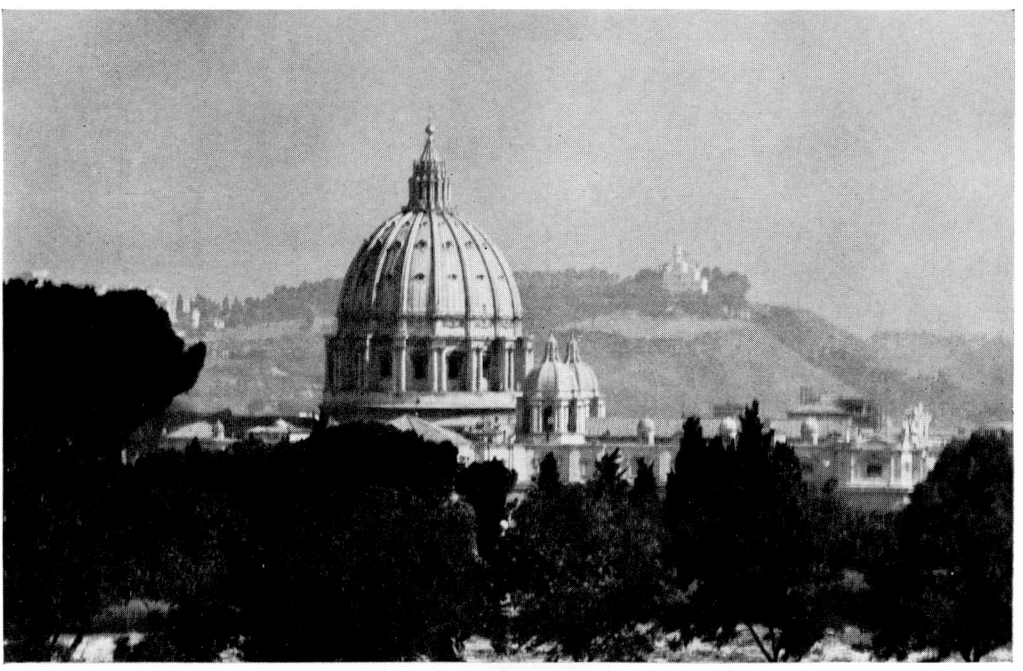

18 The dome of St. Peter's by Michelangelo

19 Sant'Andrea della Valle – façade of 1663

20 Roman domes from the Janiculum

21 Sant'Ignazio – part of façade

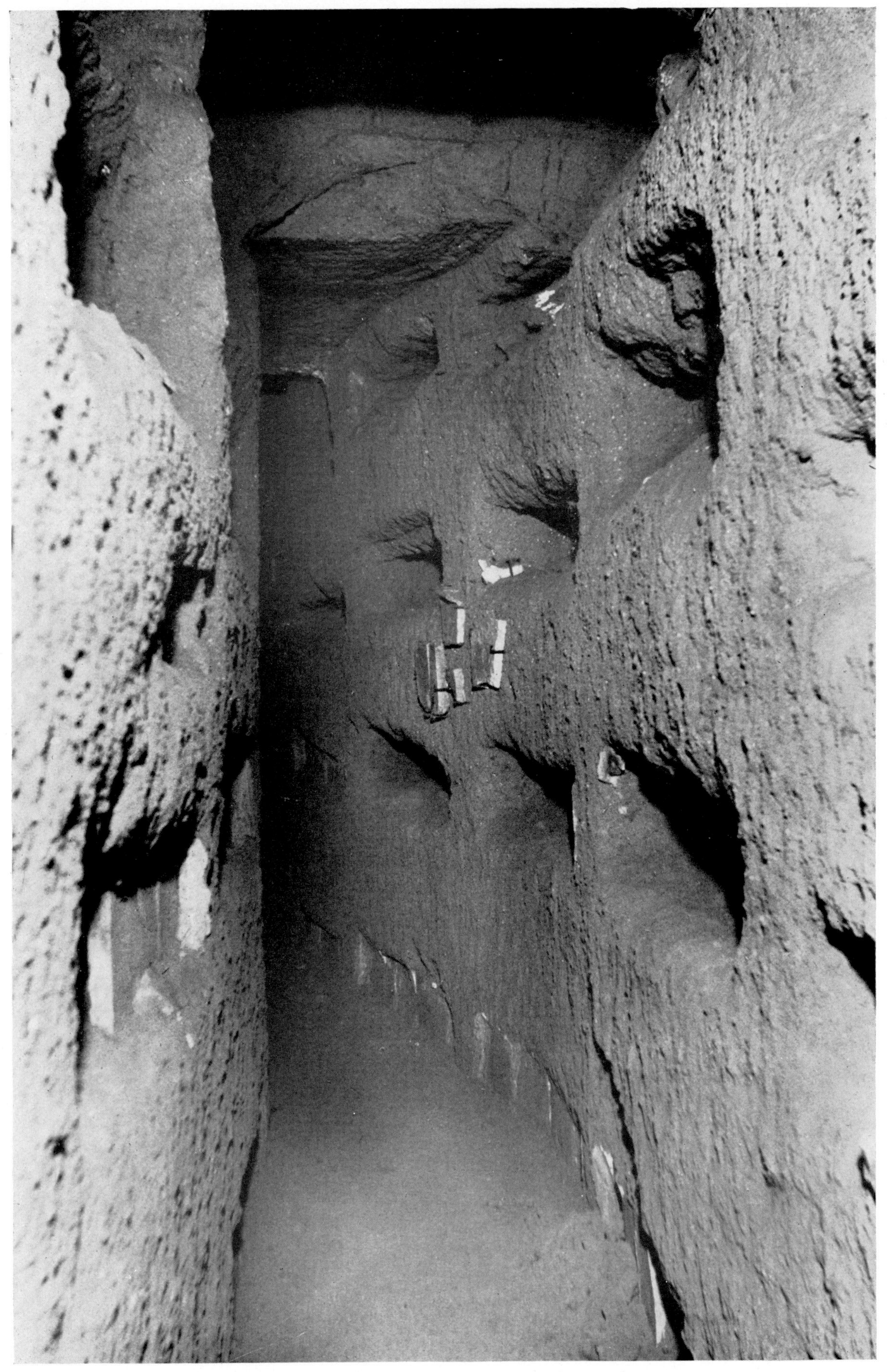

22 (*opposite*) Catacombs of Santa Domitilla

23 Fresco in the cubicolo of St. Petronilla

24 Partly subterranean basilica of late 4th century, St. Domitilla's Catacombs

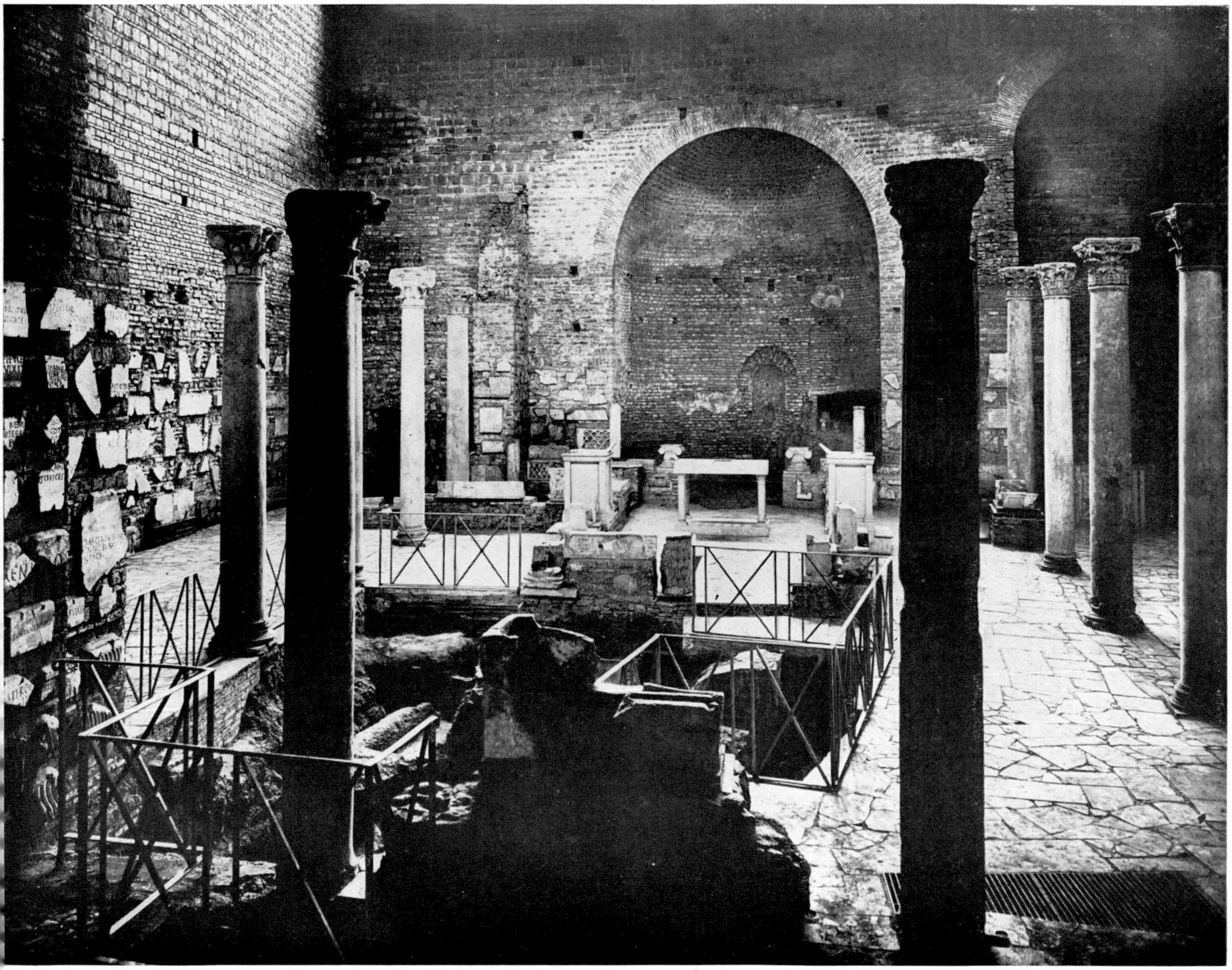

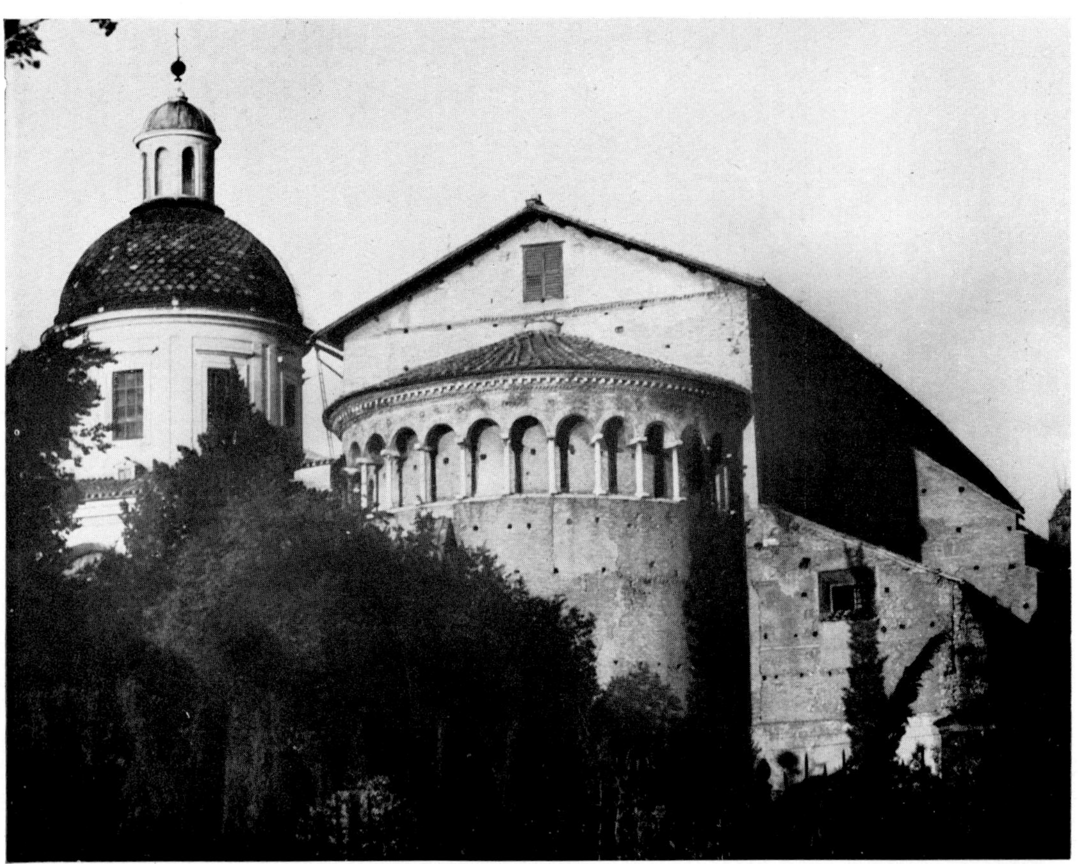

25 Santi Giovanni e Paolo – the apse

27 (*opposite*) Roman house on the Clivus Scauri, later aisle-wall of Santi Giovanni e Paolo

26 Santi Giovanni e Paolo – the façade

28 (*opposite*) Santa Sabina (early 5th century) – the restored church before insertion of ceiling

29 Santa Sabina – ceiling as restored in 1936–38

30 San Lorenzo fuori le Mura – galleried aisles of 6th century

32 Santa Sabina – 5th century mosaic

31 (*opposite*) Santa Sabina

33 Doors of Santa Sabina – Elijah's ascent into Heaven

34 Santa Sabina – Zacharias outside the Temple

5 Santa Sabina – Christ in Glory; below, SS. Peter and Paul

36 Santa Sabina – Moses and the burning bush

37 Santa Maria Maggiore – 5th-century basilica

38 Santa Maria Maggiore – mosaic of sanctuary-arch: Annunciation and Epiphany

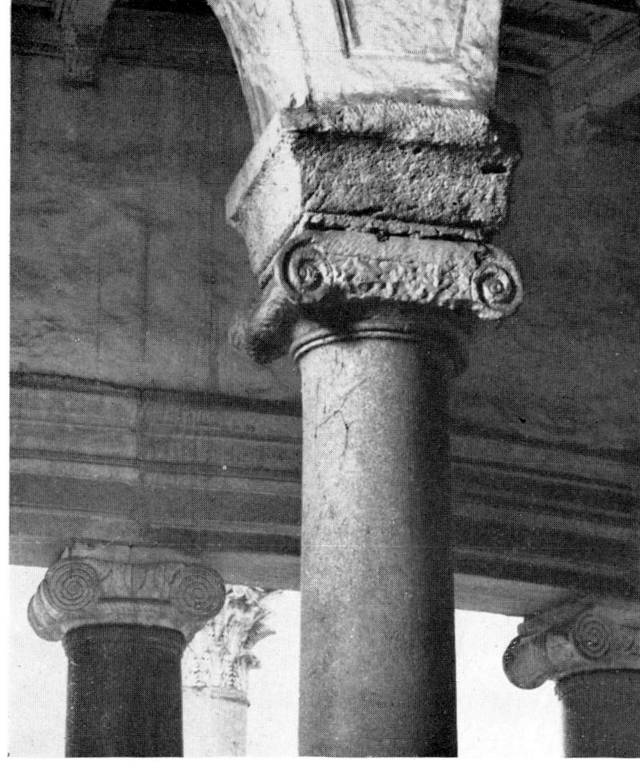

39 (*opposite*) The common Acanthus
40 Santa Sabina – Corinthian capital
41 Sant'Agata dei Goti – Ionic capital with pulvin
42 Santo Stefano Rotondo – Corinthian capital

43 Santo Stefano Rotondo (5th century)
44 Santo Stefano Rotondo – Ionic capital with pulvin
45 Santo Stefano Rotondo – Ionic capital of inner arcade

PRIMVS
FELICIANVS
CVLMINE TECTVM ASTRIF

SCS MAVRVS · SCS SEPTIMIVS · SCS ANTIOCHIANVS · SCS GAIANVS

48 Santa Maria Antiqua – 8th-century fresco of St. Julitta

49 St. Quiricus, son of St. Julitta

46 (*opposite*) Santo Stefano Rotondo – mosaic of 7th century

47 (*opposite*) Chapel of St. Venantius at the Lateran Baptistery – mosaic of 7th century

50 Santi Cosma e Damiano – 6th-century mosaic

51 Santa Prassede – 9th-century apse-mosaic inspired by Santi Cosma e Damiano

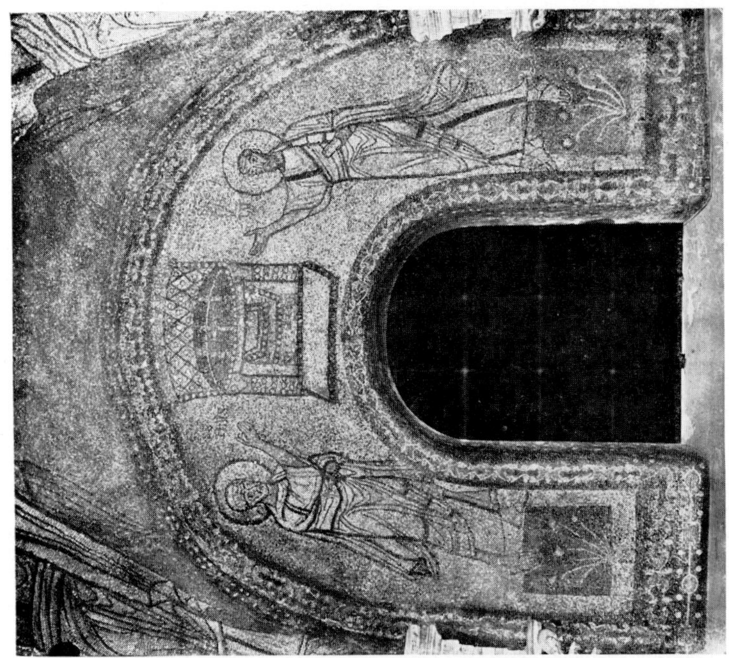

53 Santa Prassede – mosaic of SS. Peter and Paul and the empty throne, in San Zeno's chapel

52 Santa Prassede – 9th-century vault-mosaic in San Zeno's chapel

54 Santa Maria in Domnica – 9th-century mosaic

55 San Bartolomeo on the island – 17th-century façade and medieval tower

56 General view of the island with Ponte Fabricio

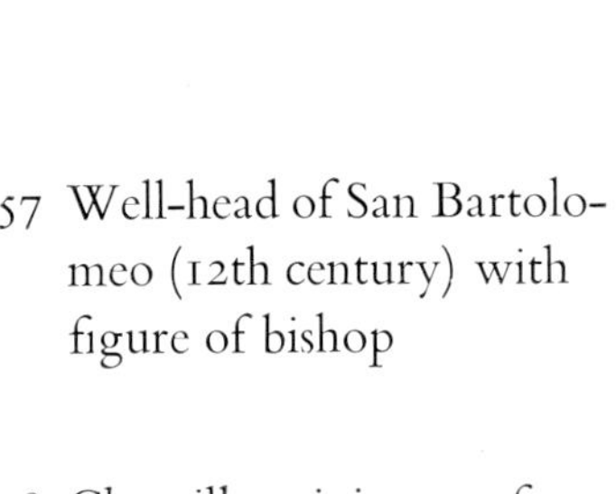

57 Well-head of San Bartolomeo (12th century) with figure of bishop

58 Chantilly miniature of Otto III (or II)

59 Otto III, founder of San Bartolomeo

60 (*opposite*) Fantastic Roman landscape by Hubert Robert, 18th century

61 Abbey of Grottaferrata – Domenichino's fresco showing the meeting of Otto III and St. Nilus

62 Castel Sant'Elia – early Romanesque church thirty miles north of Rome

63 Castel Sant'Elia and the great gorge

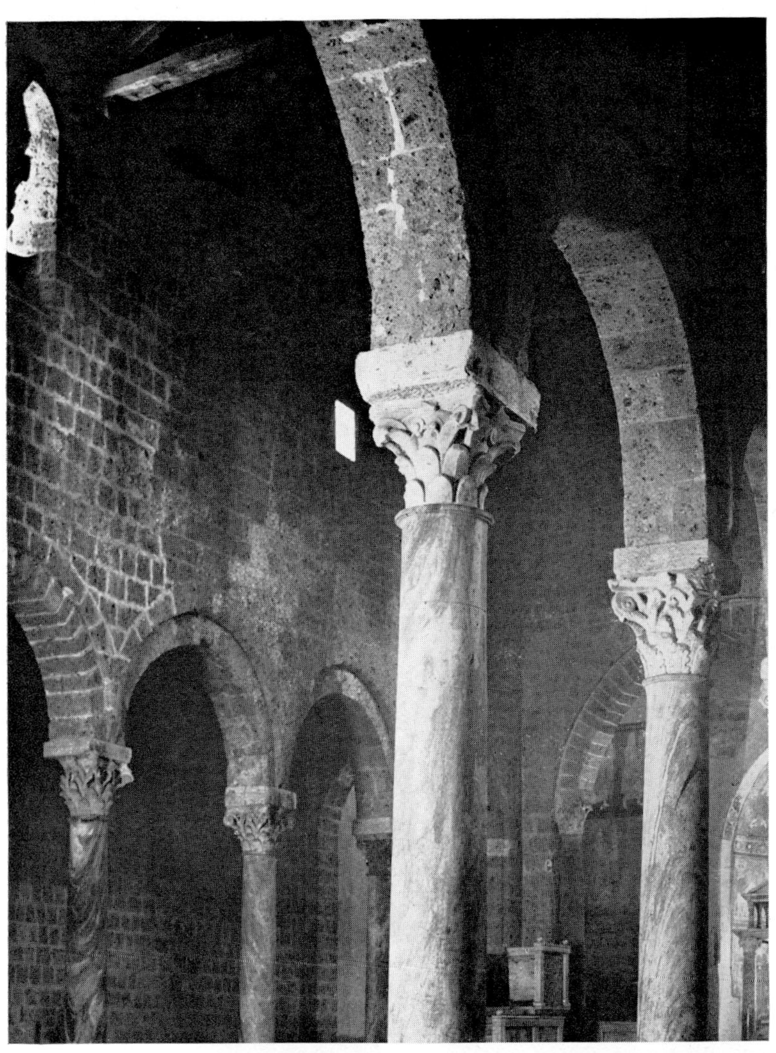

64 Castel Sant'Elia – antique columns of nave arcade

65 Castel Sant'Elia – interior, looking towards apse

69 San Sebastianello – 17th-century copy of late 10th-century fresco (Apostles raised on Prophets' shoulders)

70 Chapel of the old Lateran Palace – 16th-century sketch of 12th-century fresco (an anti-pope's defeat is symbolised)

66 (*opposite*) Apses of San Saba

67 (*opposite*) Baldaquin of Sant'Agata dei Goti (*c.* 12th century)

68 (*opposite*) Castel Sant'Elia – roofs of apse and transept

71 San Paolo fuori le Mura – 11th-century bronze door

72 Decorative band from door panel

73 St. Peter from the door

74 San Paolo fuori le Mura before the fire

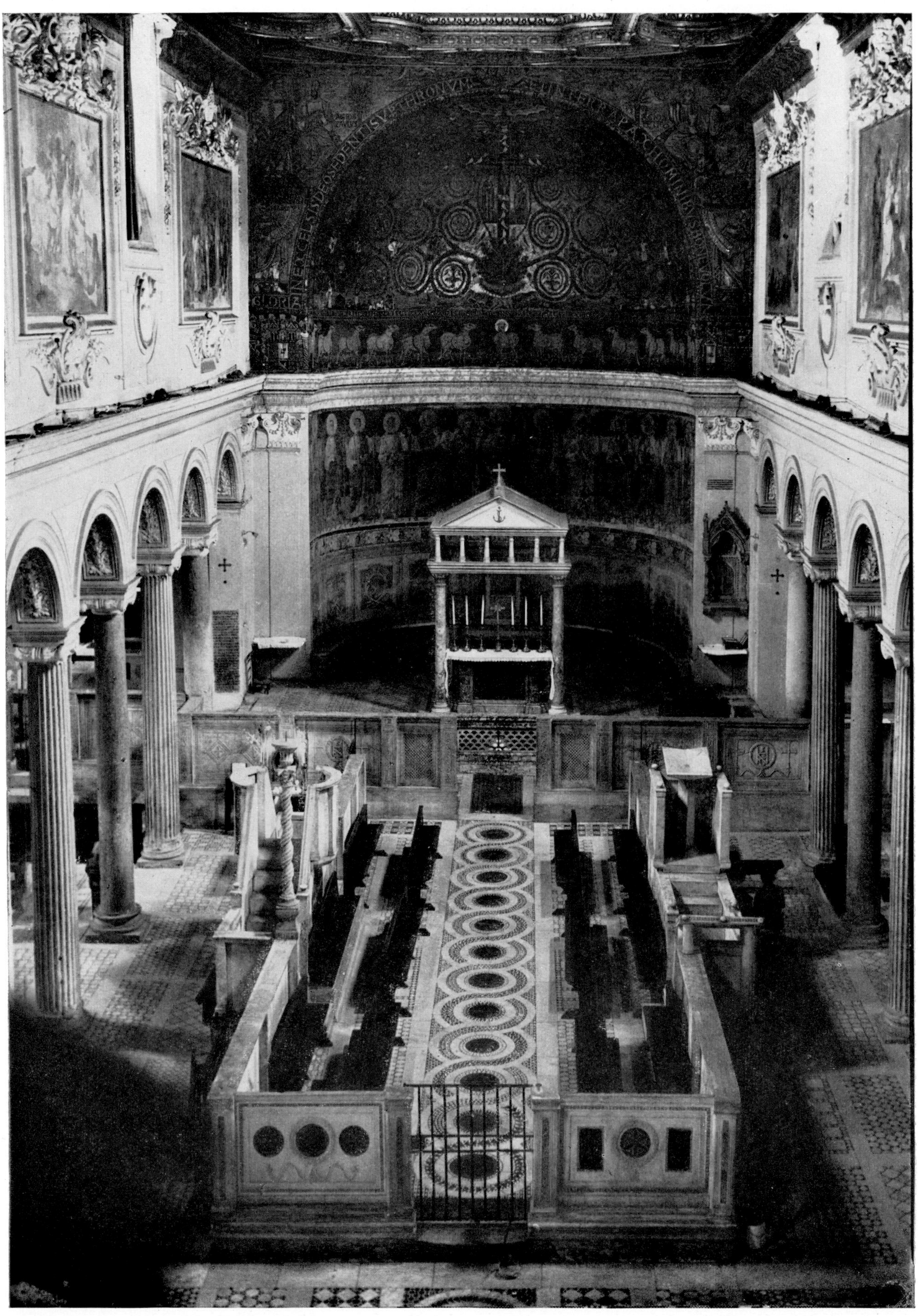

75 San Clemente (early 12th century)

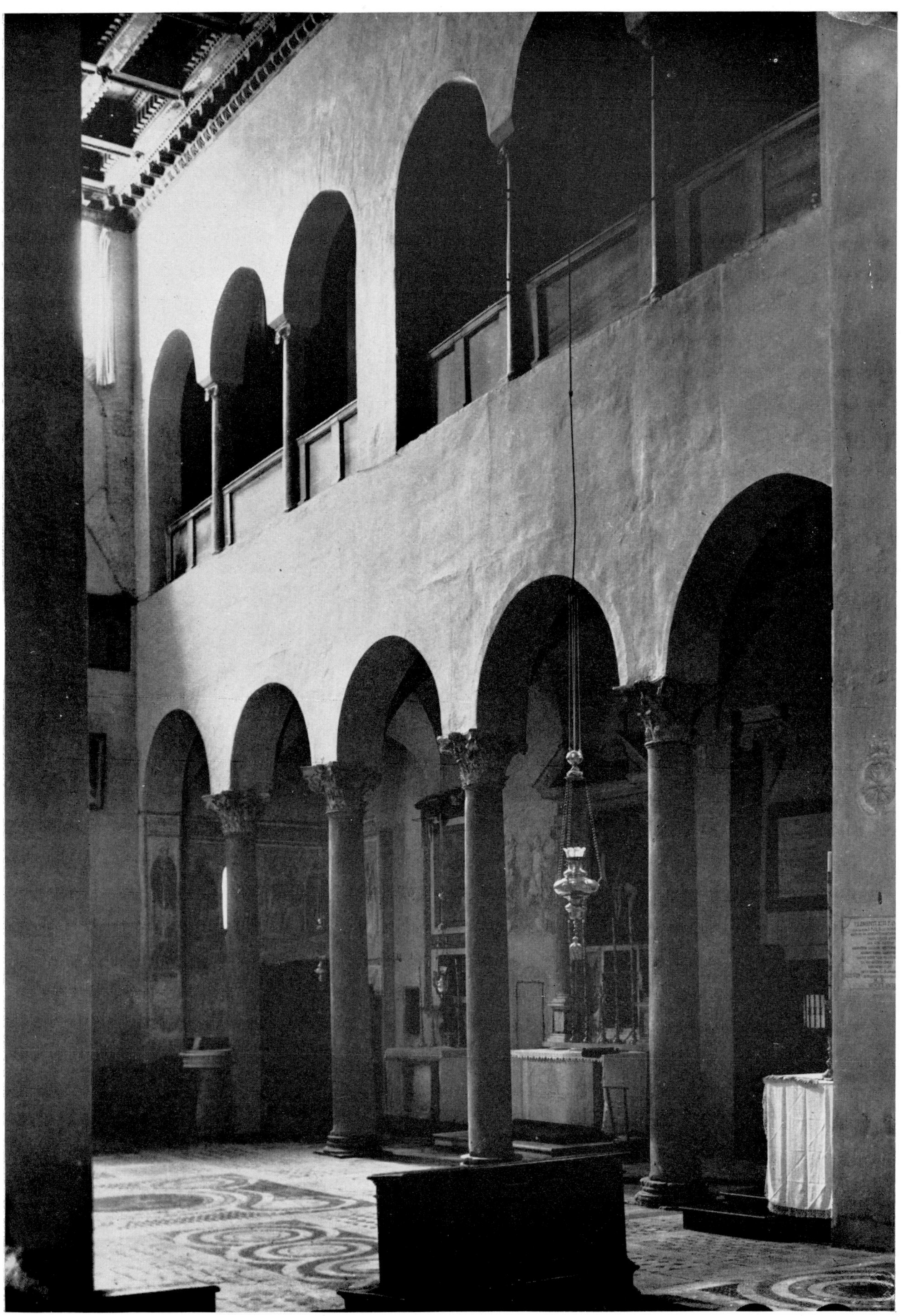

76 Santi Quattro Coronati (1110)

77 (*left*) Santa Croce in Gerusalemme – Submission of the anti-pope Victor IV, by Carlo Maratta (*c.* 1660)

78 Abbazia delle Tre Fontane – St. Bernard's vision of the heavenly ladder

79 San Giorgio in Velabro

80 Santa Maria in Cosmedin

81 Santa Maria in Trastevere (1140)

82 Santa Maria in Trastevere – interior

83 San Lorenzo fuori le Mura

84 Santa Maria in Trastevere

85 Sant'Agata dei Goti

86 Santa Maria in Trastevere – detail of 12th-century apse-mosaic showing the triumph of the Virgin

87 Santa Maria in Trastevere – mosaic of Jeremiah from apse spandrel

88 Santa Maria Maggiore – the Coronation of the Virgin: apse-mosaic by Torriti (1296)

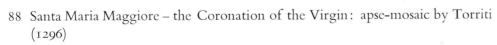

89 San Clemente – detail of mosaic (probably early 12th century)

(*opposite*)

90 San Paolo fuori le Mura – 13th-century Cosmatesque cloister

91, 92 San Paolo fuori le Mura – twin columns with mosaic-inlay

93 San Lorenzo fuori le Mura – 13th-century pavement

94 Santa Maria in Cappella (1090)
95 Santa Rufina (probably early 12th century)
96 San Lorenzo fuori le Mura – bell-tower of 11th–12th century
97 Sermoneta – 13th-century campanile

(*opposite*) 98 San Giovanni a Porta Latina
99 Velletri – Torre del Trivio (14th century)
100 Santi Giovanni e Paolo – 12th century tower (restored 1950–52)
101 Santi IV Coronati – entrance-tower

102 Santa Cecilia in Trastevere – 12th-century portico and tower

103 Santa Francesca Romana – 12th-century tower and Baroque façade

104 San Sisto Vecchio – 13th-century campanile

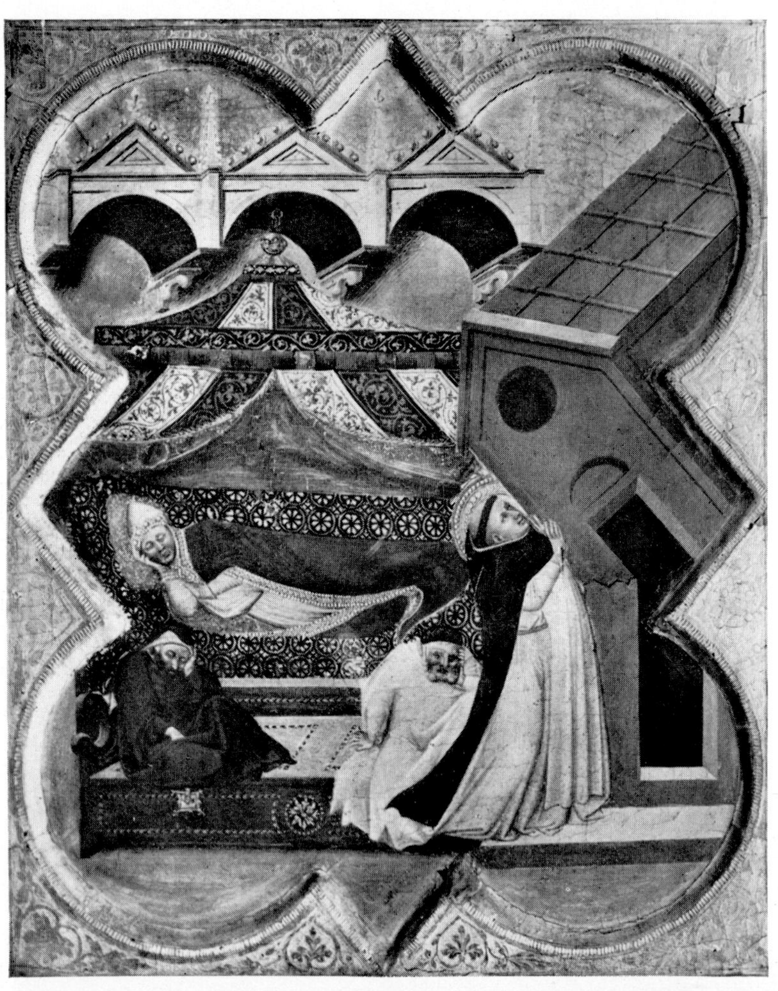

105 Pisa – panel from an altarpiece (*c.* 1345) by Traini: the dream of Pope Innocent III

106 (*below*) Cortona – panel from a predella by Fra Angelico, depicting a miracle of St. Dominic

107 (*opposite*) Santa Sabina – cloister of St. Dominic's monastery

108 (*opposite*) Abbey of Fossanova – the cloister

111 (*opposite*) Abbey of Fossanova (late 12th century)

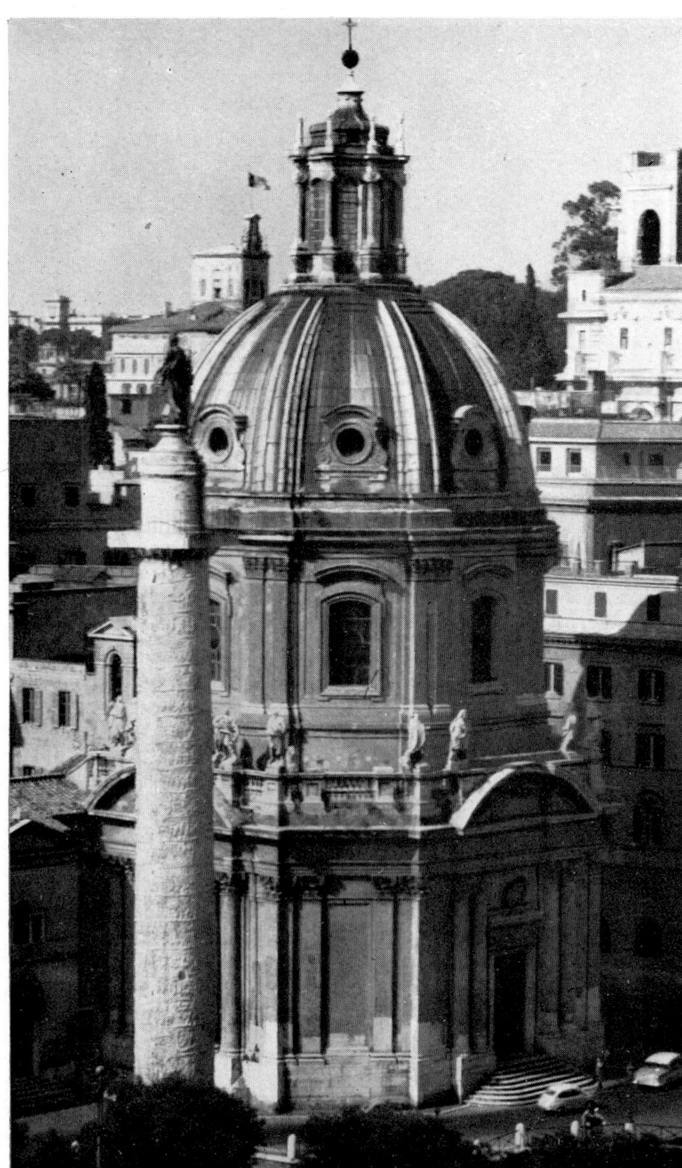

109 Church of the Santissimo Nome di Maria (1738) with Trajan's column

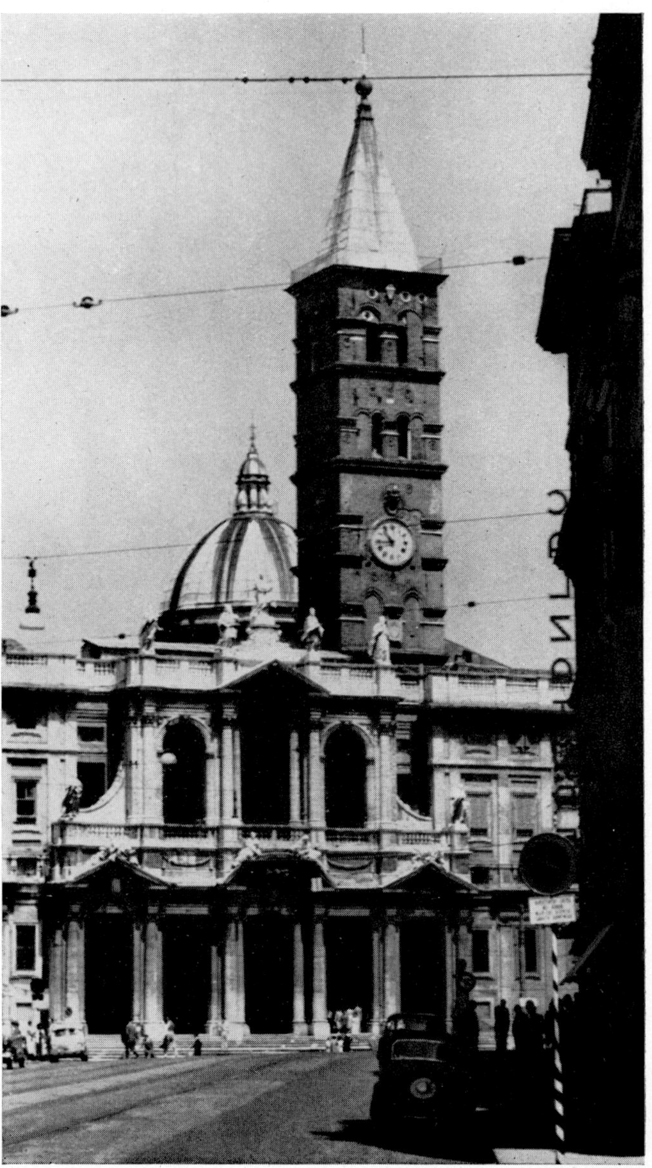

110 Santa Maria Maggiore – façade by Fuga, 1741–43

112 Fossanova – the nave

113 Fossanova – south aisle

114 Casamari (early 13th century)

115 Fossanova from the north-east

116 Casamari – western portico

117 Santa Maria Novella, Florence (1278–1350)

118 Santa Maria sopra Minerva (late 13th century)

Notes to the Illustrations

1 The Colosseum (1st century A.D. and later). It shows how the Greek orders (Doric, Ionic and Corinthian) were adapted by the Romans to adorn buildings based on other constructive principles. The photograph includes less than one-twentieth of the original outer surface of this vast amphitheatre.

2 Temple of Antoninus and Faustina (2nd century A.D.) overlooking the Forum. Transformed into a church (San Lorenzo in Miranda) in the 11th century, it was rebuilt, leaving the great Roman portico standing free, in the early 17th.

3 Via Biberatica – an ancient Roman street with shop-fronts, part of the complex of 'Trajan's markets', in the very centre of modern Rome.

4 Constantine's Arch, the most imposing of the surviving triumphal arches in Rome, belongs to the first quarter of the 4th century but incorporates many earlier reliefs and statues. It commemorates Constantine's victories and hence, by association of ideas, the triumph of Christianity.

5 Constantine's 'Basilica', started in the early years of the 4th century by Maxentius and also known by his name. The stupendous coffered vaults shown here, each 68 feet in span, represent only one 'aisle' of the original building.

6 Tomb of Cecilia Metella on the Appian Way. The engraving of 1816 shows this great Roman landmark much as it appears today. The battlements date from the time it was incorporated in medieval fortifications of the Caetani family.

7 Church of Sant'Urbano, as restored in 1634. It occupies the exact site of a temple of Bacchus, the columns of whose pronaos are incorporated in the façade. It still stands isolated in the fields, and this view is now obscured by trees.

8 Interior of the Pantheon, lit by one great eye at the summit of the dome, seen from one of the recesses (now chapels) in the walls of the rotunda. The old engraving is reproduced here, since it is virtually impossible to photograph this interior as a whole.

9 Pantheon. This huge rotunda, dating in its present form from the 2nd century A.D., was saved from spoliation through being early consecrated as a church, and is wonderfully preserved. The superfluous turrets were erected in the 17th century by Bernini and pulled down in 1893.

10 Villa dei Quintili. A picturesque and extensive series of ruins standing in open country between the old and the new Appian roads. They are fine examples of Roman brick building of the 2nd century. This great villa was served by its private aqueduct, much of which still exists.

11 The Aqua Claudia is one of the many aqueducts which traversed the plains between Rome and the Alban or Apennine hills. Though built for a utilitarian purpose with no thought of effect, they are singularly satisfying to the eye.

12 Torre Appia – a shattered medieval watch-tower standing solitary in the Campagna some six miles outside the city walls. There are many such towers in the immediate surroundings of Rome.

13 Torre delle Milizie (13th century), the most massive of the medieval towers within the city. Also visible are the bell-tower of Santa Caterina da Siena and the graceful 15th-century loggia belonging to the old Roman Priory of the Knights of Malta.

14 Monte Soratte, a conspicuous natural landmark rising in isolation about 25 miles north of Rome. The mountain forms a long, sharp ridge and appears pyramidal only when viewed, as here, end-on.

15 Civita Castellana, an ancient (originally Etruscan) city near Monte Soratte, standing between two deep, rocky ravines. This early 13th-century portico of the cathedral is one of the best works of the Roman Cosmatesque school (cf. cloister of San Paolo, pl. 90/92).

16 Norma, a cliff-top village of medieval origin and aspect. From the heights of the Monti Lepini it overlooks the abandoned city of Ninfa (whose inhabitants transferred to Norma to escape the malaria) and the once marshy Pontine plains beyond.

17 Sermoneta. This is a typical Latian hill town 35 miles south-east of Rome. Surmounting a spur of the Monti Lepini, it is itself dominated by the great medieval castle of the Caetani. For the Romanesque campanile, barely visible in this photograph, see pl. 97.

18 The splendid dome of St. Peter's, mother of all Roman domes and of countless others throughout the world, seen from the Villa Doria Pamphili. Designed by Michelangelo under the inspiration of Brunelleschi's dome at Florence, it was not completed until 1589, long after his death.

19 Sant'Andrea della Valle. One of the innumerable 17th- and 18th-century façades which give Rome a predominantly Baroque character. They are treated as independent units and seldom fit the church behind. This one dates from 1663, some years after the completion of the church itself.

20 Some Roman domes seen from the Janiculum above San Pietro in Montorio. Counting from left to right they belong to: Sant'Andrea della Valle; the Trinità dei Pellegrini; San Carlo ai Catinari; the Gesù.

21 Sant'Ignazio – part of façade. It follows the two-storeyed tradition derived from the Gesù more closely than Sant'Andrea della Valle, for the lateral scrolls, which aid the transition to the upper part of the façade, are retained.

22 Catacombs of Santa Domitilla. Apart from the slight curve, which is unusual (but a great help to the photographer), this view typifies many miles of galleries in all the Roman catacombs. These early Christian cemeteries – amazingly complex and

extensive – were excavated in the coarse-grained volcanic tufa which abounds on the outskirts of the city. Four of the *loculi* here visible (three of them at ground level) have never been disturbed.

23 Fresco in the *cubicolo* or miniature chapel of St. Petronilla, which opens off a gallery close to the basilica. The saint (on the right) is seen introducing another Christian lady, Veneranda, into heaven. There are scrolls (of the scriptures) in a receptacle on the ground.

24 The partly subterranean basilica of the late 4th century. It was found in 1874 during the exploration of St. Domitilla's catacombs and subsequently restored, but the original roofs were not reconstructed. The basilica has nave and aisles, apse, and a narthex (from which this view was taken).

25 Santi Giovanni e Paolo – the apse: the attractive arcade is a 13th-century addition unique in Rome. This basilica was originally built at the end of the 4th century on top of the house in which John and Paul, two dignitaries of the Imperial court, were executed for their faith in A.D. 362.

26 Façade of Santi Giovanni e Paolo as it now appears. The upper arcade, invisible until revealed by the restoration of 1948–52, belongs to the original 4th-century building. The portico, typically Roman, is of the mid-12th and the 'gallery' above it of the early 13th century. The *Clivus Scauri*, spanned by medieval arched buttresses, runs down to the left of the church.

27 Part of the 2nd-century Roman house on the *Clivus Scauri* which contained the *Titulus Byzantis*, a Christian domestic sanctuary probably going back to the 3rd century. This ancient house-front was retained to form the south aisle-wall of Santi Giovanni e Paolo, new windows being broken through it.

28 Santa Sabina. This is the ideal type of the simple Early Christian basilica with arched colonnades. Built early in the 5th century, it was restored (1936–38) not quite to its original but to its 9th-century aspect. The nave and aisles are separated by long unbroken rows of antique columns; there are timbered roofs and a single apse. The *schola cantorum* or choir enclosure was a characteristic addition of the 9th century.

29 Santa Sabina, showing the flat ceiling added by the restorers since the photograph on the opposite page was taken. Although there was some evidence that such a ceiling existed in the original basilica, there are those who would have preferred the open timbered roof to remain exposed.

30 San Lorenzo fuori le Mura. The eastern portion of the church offers an early (6th-century) example of galleried aisles. The floor of the choir was raised to its present rather awkward level as the result of the insertion of the crypt below. Part of the 12th-century altar-canopy is visible to the left. Compare 76 and 83.

31 Santa Sabina. A diagonal view showing the superb Corinthian columns with their well-matched but not identical capitals, probably derived from a pre-existing temple. Coloured marbles are arranged in patterns above and between the arches. The complex

window-gratings are copied from those of the 9th century of which remnants were found during the restoration.

32 Santa Sabina. The 5th-century mosaic inside the western wall consists of a gold-lettered inscription (which concerns the building of the basilica), at either end of which stands a solemn female figure. The two women symbolise the two components of the early Church: Jewish ('Eclesia ex Circumcisione') and Gentile; but the author sees in them the perfect image of some Christian ladies of the period, devout, virtuous and austere.

33 Santa Sabina. The carved cedar-wood panels of the western door are believed to be contemporary with the church and the work of Syrian sculptors. Splendidly imaginative is this scene of Elijah's ascent into heaven, witnessed (according to a Palestinian legend) by some young woodcutters with their axes. A lizard and a snail provide charming touches of realism. Of the eighteen surviving panels four are illustrated.

34 A church with twin towers (indicating a Syrian architectural model) before which stands a figure accompanied by an angel. The author identifies the figure as Zacharias, emerging from the Temple after his vision, struck dumb for his unbelief. Onlookers stand below.

35 Above, Christ in Glory in a circular aureole, surrounded by the symbols of the Evangelists. Below, Peter and Paul holding a star above the head of a woman, who personifies the Church.

36 Moses, shown young and beardless, takes off his sandals before the burning bush, and God speaks to him through the mouth of an angel.

37 Santa Maria Maggiore (5th century). The very broad nave and Ionic colonnade with architrave, all of Vitruvian proportions, once led to the belief that this was a pagan basilica later adapted for Christian purposes. The pure classicism of the interior is, however, largely due to Fuga's 18th-century restoration. The coffered ceiling is of the end of the 15th century, gilded, it is said, with the first gold brought by the Spaniards from America.

38 Santa Maria Maggiore. Mosaics of the 'triumphal' or sanctuary-arch, contemporary with the basilica itself. The subjects are all treated in a most unusual manner. *Above:* Annunciation, with the Archangel Gabriel floating in the air; on the right, St. Joseph's vision. *Below:* Epiphany scene. The Child (no longer an infant) is seated on a broad throne. Two of the Magi, in Persian costume, approach from the right, the third (not included in the photograph) from the left.

39 A modest specimen of the common acanthus, which is believed to have inspired the foliage of the Corinthian capital. It abounds in shady places among the ruins of the Forum and in parks and gardens in Rome, well-grown specimens growing almost as tall as a man with leaves four to five feet long.

40 Santa Sabina. One of the exquisite antique Corinthian capitals re-used, with the corresponding fluted columns, in the 5th-century basilica.

41 Sant'Agata dei Goti. Ionic capital with pulvin. The simple original pulvins remain in position but were overlaid with moulded stucco in the course of the 17th-century restoration.

42 Santo Stefano Rotondo. Corinthian capital with uncut foliage (originally, the acanthus pattern was probably painted on). Like all the capitals of the outer colonnade, it carries a pulvin.

43 Santo Stefano Rotondo, a Roman version of the Church of the Holy Sepulchre at Jerusalem. The great 5th-century rotunda remains immensely impressive, even though it has lost the outer of the two circular aisles which once surrounded the central space. The tall transverse arcade was inserted in the 12th century to improve stability.

44 Santo Stefano Rotondo. Ionic capital, with pulvin, of the outer colonnade, most of which is now walled-up.

45 Santo Stefano Rotondo. Ionic capital of the inner colonnade, without pulvin. The columns are antique, but the capitals were made for the church.

46 Santo Stefano Rotondo. Mosaic dedicated by the 7th-century pope, Theodore I, to SS. Primus and Felician, whose remains he had brought from the catacombs. The richly ornamented cross standing between them appears to represent the one set up by Constantine on Golgotha; it was here intended to commemorate the tragic destruction of Jerusalem by the Persians in 614 and its final loss to the Arabs in 638.

47 Chapel of St. Venantius at the Lateran Baptistery. The mosaic does honour to a number of Dalmatian martyrs. It was made by Pope John IV (640–642), himself a Dalmatian, at a time when his Christian countrymen were again suffering persecution – by the invading Slavs.

48 Santa Maria Antiqua, the ancient Christian sanctuary re-discovered in 1900 in the Forum. The remarkable array of 8th-century frescoes, many of which have unfortunately faded, appear to be the workmanship of Greek artists who had fled from the iconoclastic persecution in the Eastern Empire. St. Julitta is represented here alongside her son, St. Quiricus.

49 St. Quiricus. According to the best-known form of the legend he was Julitta's three-year-old son who persisted in affirming his faith at his mother's trial so that both were martyred together (in Tarsus, under Diocletian). He is represented here, however, as a young man.

50 Santi Cosma e Damiano. The splendid 6th-century mosaic which served as a model for the Roman mosaic-makers and fresco-painters for centuries. The dominating figure of Christ is accompanied by SS. Peter and Paul, by three martyrs including Cosmas and Damian, and by Pope Felix IV (on the left, with model of the church). The Phoenix is perched in the palm-tree on the left. Below, the twelve apostles are shown as sheep approaching the Mystic Lamb in the centre (hidden by the canopy).

51 Santa Prassede. This apse-mosaic shows how the 6th-century model at SS. Cosma e Damiano (opposite) was interpreted three hundred years later. The lateral figures,

rigid and unworldly, represent Peter and Paul who each place a hand on the shoulder of the two saintly women, Praxedes and Pudentiana. The outer figure to the left shows Pope Paschal I with the square halo reserved for persons still alive. The palms and Phoenix, and the two processions of sheep (issuing respectively from Jerusalem and Bethlehem) are duly repeated.

52 Santa Prassede. Vault-mosaic in San Zeno's chapel. It is a jewel of 9th-century mosaic decoration, unique in Rome.

53 Santa Prassede. Mosaic above the door in San Zeno's chapel. Here SS. Peter and Paul stand on either side of an empty throne; this represents the judgment-seat which awaits the coming of the Lord on the Last Day.

54 Santa Maria in Domnica. This is perhaps the most beautiful 9th-century mosaic in Rome and, like others of the iconoclastic period, was the work of fugitive Greek artists from the Eastern Empire. The Virgin here occupies the place of honour in an apse for the first time. The Child sits on her knees looking directly forward; a multitude of attendant angels stand behind. The figure with square halo, kneeling at the Virgin's feet, is Pope Paschal I, who commissioned the mosaic.

55 San Bartolomeo on the island in the Tiber: 17th-century façade and medieval tower. The church was founded by Otto III towards the end of the 10th century, on the site of a temple of Aesculapius. Though repeatedly damaged by floods and restored from time to time it retains its basilican plan and antique columns.

56 General view of the island. It is linked with both banks of the Tiber by ancient bridges, the one here shown, the Ponte Fabricio, dating from 62 B.C. Of the two medieval towers visible, that on the left belongs to San Bartolomeo.

57 The well-head of San Bartolomeo, a 12th-century work, is curiously placed half-way up the sanctuary steps. The four figures represent Christ, Otto III, and the two saints whose relics he brought here – St. Bartholomew and St. Paulinus of Nola. This is the last-named, represented as a bishop.

58 The well-known Chantilly miniature representing Otto III (or his father Otto II) as a handsome, beardless young emperor to whom the nations are doing homage. Unlike the relief on the well-head, this miniature was probably intended as a portrait.

59 Otto III himself, carrying a disk which bears a miniature representation of the church he founded. Otto is elderly and bearded, showing that little but his name was remembered in Rome when these figures were carved.

60 Landscape with imaginary ruins by Hubert Robert (1733–1808). It was formerly attributed to G. P. Pannini. Whether or not this is the painting the author had in mind in Chapter 7, it certainly calls up a vivid picture of the decaying magnificence of Rome in the times of Otto III, about the year 1000.

61 Abbey of Grottaferrata. Fresco by Domenichino (1610) showing the meeting of Otto III, the young Holy Roman Emperor, with the aged St. Nilus. The scene con-

jured up by the artist from various elements of fact and fancy is compared by the author to Shakespeare's story-telling.

62/63 Castel Sant'Elia. The early Romanesque church in its romantic setting among the gorges between Nepi and Civita Castellana. Though only thirty miles north of Rome it owes little or nothing to Roman influence and appears to be the work of a Lombard architect. Originally a Benedictine foundation, it is now served by German Franciscans.

64/65 Castel Sant'Elia. Antique columns were used to support the arches of the nave arcades which are recessed in two orders, and so match the doorways of the west front. The high, bare nave walls carry an open timber roof. There is a very fine fresco cycle mostly of the 11th century, while the pulpit and ciborium date from the 12th.

66 San Saba. Typical plain Roman apses. The small lateral apses reflect eastern influence, for this church was built by Greek monks in the late 9th or early 10th century.

67 Sant'Agata dei Goti. One of the beautiful Cosmatesque ciboria or altar-canopies, dating from about the 12th century, with which the apses of Roman basilicas are nearly always furnished.

68 Castel Sant'Elia. Roofs of apse and transept. Their pleasing texture is due to the alternating flat and arched tiles, a very ancient roofing technique still commonly in use.

69 San Sebastianello. A strange and rare subject from the destroyed portion of the late 10th-century fresco-cycle: it shows the Apostles raised up on the shoulders of the Prophets. These 17th-century copies, exhibited on the choir walls, form a precious record, but have obviously played havoc with the style of the originals.

70 Chapel of the old Lateran Palace: 16th-century sketch of a 12th-century fresco. It represents Pope Calixtus II triumphing over the anti-pope Bourdain and at the same time concluding the Concordat of Worms (1122) with the Emperor Henry V. The Palace, with its chapel and all the frescoes, was destroyed in 1747.

71 San Paolo fuori le Mura. Part of the great 11th-century bronze door, irreparably damaged in the fire of 1823 and now preserved in the sacristy. The partly obliterated subjects of these six panels are: Crucifixion; Deposition; Resurrection; Appearance to the Apostles; Ascension; Descent of the Holy Ghost.

72 Decorative band from one of the raised bars which frame the panels.

73 St. Peter, from the same bronze door. The characteristic outline of the head would identify him, even without the inscription. The key of heaven, slung from his right elbow, is unfortunately broken away, as are his feet.

74 San Paolo fuori le Mura. This engraving shows the immense five-aisled early-Christian basilica still standing in its original form. Its destruction by fire in 1823 was one of the greatest architectural tragedies of all time. The basilica was rebuilt on the identical plan but with smooth granite columns instead of the beautiful antique fluted ones seen in the engraving. The open timbered roofs were replaced by flat gilded ceilings of complicated design. It remains a magnificent monument. See also 90/92.

75 San Clemente. Built at the beginning of the 12th century on top of the nave and one aisle of the earlier structure, which the Normans had burnt down in 1084. The very early choir enclosure or *schola cantorum*, with pulpits and lectern, was brought up from the lower church. The Cosmatesque pavement, ciborium and paschal candlestick, as well as the mosaic in the conch of the apse, date from the 12th century. See 89 for detail of mosaic.

76 Santi Quattro Coronati. One of the few Roman churches with galleried aisles (cf. 30). The present building (*c.* A.D. 1110) occupies no more than half the nave of the vast pre-existing basilica, partially destroyed by Robert Guiscard in 1084. The original aisles were abandoned, the colonnades which divided them from the nave being incorporated in the new outer walls. In this view, part of a column with Ionic capital is visible in the far wall.

77 Santa Croce in Gerusalemme. Painting by Carlo Maratta above an altar in the right aisle (*c.* 1660). St. Bernard leads the repentant anti-pope Victor IV to the feet of the legitimate pope, Innocent II.

78 Abbazia delle Tre Fontane: 16th-century picture showing St. Bernard's vision of the heavenly ladder. It forms the altarpiece of Santa Maria Scala Coeli, the chapel which commemorates this legendary incident.

79 San Giorgio in Velabro. The bell-tower and the Ionic portico (both of the 12th century) are characteristically Roman. The church itself, of far earlier origin but often altered, was restored to its medieval condition in 1926. These two churches, together with two Roman temples, a Roman arch, a medieval house and a Baroque fountain, make up a splendid monumental group at the foot of the Aventine.

80 Santa Maria in Cosmedin. Assumed substantially its present appearance in the 8th century, when it became a refuge for Greek monks fleeing from iconoclasm. In the early 12th century many alterations and internal embellishments were undertaken, and the exceptionally fine campanile was added. All 16th-century and subsequent additions were removed in the course of a radical restoration in 1894–99.

81 Santa Maria in Trastevere. Though a very early foundation the present church was built as late as 1140 and well illustrates the extraordinary strength of the Early Christian architectural tradition in Rome, where neither Romanesque nor Gothic ever gained acceptance. The bell-tower, and the plain façade with projecting portico, are unmistakably Roman.

82 Santa Maria in Trastevere. The broad nave with trabeated colonnades, purely classical in effect, would be impossible in a 12th-century building anywhere but in Rome. The plan is a transeptal basilica in the tradition of old St. Peter's and St. Paul's Outside the Walls; hence the sanctuary arch (or 'triumphal' arch) dividing nave from transept. There are important mosaics of the 12th and 13th centuries (see 86/87).

83 San Lorenzo fuori le Mura. Illustrates the casual manner in which classical spoils were re-used in early-Christian architecture of about 580. Over some magnificent Corin-

thian capitals an entablature of beautifully carved but imperfectly matched elements has been set.

84 Santa Maria in Trastevere. Six hundred years later classical columns of varying length, miscellaneous capitals and quaintly re-arranged modillions are still being employed in Rome – but without detriment to the general effect.

85 Sant'Agata dei Goti. A simple type of basilica without transept, for comparison with Santa Maria in Trastevere. The Ionic capitals carry pulvins (cf. 41) and the colonnades are arched. The Cosmatesque ciborium is of 12th-century and the typically Roman flat coffered ceiling of 17th-century date.

86 Santa Maria in Trastevere. Detail of the 12th-century apse-mosaic depicting the Triumph of the Virgin. Christ's hand is placed on the Virgin's shoulder – an iconographic novelty. Compare the more usual 'Coronation' shown on the opposite page.

87 Santa Maria in Trastevere. Mosaic of Jeremiah from spandrel of the apse. The inscription on the prophet's scroll gives a clue to the meaning of the caged bird. It symbolises Christ's sacrifice in imprisoning himself in the flesh so as to expiate the sins of mankind.

88 Santa Maria Maggiore. Apse-mosaic by Torriti (1296). This Coronation fittingly completes the Early Christian mosaic sequence devoted to the praises of the Virgin. The subject is rare in Italy and was certainly inspired by French models.

89 San Clemente. Detail of the superb mosaic (probably early 12th century) in the conch of the apse. The vine-scroll is based on 4th-century or earlier Roman models, but the cross adorned with doves, and the miniature figures of men, beasts and birds (all of symbolic significance) are probably late medieval innovations. Compare 75.

90 San Paolo fuori le Mura. The early 13th-century cloister, which escaped destruction in the fire of 1823. It is perhaps the finest work of the medieval Roman *marmorari* or marble-workers, often collectively referred to as the Cosmati.

91/92 Cloister of San Paolo fuori le Mura. The twinned columns may be straight, spiral, corkscrew-shaped (like sticks of barley-sugar) or may have two shafts twined together. Many of them are adorned with multi-coloured Cosmatesque mosaic-inlay.

93 San Lorenzo fuori le Mura: 13th-century pavement. It is a very typical (but late) example of the numerous Roman church-pavements associated with the name of the Cosmati. The characteristic geometrical patterns are carried out in coloured stones forming a coarse mosaic. The large disks are usually of green marble or red porphyry.

94 Santa Maria in Cappella (A.D. 1090). A modest precursor of the later Roman bell-towers, with plain, completely separate, openings.

95 Santa Rufina. Another attractive small tower in Trastevere, probably early 12th century. The windows are now coupled, and share a central colonnette.

96 San Lorenzo fuori le Mura. The free-standing bell-tower, late 11th or early 12th century. Almost as simple as 94, though of much more imposing proportions.

97 Sermoneta. A 13th-century stone-built campanile belonging to the same class as the Roman towers. The twin windows are divided by coupled colonnettes.

98 San Giovanni a Porta Latina. 12th-century tower with triple windows in the upper storeys. The ensemble is one of the most picturesque in Rome.

99 Velletri. The tall, isolated Torre del Trivio, which has Gothic details, illustrates the persistence of the same tradition into the 14th century.

100 Santi Giovanni e Paolo. A splendid example of the later 12th-century towers which have two pairs of windows in each face of each storey. Restored and partly detached from adjoining buildings in 1950–52.

101 Santi Quattro Coronati. 13th-century entrance-tower with quadruple windows.

102 Santa Cecilia in Trastevere. The 12th-century Ionic portico, tower of the same epoch (1113) and Baroque façade combine to form a typically Roman composition. The interior, though remodelled in the 18th century, retains a graceful Gothic altar-canopy and a 9th-century apse-mosaic. The adjoining convent contains a famous fresco, originally in the church, by Cavallini (*c.* 1293).

103 Santa Francesca Romana. It is also known as Santa Maria Nova, having been built in the 10th century to replace Santa Maria 'Antica' on the other side of the Forum. The façade is Baroque (1615). The 12th-century tower is a fine example of the more evolved Roman type, with two pairs of windows at each level.

104 San Sisto Vecchio. The campanile was built early in the 13th century and is thus contemporary with St. Dominic, with whom the church is very closely associated. Its present aspect is due to a reconstruction about 1725.

105 Pisa. Panel from an altarpiece (*c.* 1345) by Francesco Traini. Pope Innocent III sees in a dream the falling Lateran, supported by St. Dominic. As a result of the vision he authorised the foundation of the Dominican Order.

106 Cortona. Panel from a predella by Fra Angelico (1387–1455), very similar to one now in the Louvre. Two angels bring bread to the brethren, when all their food had been given to the poor. The monastery of San Sisto was the scene of this miracle.

107 Santa Sabina. The cloister of St. Dominic's own monastery, founded by him in 1220 when the community was transferred from San Sisto. The saint planted an orange tree here, which survived until recently. The columns are alternately single and paired – an unusual feature. (See also 28–36.)

108 Abbey of Fossanova. The cloister. Three sides of it are Romanesque of extreme simplicity, befitting a Cistercian abbey. The fourth side, including a charming pavilion jutting out from it, is ornate Gothic of the late 13th century. This corner illustrates the transition. (See also 111–116.)

109 Church of the Santissimo Nome di Maria (1738) by the French architect Dérizet, seen from the Victor Emmanuel monument. Close by stands Trajan's column (A.D. 114) with its spirally ascending reliefs of the Dacian wars and surmounted (since 1587) by a statue of St. Peter.

110 Santa Maria Maggiore. Externally, the ancient basilica has almost completely disappeared from view. The principal façade seen here is due to Fuga (1741–43). The

campanile, though Romanesque in style like practically all Roman towers, dates from 1377 and is the tallest in Rome. (See also 37.)

111 Abbey of Fossanova. View across the nave from aisle to aisle. Built by the Cistercians at the end of the 12th century in the earliest Gothic style, it is almost indistinguishable from contemporary Burgundian churches. Though the new style had a wide influence in Italy it went quite unheeded in Rome, only 50 miles to the north-west.

112 Fossanova. The nave, looking westwards from the crossing. The nave-vault, otherwise unribbed, is strengthened by means of transverse arches. These are carried on long semi-columns which, however, stop short before reaching the ground.

113 Fossanova. View westwards in the south aisle. It has slightly stilted transverse arches matching those of the nave, and groined vaults showing between. The capitals, of Corinthian derivation, are the only form of ornament.

114 Casamari. This neighbouring Cistercian abbey was built early in the 13th century. Though very similar to Fossanova it is slightly later and faithfully reflects the progress made in French Gothic in the intervening years. Both nave- and aisle-vaults are now furnished with ribs, as in contemporary French churches.

115 Fossanova. The church from the north-east. Except for the characteristic lantern over the crossing it is severely plain, both inside and out. There are simple, but no flying buttresses. Originally Cistercian, Fossanova has passed to the Franciscans.

116 Casamari. The western portico, probably similar to that of Fossanova which no longer exists. A central round arch flanked by pointed ones is a Burgundian arrangement reappearing later in the cathedrals of Siena and Orvieto. Casamari remains a Cistercian abbey.

117 Santa Maria Novella, Florence. A splendid example of Florentine Gothic, begun in 1278 but not completed until about 1350. Owing to the slenderness of the pillars and great span of the arches (increasing westwards) the interior gives the impression of a vast uninterrupted space.

118 Santa Maria sopra Minerva. A not very inspired copy (late 13th century) of Santa Maria Novella in Florence; it is interesting nevertheless as the only Gothic church ever built in Rome. Its Gothic purity was adulterated in the 17th century but recovered, in some degree, as the result of a restoration in 1847.

Index

[Illustrations are indicated by their serial numbers which are given in bold type, e.g. **90–93**.]